Social Work and the Law in Scotland

Edited by

Deborah Baillie
Kathryn Cameron
Lesley-Anne Cull
Jeremy Roche
and
Janice West

in association with

First published 2003 by
PALGRAVE MACMILLAN
Houndmills, Basingstoke, Hampshire RG21 6XS and
175 Fifth Avenue, New York, N.Y. 10010
Companies and representatives throughout the world

PALGRAVE MACMILLAN is the global academic imprint of the
Palgrave Macmillan division of St. Martin's Press, LLC and of
Palgrave Macmillan Ltd. Macmillan® is a registered trademark
in the United States, United Kingdom and other countries.
Palgrave is a registered trademark in the European Union and
other countries.

ISBN-13: 978-1-403-91288-6 (paperback)
ISBN-10: 1-403-91288-2 (paperback)

The book is printed on paper suitable for recycling and made
from fully managed and sustained forest sources. Logging, pulping
and manufacturing processes are expected to conform to the
environmental regulations of the country of origin.

A catalogue record for this book is available from the British Library.

10   9   8   7   6   5
12   11   10   09   08   07

Typeset by Cambrian Typesetters, Frimley, Surrey

Printed and bound in Great Britain by
Creative Print & Design (Wales), Ebbw Vale

Contents

PART III SERVICE USER AND PRACTICE PERSPECTIVES

Notes on the Contributors

Deborah Baillie is Associate Lecturer with the Open University on K267 and an independent consultant and trainer for the public and voluntary sector in the fields of health and social work law. She is a director of Advocacy Service Aberdeen and the Scottish Alliance for Children's Rights and administers web sites for both organisations. She is also the author of *The Law Reference Manual* published by Camphill Scotland and co-author of *An Essential Guide to Legal Issues for Health Professionals in Scotland* published by Grampian Primary Care NHS Trust. From September 2003 she will be the visiting lecturer in social work law at Dundee University.

Kathryn Cameron is Senior Lecturer in the Department of Social Work at the University of Strathclyde. She is qualified in both social work and law. She has played a significant role in the development of the curriculum for the teaching of law on the Diploma in Social Work in Scotland and is a co-author of *Social Work and the Law in Scotland*. She has a particular interest in law and practice in relation to children and families.

Elizabeth Craigmyle is Principal Solicitor at ENABLE legal services and Manager of ENABLE Trustee Service. She is a member of the Law Society of Scotland's Mental Health and Disability Committee.

Lesley-Anne Cull is Dean of the School of Health and Social Welfare at The Open University and a lecturer in law. She is a practising barrister and has researched and written widely in the areas of child and family law. She is co-editor of *The Law and Social Work: Contemporary Issues for Practice* (2001).

Mike Dailly has been principal solicitor at Govan Law Centre since September 1999. He is co-annotator of Current Law Statutes *Housing*

(Scotland) Act 2001, consultant editor of Butterworth's *Housing Law Statutes* and author of *Housing Law in Practice* (2003). He has assisted members of the Scottish Parliament from four political parties in drafting legislation. He has written, lectured and broadcast extensively on housing and debt law, and undertakes a large volume of court work within these fields.

Iain Ferguson is Lecturer in Social Work at the University of Stirling. He has written widely on issues of service user involvement (particularly in the area of mental health), participatory and emancipatory research, asylum seekers and social welfare theory. Prior to moving into academic life, he worked for many years as a social worker and community worker and is a qualified Mental Health Officer.

Alan Ferry is Lecturer in Division of Social Work at Glasgow Caledonian University, specialising in issues of poverty and exclusion, and in community care and working with older adults. Prior to working on these issues he was the coordinator of a drug project in Glasgow and served as the adviser on drug issues for the Scottish Aids Monitor (SAM) and as the chair of Realise, a local voluntary service for drug users and their families in Glasgow.

Angela Forbes is the manager of Advocacy Service Aberdeen (ASA), an independent advocacy service based in the City of Aberdeen. She has worked in independent advocacy since early 1994. Prior to this she worked in further and higher education. For more information about ASA visit their website www.advocacy.org.uk.

Moyra Hawthorn worked in residential childcare and in various childcare settings in Liverpool and Scotland - area teams, family placement and child protection. In 1993, she moved to the voluntary organisation NCH to run a counselling project for sexually abused children and their families. She currently works in a family support project which offers an outreach and residential short break service for disabled children and their families. Since 2001, she has also worked part-time at the Scottish Institute for Residential Child Care at the University of Strathclyde.

Brian Kearney was a solicitor in private practice, 1960–74. He was appointed a 'floating' sheriff in 1974 and transferred in 1977 to Glasgow, where he is still sitting and is now senior Sheriff in Glasgow.

He published *Ordinary Procedure Court* in 1987 (second edition 2000). He is Honary President of the Glasgow Marriage Counselling Service and the Family Law Association. He was for a time a member of the Child Care Law Review until seconded to preside over the Inquiry into Child Care Services in Fife in 1989 (report published in 1992). He has spoken and written about children's law on many occasions at home and abroad and is a member of the Judicial Studies Committee of Scotland.

Andrew Kendrick is Professor of Residential Child Care in the Department of Social Work at the University of Strathclyde. He is closely involved in the work of the Scottish Institute for Residential Child Care (SIRCC) and in coordinating SIRCC's research activities. He has particular research interests in residential childcare; decision-making in childcare; interdisciplinary work, particularly the relationship between education and social services; the safety of children in residential and foster care; and the residential treatment of sexually aggressive young men.

Katy Macfarlane is the Policy and Education Officer for the Scottish Child Law Centre. Her work involves the promotion of the rights of children and young people in Scotland. This is done through the delivery of training sessions to children, parents, carers and professionals working with children, as well as through the Centre's free telephone advice service. Her particular interest is in education law, especially the law relating to children with additional support needs. She is also a trained mediator.

Janice McGhee is Social Work Lecturer in the School of Social and Political Studies at the University of Edinburgh. She is responsible for teaching law on the Master of Social Work and BSc (Social Work) programmes. Her research interests are in child welfare policy and law, including the children's hearings system in Scotland. She completed a study of the characteristics and outcomes of 1,155 children referred in 1995 to the children's hearings system (L. Waterhouse, J. McGhee, B. Whyte, N. Loucks, H. Kay and R. Stewart (2000) *The Evaluation of Children's Hearings in Scotland, Volume 3: Children in Focus.*

Kathryn MacKay is a Teaching Fellow in Social Work with the Department of Applied Social Science at the University of Stirling. She was a Mental Health Officer prior to moving to the university. She is currently appointed by the Scottish Social Services Council as an External Assessor for approved MHO training courses.

Robert MacKay has practised as a criminal justice social worker and as a lecturer on a Scottish DipSW programme. He served on the Consultation Group for the original *National Objectives and Standards for Social Work in the Criminal Justice System*. He set up the first Restorative Justice programme in Scotland with SACRO. He has extensive involvement with the Restorative Justice movement, and has published extensively in this field. At the time of writing he is Youth Justice Co-ordinator with Perth and Kinross Council.

Anne MacKenzie is Coordinator of Aberdeen Welfare Rights, a service of Aberdeen City Council. As such she has considerable experience of welfare rights work, including representing clients at tribunal. A graduate of Edinburgh University, she graduated with a BA in 1977 and LLB in 1979. In addition she completed a research degree on Mediation in Child Custody Disputes, graduating as LLM in 1995 from the University of Aberdeen where she has previously taught in the Law Department on a part-time basis.

Marion McLarty has been a Senior Lecturer in the Department of Educational Support and Guidance at the University of Strathclyde since 1993. Prior to this she had a teaching career of over twenty years spent in various areas in Special Education in the west of Scotland, culminating in the post of Head Teacher in Carnbooth School, Glasgow, the only school in Scotland which caters specifically for Deafblind Children and young people.

Kathleen Marshall is a solicitor, child law consultant and Visiting Professor to the Centre for the Child and Society, University of Glasgow. She was formerly Director of the Scottish Child Law Centre. She chaired the Edinburgh Inquiry into Abuse and Protection of Children in Care, reporting in February, 1999. She is the author of *Children's Rights in the Balance: The Participation-Protection Debate*, published in 1997, co-author of the law module of Dundee University's Child Protection Certificate, and has undertaken research on many matters associated with children.

Iain Nisbet is the Associate Solicitor at Govan Law Centre where he is the coordinator of its Education Law Unit. He has provided training for the Disability Rights Commission advice and legal personnel on discrimination legislation and its interaction with Scots education law and was the legal adviser in Scots law for the statutory Codes of Practice on Part 4 (Chapters 1 and 2) of the Disability Discrimination Act 1995.

Alison Petch has been Director of the Nuffield Centre for Community Care Studies based at Glasgow University since 1993 and prior to that worked at the Social Work Research Centre at Stirling University. She has professional training in planning and in social work and has carried out research across a broad range of social work, health and housing issues. The Nuffield Centre is committed to a multidisciplinary and multi-agency perspective.

Jackie Robeson enrolled as a solicitor in 1982 and worked initially in local government legal services. She became a Children's Reporter in 1986 and is presently Head of Practice within Scottish Children's Reporters Administration with responsibility throughout Scotland based at SCRA's Headquarters in Stirling.

Jeremy Roche is Senior Lecturer in Law in the School of Health and Social Welfare at The Open University. He writes and researches in the field of children's rights and the law, and is co-editor of *The Law and Social Work: Contemporary Issues for Practice* (2001).

Kay Tisdall is Lecturer in Social Policy at the University of Edinburgh. She is Programme Director of the multi-disciplinary postgraduate degree, the MSc/Diploma in Childhood Studies. Current and recent research projects include girls and violent behaviour, implementation of disability rights legislation in schools, integrated services for children and their families, and the 'voice of the child' in Scottish family law.

Janice West is Senior Lecturer in Social Work at Glasgow Caledonian University. This post was preceded by a 20-year career in social work practice, specialising in child care issues. She teaches and has written on social work law, social work practice and residential childcare and is a co-author of *Social Work and the Law in Scotland*. She has been a curator *ad litem* and Reporting Officer for twenty years and is the co-founder and coordinator of the Social Work Law Association in Scotland.

Foreword

Social work and the law

Social work has been at the centre of much debate since the 1980s and the consequences have included a new emphasis on the law in social work education and the creation of new relationships of accountability to service users. The law regulates social work practice, holding it to account and providing social workers with the powers and duties they need to do their job properly; it provides social workers with the authority they need as professionals. The law also structures their discretion through providing them with legal powers and duties in a range of situations and with 'advice' in the form of guidance. This said, individuals working in social work are still faced on a daily basis with dilemmas as to what they can and should be doing, and the law does not, and cannot, provide an answer to the complex human and social questions which lie at the centre of the social work task.

Thus the law provides authority and a structure for decision-making, not solutions; it provides the framework within which individual social workers have to act. In other words, while social workers have discretion in the action they decide to take, this is not an unconstrained discretion. Social workers have to act within the law and in the light of their contractual obligations as employees. They should also work within a framework that enables them to treat all service users with an equality of concern and respect. Social workers are in a position to make a judgement about the needs of service users by virtue of the fact that it is the social worker who engages with the service user about such matters. This raises issues concerning how the social work task is accomplished as well as the scope of social work powers and duties. So it is not simply a matter of deciding whether the action taken is lawful – that is the very least one can expect – or whether the social worker was acting within their powers and duties.

It also entails a concern with the process whereby decisions are made and action taken.

Effective and ethical practice relies upon a commitment to develop and consolidate legal knowledge. It can also make a crucial difference to a social worker's ability to act as an effective advocate for service users if he or she is up to date and confident about their knowledge of the law. This knowledge may also be important because it can impact on the choices available to them as professionals. This entails being clear about the legal principles which inform an area of practice as well as knowing where to go for more specialist advice.

One of the challenges facing practitioners as well as any student of law is the need to keep up to date with changes in the law. The difficulty of accomplishing this is compounded by the fact that legal change takes a number of forms and is the result of quite different kinds of activity. For example, the courts as well as parliament develop the law. Some of these changes have their origins in forces external to the world of social work while others are internal. For example, demographic changes whereby more people are living longer and are in need of care and medical services, how care and medical services for the elderly are to be financed and the proper balance to be struck between private responsibility and public welfare are key issues in contemporary social care debates. Finally voluntary sector organisations and service users are increasingly expressing their political demands for improvements in services in the language of rights rather than simply welfare or needs; there are demands not only for different procedural and substantive rights but also for fair and respectful treatment.

In editing this collection we have been conscious of the breadth as well as the complexity of the legal issues which impact on the world of social work. This collection is divided into three sections exploring conceptual and thematic issues, providing an overview of areas of law and social work practice and first-hand practitioner accounts.

Part I is concerned with the conceptual and thematic issues which shape law's engagement with social work practice at the beginning of the twenty-first century. As such the contributions cover a range of issues, including the changing and contingent character of the idea of welfare, emergent forms of accountability and the impact of human rights discourse on social work. Overall this section seeks to set the intellectual and policy scene within which contemporary social work practice takes place.

Part II has a different rationale, focusing on the relationship between social work practice and the law in a number of specific environments.

The chapters in this section are varied and either provide an overview of an area of law and social work practice, such as community care law, or raise questions about particular legislation.

Part III consists of personal accounts of the practice experience. These provide an insight into the daily dilemmas experienced by social welfare professionals and others. Thus this section is concerned to complement Part I's theoretical analyses of law and Part II's consideration of law in practice contexts with the voices of professionals working in different ways in the social work and social care system.

Acknowledgements

The editor and publishers wish to thank the following for permission to reproduce copyright material:

SCRA for Table 8.1 *'Children's hearings statistics: comparison between 1990 and 2000/01'*.

Scottish Social Services Council for Chapter 26: *'Code of Practice for Social Service Workers and Code of Practice for Employers of Social Service Workers'*.

List of Abbreviations

ASA	Advocacy Service Aberdeen
ASBO	Antisocial behaviour order
BMA	British Medical Association
CCETSW	Central Council for Education and Training in Social Work
CSDPA	Chronically Sick and Disabled Persons Act
CSP	Coordinated Support Plan
CTO	Compulsory treatment order
DLA	Disability Living Allowance
DWP	Department of Work and Pensions
ECHR	European Convention on Human Rights
ECT	Electroconvulsive therapy
HMI	Her Majesty's Inspectors of Schools
HRA	Human Rights Act
MHO	Mental Health Officer
MIG	Minimum Income Guaranteed
NASS	National Asylum Support Service
RMO	Responsible medical officer
RoN	Record of Needs
SACRO	Scottish Association for the Care and Resettlement of Offenders
SALC	Scottish Association of Law Centres
SAMH	Scottish Association for Mental Health
SCRA	Scottish Children's Reporter Administration
SEN	Special Educational Needs
SiSWE	Standards in Social Work Education
SSSC	Scottish Social Services Council
UNCRC	United Nations Convention on the Rights of the Child

Part I

The Law and Social Work

1

Critical Perspectives on Welfare: The Example of Childcare Services

KAY TISDALL

The concept of 'welfare' is core to social work services' mandate, institutional base and principles. Social work services emerged, first in the voluntary and then in the statutory sectors, to meet social needs, to compensate for 'diswelfares' and to promote social justice (Parton, 1999). Social work services are a component of the British 'welfare state', which can be defined as

> a society in which the government accepts responsibility for ensuring that all its citizens receive a minimum income, and have access to the highest possible provision in the fields of health care, housing, education and personal social services. (Deacon, 2002, p. 4)

The 'welfare principle' is a standby of current social work legislation and practice. The foundational Act for social work, the Social Work (Scotland) Act 1968, introduced a duty 'to promote social welfare'. The 'welfare principle' for children has a long history in statutory requirements for state intervention to be 'in the child's best interests'. It has a newer history in Article 3 of the UN Convention on the Rights of the Child (UNCRC), where the best interests of the child must be a primary consideration in all actions concerning children.

Despite – or perhaps because of? –the centrality of 'welfare' to the welfare state in general and social work services in particular, 'welfare' is one of the most inconsistently used words in the social sciences

(Deacon, 2002). It, and its associated concepts of needs and social rights, are also some of the most contested both theoretically and in their implementation. Part of this contestation arises because the welfare state establishes particular spaces, relationships and tensions between the 'public' and 'private' spheres, between where the state does and does not intervene. Social services are commonly on the cusp of these, seeking to support families and individuals whilst avoiding undue state intervention.

Consideration of children's social services – their history, their definitions of welfare and their debates – provides a particularly searching exploration of the concept of 'welfare', the welfare principle and the development of the 'welfare state'. Children are currently some of the highest users of welfare state services. Reforms for children have spearheaded many developments in the welfare state, from the Factory Acts in the nineteenth century to preventive child health policies in the twentieth and twenty-first centuries. This chapter considers the concept of 'welfare' through three lenses. First, it looks at meanings historically, through the development of state intervention in childcare. Second, it examines how welfare and the welfare state are defined through gatekeeping criteria for childcare services/intervention. Third, the chapter considers complementary and alternative concepts, that is, needs, rights and risks. It concludes with reflections on the pertinence of 'welfare' in the New Labour policy agenda.

Developing ideas of welfare and the welfare state through history: from the Poor Law to the Children (Scotland) Act 1995

Several trends are typically described in the history of the welfare state up until the early twentieth century and for children's services in particular. First, the state increasingly took on responsibility to ameliorate 'social problems' and provide for those in need. Second, stigma, harsh eligibility criteria and poor provision served to deter people from relying on state provision. Third, the perception gradually grew that children should receive state help and protection and not be subsumed solely in the family as their parents' responsibility. Fourth, and related, increasingly children were given additional and different protections, in comparison to adults, because of their status as children.

Poor relief, and its formalisation into the Poor Law, exemplifies these first two trends. In the 1500s, poor relief was available but was a harsh and punishing system. Poor people were classified into undeserving and deserving categories. Those considered lazy and able-bodied were punished while those deemed poor through no fault of their own (such as disabled people, orphans, elderly people) were assisted through charitable donations. The concepts of 'less eligibility' and the 'workhouse test' sought to maintain the residual nature of public provision (Hill, 1997). The concept of 'less eligibility' meant that those who received help had to be worse off than the poorest at work. The 'workhouse test' required conditions in the public workhouses to be worse than those living outwith them.

Gradually, poor relief became standardised and the responsibility shifted from voluntary donations and voluntary providers to statutory provision. The various Poor Laws from 1579 onwards required each parish to provide poor relief. In the eighteenth century, the Scottish Poor Law continued to be administered mainly by the Kirk and magistrates and Scottish funding continued to come from voluntary contributions and subscriptions. In 1845, the responsibility transferred to a national Board of Supervision, parochial boards and paid inspectors. Accusations of unfairness and variation in the Poor Law system then led to change in the 1890s. The national Board of Supervision was replaced by the Local Government Board for Scotland, the powers and duties were transferred from parish boards to elected parish councils, and these were inspected by Inspectors of the Poor.

Children were primarily seen as a parental responsibility, prior to the 1800s, with their needs to be met through their parents. The British Factory Acts at the start of the nineteenth century, however, gradually regulated and restricted children's employment hours and the type of work they could undertake, and established minimum ages for employment. A Sheriff's decision in 1848 ruled that children of 'undeserving' parents could themselves be eligible for poor relief (Ferguson, 1948; Hill *et al.*, 1991). Gradually, then, the state was taking on some responsibility for children's well-being, separate from parental responsibility. This was complemented by an emerging protectionist approach to children, which perceived children's needs as different from those of adults and requiring additional protection. This is exemplified by the Factory Acts, increasing separation of juvenile justice from the adult justice system, and the introduction of compulsory state education. Children's legislation gradually extended protection to children from abuse and ill-treatment by their parents and care-givers. (For discussion, see Hill *et al.*, 1991.)

After the Second World War, the British welfare state took on increasing responsibility for policy planning, administration and provision of services. State childcare services were amalgamated into unitary children's departments with specialist staff by the Children Act 1948. Preventive and supportive work was increasingly emphasised. State responsibilities were extended in child protection and substitute care. Services were increasingly professionalised and coordinated.

The Social Work (Scotland) Act 1968 created two cornerstones of the modern Scottish welfare system for children: the children's hearings system and local government social work services. The children's hearings system (see Chapter 8 for more detail) is based on the welfare principle: that is, whether children are in need of care or protection or have offended, their welfare should be the paramount consideration (subject to public safety) in making decisions. A separation is made between legal determinations of fact, which are heard in the court system, and decisions in relation to welfare, which are largely dealt with by the children's hearings. The Social Work (Scotland) Act 1968 created local authority social work departments. As mentioned in the introduction, a revolutionary feature of the Act was the wide-ranging 'duty of every local authority to promote social welfare by making available advice, guidance and assistance' (s.12). This duty was further specified for children (that is, under 18 years) to diminish the need for taking in or keeping a child in local authority care or for referring a child to a children's hearing. Local authorities had the power to provide assistance not only 'in kind' but also in cash.

For over twenty years, the 1968 Act remained the foundation of childcare services in Scotland, although the Children Act 1975 and the Adoption (Scotland) Act 1978 made significant changes in planning for young people in local authority care and adoption and the Children Act 1989 introduced early years reviews and childcare inspections. It was not until 1995 that new children's legislation was introduced that substantially revised childcare legislation: that is, the Children (Scotland) Act 1995.

The 1995 Act was parallel, but substantially different, legislation to the English and Welsh Children Act 1989 and the Children (Northern Ireland) Order 1995 (see Tisdall, 1997). It brought together aspects of family, childcare and adoption law. The Act began with a concept of parental responsibilities, to emphasise that children were not the property of their parents. Child protection proceedings were revised to meet stricter timescales and judicial requirements while the children's hearings system was updated. The references to children were deleted from s.12 of the Social Work (Scotland) Act 1968 and a new duty placed on local authorities towards the welfare of children in need. The paramountcy of children's best interests (the 'welfare principle') in legal decision-making was reinforced, along with the addition of the principles of minimal intervention and the requirement for 'due regard' to children's views in decision-making.

Meanings of welfare and the welfare state: gatekeeping criteria and assessment

Gatekeeping of scarce resources has arguably long been a feature of welfare services, as evidenced by the historical description of the Poor Law above. Even when the Social Work (Scotland) Act 1968 was implemented, the revolutionary capacity of the general welfare duty was curtailed by resource constraints (Cooper, 1983). Two key and interrelated gatekeeping methods in the social work services are eligibility criteria and assessment (Barnes and Prior, 2000; Kemshall, 2002) – both of which are strongly emphasised in current children's legislation and practice.

The Children (Scotland) Act introduced a new category to Scottish childcare: 'children in need'. Section 22 requires local authorities to safeguard and promote the welfare of children in their area who are in need, by providing a range and level of services appropriate to the children's needs. The upbringing of such children by their families should be promoted, so far as is consistent with this duty. Section 93 (4) (a) then defines a 'child in need' as being under 18 and the child is 'in need' because:

(i) the child is unlikely to achieve or maintain, or to have the opportunity of achieving or maintaining, a reasonable standard of health or development unless there are provided for him, under or by virtue of this Part, services by a local authority;

(ii) his health or development is likely significantly to be impaired, or further impaired, unless such services are so provided;

(iii) he is disabled; or

(iv) he is affected adversely by the disability of any other person in his family.

The vagueness of this definition does provide local authorities with the possibility of providing flexible and effective services that best meet the needs of children in their communities. It also means, however, with 32 local authorities across Scotland, that children in one area could be offered vastly different services to those that children in another area might receive. How has 'children in need' been defined in local planning and practice? No comprehensive research has yet been undertaken on the implementation of 'children in need' in Scotland. Research on the first children's services plans, which provided an opportunity for local authorities to define 'children in need' locally, had poor information bases by which to do so and largely repeated the legal definition without elaboration (Wheelaghan *et al.*, 1999). Research in three Scottish social work departments (Wright, 2002) shows poor knowledge of local children's services planning by fieldworkers and little knowledge of the law on 'children in need'.

A very similar duty and definition exists in the Children Act 1989. Early research in England (Tunstill, 1995) and in Wales (Colton *et al.*, 1995) found many local authorities identifying the same priority service groups as those they would have done pre-1989 legislation, rather than basing their priorities on new empirical data. Disabled children were rarely identified as a 'children in need' group, even though they are legally part of the 'children in need' definition (Tunstill, 1995; Wright, 2002). Six of the eight Welsh social services departments surveyed did not provide guidance to social workers on how the concepts ought to be interpreted when dealing with clients (Colton *et al.*, 1995). A major concern has been that family support services have been sidelined by concentrating on the crisis needs of child protection, thus not delivering on the potential to prevent child abuse in the first place (Department of Health, 1995).

Child protection and children's hearings systems have further gate-keeping criteria. The Children (Scotland) Act 1995 copied the Children Act 1989's use of 'significant harm'. Different thresholds pertaining to 'significant harm' are introduced for the three different orders that can be requested from the courts.[1] The Children (Scotland) Act 1995 outlines the twelve grounds of referral to a children's hearing. These can be encapsulated into four main types: if the child is alleged to have committed an offence; if the child has been truanting from school; if the child needs 'care and protection', for reasons such as parental neglect, substance abuse, falling into 'bad associations' or risk of harm in a household; or if the child is 'out of control' of the parent or whoever is looking after the child. The child can be referred to protect others' interests under certain circumstances when the local authority is 'looking after' them. These criteria are thus establishing boundaries between when the state can and cannot intervene in family life and interpreting what is salient in protecting children's welfare.

Assessment is critical in applying these gatekeeping criteria. Guidance recommends assessment for 'children in need'. A particular duty is placed on a local authority if the child is affected by a disability of a family member – the local authority must undertake an assessment of the child's needs. Local authorities must provide sufficient evidence to the judiciary to obtain a child assessment, child protection or exclusion order. There are numerous other examples where professional assessments are subject to judicial scrutiny. In the children's hearings system, reporters must make a judgement whether one or more of the grounds of referral is met and a child is in need of statutory measures of supervision. Ultimately, the grounds of referral could be tested in the Sheriff Court should a child or parent not accept them (or the child is too young to do so). The children's panel itself must assess whether a supervision order is needed, considering the paramountcy of a child's welfare and the minimal intervention rule and taking into account the child's views. The decision of the children's hearing can be appealed to the Sheriff, who in turn can replace his or her own disposal for that of the children's hearing. Thus both child protection and children's hearings procedures exemplify the increasing influence of the judicial system in ultimately determining welfare criteria. They also demonstrate the lines drawn when state intervention or state support can be justified (Barnes and Prior, 2000).

Meanings of welfare and the welfare state: challenging concepts

The use of 'need' within the category 'children in need' demonstrates the reliance of welfare and the welfare state on the concept of need. As Plant (1991) describes:

> There is one area of modern society in relation to the nature and limits of social action to which the theory of needs is directly and acutely relevant and that is the welfare state. Without the idea of need and the nature of the claims on society which needs make, it would be very difficult to understand the nature and normative underpinnings of the welfare state just because it is often thought that needs

characterize the sphere of welfare independently of the sphere of markets. (Plant, 1991, p. 186)

Theories of needs can be broadly divided into those that assert objective, universal needs and those that argue that needs can only be considered subjectively and in context. Doyal and Gough's seminal work on *A Theory of Human Needs* (1991) is a modern exemplar of a universal need theory. Physical health and autonomy are the two basic human needs they identify, in order for humans to avoid serious harm so people can effectively participate in their society. The authors then enumerate eleven intermediate needs necessary for the fulfilment of physical health and autonomy. The fulfilment of these is considered to be culturally relative. Smith (1980), in contrast, argues that there is 'no objective', universally applicable criteria by which to define need (p. 196). 'Need' is socially constructed, inseparable from the context in which need is defined and thus ultimately subjective. Smith, therefore, is interested in how 'need' is used as a resource for and a discourse by welfare professionals.

Those supporting subjective theory draw out the power of those who define need. Bradshaw (1972), for example, develops a much-quoted taxonomy of need:

1. Normative needs: those defined by experts or professionals, based upon an agreed standard.
2. Felt need: those identified by individuals themselves, although not necessarily expressed publicly.
3. Expressed need: when individuals do express their felt needs publicly.
4. Comparative need: when people are not receiving a specific service, although they share relevant characteristics with those who are receiving that service.

The power of the professional to define and then determine needs, using the assessment as a tool of control, is brought out in this taxonomy. Bradshaw, however, ultimately abandons his taxonomy and the concept of need as 'too imprecise, too complex and too contentious to be a useful target for policy' (1994, p. 96). Needs, then, may be questioned for their objectivity and thus their ability to justify state intervention through the welfare state.

In social work, and specifically in children's services, a rights discourse has gained ground in recent years. The Children (Scotland) Act 1995 is held up by the UK government as putting the UNCRC into practice. The overarching principles of the Act (see Chapter 4) institute certain of the key articles of the UNCRC – for example, the welfare principle and due regard to children's views. The European Convention on Human Rights had a strong influence on the 1995 Act (for example, in appeals to child protection orders) and an increasing one in social work due to the incorporation of the Convention into domestic law (Human Rights Act (HRA) 1998).[2]

A rights discourse does not escape from difficulties in determining welfare, when it incorporates the subjectivity of 'best interests':

> the operation of a best interests principle should not be seen as inherently beneficial to children. It can be, on the contrary, a powerful tool in the hands of adults, which can be used to justify any of their actions and to overrule the wishes and feelings of children. (Lansdown, 1994, p. 41)

Several questions can be asked. On what basis is the welfare principle decided? Harding (1999) describes the 'future-oriented consent' – based on the interests of the adult person that the child will in time become – of much present decision-making. This may ignore, however, the children's perspective in the present and their current concerns. It ignores how a decision now can mould the adult of the future into supporting that decision. Parker (1994) notes how 'the open-endedness of the standard can legitimate practices in some cultures which are regarded in other cultures as positively harmful' (p. 26). Equally, the welfare principle could be applied with cultural insensitivity. How does the decision-maker balance different perspectives or contradictory elements? Who should be the decision-maker on what is in someone's welfare interests – the person themselves, those responsible for them, a professional, the court?

The court is the ultimate decision-maker in the UK, should there be disputes over, or failures to meet, rights expressed in legislation. Unlike England, there is no statutory checklist of factors that the court must consider in regard to the welfare principle. Sutherland (1999) summarises key elements used to justify Scottish court decisions on parental responsibilities and rights to date:

- the child's physical, emotional, spiritual and educational welfare;
- the (adult) applicant's behaviour which affects the child;
- some adherence to the 'maternal preference' (that is, very young children needing their mother more than their father);

- links with other family members and continuity of established relationships.

These sit beside the other principles of the 1995 Act: that is, due regard to the child's views and the principle of minimal intervention.

With the court as the ultimate decision-maker, King and Piper (1990) argue that legal conceptualisations of (child) welfare have come to dominate social (work) services. King and Piper explain that law has certain tendencies: to individualise; to exclude context; to encourage distortion and exaggeration when adversarial; to compartmentalise; and to 'enslave child welfare science'. Law does not address fundamental structural issues, such as war, poverty, natural disasters and family breakdown, but excludes them as irrelevant (see King and Piper, 1990; King, 1997). Such criticisms are akin to those particularly expressed by commentators on child protection, that is the dominance of the socio-legal discourse:

> While in the 1960s child abuse was constituted as essentially a medico-social problem, increasingly it has been constituted as a socio-legal problem, where legal expertise takes pre-eminence. Previously the concern was with diagnosing, curing and preventing the 'disease' or syndrome; increasingly the emphasis has become investigating, assessing and weighing the 'evidence'. (Parton and Otway, 1995, p. 600)

This dominance is problematic because it excludes other concerns, non-forensic expertise is undervalued, and work is focused on investigation rather than supporting children and their families. The focus of child protection work, then, is to ascertain whether children reach the thresholds for state intervention and whether there is evidence for a criminal case against the offender. How to judge what is 'significant harm' is thus critical. Provision of support services, either to prevent child abuse occurring or to support children and families when it has happened, are given less priority (see above for references). The socio-legal discourse can lead to focusing on the rights of 'due process' to the exclusion of 'substantive rights' to well-being.

'Nonsense on stilts'?

'Needs' and 'rights' have been posed as alternative discourses for social work service provision (Oliver, 1996). But both discourses can be subject to similar questions about their concepts' subjectivity, biases and premises. Bentham (1970) famously quipped in the nineteenth century that rights not established in law are 'nonsense on stilts' and simply have no philosophical justifiable claim. 'Needs' theory can be similarly insulted, as only having justification when needs are established in law. Otherwise, 'needs' and their accompanying concept of welfare can be accused of being ultimately subjective and without moral claims.

New Labour has introduced a variation of the needs and rights debate by basing its welfare reform on the concepts of social inclusion and social exclusion and seeking to encourage a particular type of citizen and society. New Labour's 'third way' is based on four elements: an active, preventative welfare state; the centrality of paid work; the distribution of opportunities rather than income; and the balancing of rights and responsibilities (Dwyer, 2000). There is to be a new practice of welfare citizenship, with responsible citizens recognising and fulfilling their obligations to society by being in education or employment and involved in and contributing to their families and their communities (Barnes and Prior, 2000). Individuals are expected to exercise informed choice and avoid risk (Kemshall, 2002). If they do not, the state may intervene negatively (for example, fining parents for children's offences or truancy) or individuals can find themselves without state support (for example, young adults who do not participate in employment, training or further education).

Children and their families are absolutely central to the New Labour welfare agenda and policy reform. Their welfare will be promoted by prevention. Childhood is a prime time for distribution of opportunities, with preventive measures to ensure good health and good learning, and for children to learn responsibility. The education of children – and their continuation in education post-16 – is critical for future inclusion in work. Childhood and its accompanying welfare state structures are key sites for intervention. Children are already one of the biggest client groups for welfare state services. Government agendas can be implemented through the health visitors and children's medical check-ups, through their use of education and care services (such as Sure Start and New Community Schools) and through youth work and leisure.

Children's welfare, then, continues to be a central concern of state intervention and social work services. A historical perspective suggests that themes of the Poor Law system continue to be debated: questions on eligibility and appropriate levels and type of state intervention; inequities of service provision and constraints on resources. A historical perspective also suggests that state intervention has gone through 'pendulum swings', in arguing for more state intervention or less successively. It suggests that a socio-legal discourse in social work has gained predominance. Such a discourse can enhance and support children's rights but has an accompanying danger of excluding certain aspects of these rights as irrelevant. How 'welfare' is defined, reoriented and utilised to make claims for resources may have changed over time; what remains constant is that it is a highly contested concept.

Notes

1. Orders that can be requested are: child assessment orders, child protection orders and exclusion orders (for an alleged abuser).
2. Norrie (2001) suggests that the paramountcy of the welfare principle will be qualified by the HRA 1998, because it will require a balance of a child's welfare right with other legitimate interests.

References

Barnes, M. and Prior, D. (2000) *Imagining Welfare. Private Lives as Public Policy*, Birmingham, Venture Press.

Bentham, J. (1970) 'Anarchical fallacies', in A.I. Melden (ed.) *Human Rights*, Belmont, Calif., Wadsworth Publishing, pp. 28–39.

Bradshaw, J. (1972) 'The concept of social need', *New Society*, vol. 19, pp. 640–3.

Bradshaw, J. (1994) 'The conceptualization and measurement of need: a social policy perspective', in J. Popay and G. Williams (eds) *Researching the People's Health*, London, Routledge.

Colton, M., Drury, C. and Williams, M. (1995) 'Children in need: definition, identification and support', *Social Work*, vol. 25, pp. 711–28.

Cooper, J. (1983) 'Scotland: the management of change', in J. Cooper (ed.) *The Creation of the British Social Services 1962–1974*, London, Heinemann Educational Books, pp. 33–53.

Deacon, A. (2002) *Perspectives on Welfare*, Buckingham, Open University Press.

Department of Health (1995) *Child Protection. Messages from Research*, London, HMSO.

Doyal, L. and Gough, I. (1991) *A Theory of Human Needs*, London, Macmillan – now Palgrave Macmillan.

Dwyer, P. (2000) *Welfare Rights and Responsibilities: Contesting Social Citizenship*, Bristol, The Policy Press.

Ferguson, T. (1948) *The Dawn of Scottish Social Welfare*, London, Thomas Nelson & Sons.

Harding, L. (1999) 'Children's rights', in O. Stevenson (ed.) *Child Welfare in the UK*, Oxford, Blackwell, pp. 62–76.

Hill, M. (1997) *Understanding Social Policy*, 5th edn, Oxford, Blackwell.

Hill, M., Murray, K. and Rankin, J. (1991) 'The early history of Scottish child welfare', *Children and Society*, vol. 5, no. 2, pp. 182–95.

Kemshall, H. (2002) *Risk, Social Policy and Welfare*, Buckingham, Open University Press.

King, M. (1997) *A Better World for Children: Explorations in Morality and Authority*, London, Routledge.

King, M. and Piper, C. (1990) *How the Law Thinks About Children*, Aldershot, Gower.

Lansdown, G. (1994) 'Children's rights', in Mayall B. (ed.), *Children's Childhood: Observed and Experienced*, London, Falmer Press, pp. 33–44.

Norrie, K. (2001) 'A child's right to care and protection', in A. Cleland and E. Sutherland (eds) *Children's Rights in Scotland*, 2nd edn, Edinburgh, W. Green, pp. 131–57.

Oliver, M. (1996) *Understanding Disability: From Theory to Practice*, London, Macmillan – now Palgrave Macmillan.

Parker, S. (1994) 'The best interests of the child – principles and problems', in P. Alston (ed.) *The Best Interests of the Child: Reconciling Culture and Human Rights*, Oxford, Oxford University Press, pp. 26–41.

Parton, N. (1999) 'Ideology, politics and policy', in O. Stevenson (ed.) *Child Welfare in the UK*, Oxford, Blackwell, pp. 3–21.

Parton, N. and Otway, O. (1995) 'The contemporary state of child protection policy and practice in England and Wales', *Children and Youth Services Review*, vol. 17, no. 5/6, pp. 599–617.

Plant, R. (1991) *Modern Political Thought*, Oxford, Blackwell.

Smith, G. (1980) *Social Need: Policy, Practice and Research*, London, Routledge.

Sutherland, E. (1999) *Child and Family Law*, Edinburgh, T. & T. Clark.

Tisdall, E.K.M. (1997) *The Children (Scotland) Act 1995 – Developing Law and Practice for Scotland's Children*, Edinburgh, The Stationery Office.

Tunstill, J. (1995) 'The concept of children in need: the answer or the problem for family support?', *Children and Youth Services Review*, vol. 17, no. 5/6, pp. 651–64.

Wheelaghan, S., Hill, M. and Tisdall, K. (1999) *Children's Services and the Voluntary Sector*, www.spsw.gla.ac.uk/centreforthechildandsociety/Baring.htm.

Wright, A. (2002) 'Children in need: an examination of the conceptual and applied definition in Scottish social service organisations', PhD thesis, University of Glasgow (forthcoming).

2

Legal Values and Social Work Values

JEREMY ROCHE

Introduction

Since the 1980s there has been much debate around the proper relationship between local authority social services decision-making and the law. This has been fuelled, in part at least, by a number of high-profile scandals which have raised questions about the quality of local authority decision-making as well as the rights of service users (Clyde Report, 1992). Major legislative changes in this period, for example the Children (Scotland) Act 1995 and the Social Work Scotland Act 1968 as amended by the National Health Service and Community Care Act 1990, have drawn on these debates and given rise to new ones. One result of this legislative activity and concern over social work practice has been a change in the place of law in social work education and training. The law used to be seen as only marginally relevant to social work education and practice whereas it has now become an issue of central importance.

In addition, despite the very different images associated with 'the law' on the one hand and social work on the other, there is significant common ground between the values underpinning social work practice and those values underpinning the law. These legal values include a respect for the individual, a commitment to formal equality, the ending of prejudice and discrimination and a concern with procedural fairness. While these are not the only legal values, increasingly issues of individual liberty and human rights are being highlighted within the legal agenda. This concern echoes that of social work's concern for the rights and interests of service users and its acceptance of the legitimacy of proper forms of accountability.

Thus I argue that there is much in the law, in terms of its rules and procedures, that can be supportive of social work; this includes the law's insistence on certain forms of accountability. The law, and the associated language of rights, should be seen by social work as a critical friend or partner. In this chapter I consider the recent history of the relationship between the law and social work before moving on to explore social work values and images of law. I then analyse the importance of the language of rights and conclude via a consideration of why law and the language of rights should be seen as valuable by social workers and service users alike.

Social work and the law

There are three aspects of the social work and law relationship which require some introductory comment. First, the law provided the mandate for social work practice in that it accorded the local authority wide-ranging discretionary powers to intervene and regulate family life, for example to protect children. In relation to social work education however the law was not seen as important (Vernon *et al.*, 1990) and 'good practice' did not see the law as a key reference point. In other words the law provided the authority upon which professional social work activity took place and within which professional discretion could be exercised, yet the law itself and knowledge of the law were not seen as integral to social work practice on a day-to-day basis.

Second, as noted above, in the 1980s and 1990s, in part as a result of a series of scandals about the ways in which local authorities discharged their social service functions, the relationship between social work and the law was radically redrawn. Now knowledge of the law was seen as fundamental to good practice. The law thus acquired an ever-increasing importance within social work education as well as day-to-day professional practice. However, many social workers see the law as complicated, lawyers as unsympathetic if not hostile and the courts as unwelcoming and inappropriate environments for dealing with the complex human problems which lie at the centre of social work practice (King and Trowell, 1992). Nonetheless the ways in which professional social workers see and understand the law is important to their practice.

Third, the courts are in the position of standing in judgement on social work decision-making. It is important to acknowledge that the calling of social work practice to account, which is integral to many cases, can be very unsettling and uncomfortable for the social work professionals involved. However, from the service user perspective legal accountability might bring some benefits: for example, as a result of making a complaint an earlier decision might be reversed and much-needed services received, services which the service user believed they were entitled to in the first place. This positive aspect of the law is important and it is not just about increased local authority accountability. Some social workers have acquired a competence in operating in the court system and in acting as advocates, and are thus better able to advance the interests of service users.

So the law has come to assume a significance to social work practice that would have been hard to predict in the early 1980s. Social work students are now required to demonstrate their competence in applying the law and the Scottish Social Services Council Code of Practice for Social Service Workers refers to social service workers being required to 'protect the rights and promote the interests of service users and carers'. The argument of this chapter is that this is not merely a technical activity but an ethical one: an ethical activity framed by disagreements over values both within social work and the law.

Social work values

There are a number of different ways in which social work values are written about in the social work literature. In the CCETSW *Revised Rules and Requirements* (1995) the section on 'Values of Social Work' made it clear that meeting the core competences could only be achieved through the satisfaction of the value requirements. The position was that 'values are integral to rather than separate from competent practice' (p. 18) and 'practice must be founded on, informed by and capable of being judged against a clear value base'. The values requirements included the requirement that students 'identify and question their own values and prejudices and their implications for practice' and 'promote people's rights to choice, privacy, confidentiality and protection, while recognising and addressing the complexities of competing rights and demands'. These are self-evidently complex and contradictory tasks; for example, the promotion of the client's right to privacy may conflict with another client's right to protection and both may be shaped by the social worker's own values.

The Scottish Social Services Council Code of Practice for Social

Service Workers resembles the CCETSW *Rules and Requirements* (Scottish Social Services Council, 2002). While the language is at times different it is clear that a positive respect for the rights and interests of service users is common to both documents, as is the promotion of the independence of service users whilst ensuring they are protected. The Code of Practice also emphasises the issue of public trust and confidence in social services. What is distinctive about the Code of Practice is the possibility that a social services worker might be deregistered as a result of failing to comply with the code. Yet the code, like the CCETSW text, is written at such a level of generality that its scope is not clear and there is little recognition of the potential conflict within the code's own professional conduct and practice requirements. For example, the meaning of respecting 'the rights of service users while seeking to ensure that their behaviour does not harm themselves or other people' is not straightforward and rapidly assumes complexity when considered in a particular instance.

Braye and Preston-Shoot (1997) see the value base as central to social work but also see its definition as open. It might refer to 'a commitment to respect for persons, equal opportunity and meeting needs' or more radically as a 'concern with social rights, equality and citizenship' (p. 59). They are not the only commentators who have identified an uncertainty in the meaning of social work's value base. Banks has observed that 'values' is 'one of those words that tends to be used rather vaguely and has a variety of different meanings' (1995, p. 4). However, Shardlow (1998) takes the argument further. It is not just a question of the openness or vagueness of the word 'values'; he argues (1998) that 'no consensus exists about value questions in social work' (p. 23). He refers to debates within social work over whether the contract culture empowers clients, the extent to which social work is predicated on a respect for the individual person, the significance of ideology in social work (for example, the impact of feminism on social work knowledge and practice in the 1980s and 1990s) and the extent to which social workers should be held responsible when something goes wrong (p. 24). Shardlow writes:

> These debates are inevitably open-ended where social work itself is intrinsically political, controversial and contested, and where the nature of practice is subject to constant change. (1998, p. 24)

The controversial and changing nature of social work's value base is taken up by Smith (1997), who argues that the application of values is not without difficulty and notes the change in 'values talk' that has taken place, for example the reference to service users rather than clients. Nonetheless whatever the significance of such shifts in language Smith argues it is still the case that respect for persons and self-determination remain central to social work practice (1997, p. 5). The complexity of the social work task relates in part to how the professional social worker negotiates the tension between these values and the decision-making dilemmas that are integral to social work. Smith's concern is that 'rights are in danger of becoming dislocated from values' such that values become invisible; what is required is a confirmation of the relationship in particular terms (1997, p. 6). While Smith sees values and rights as conceptually distinct she also sees in the idea of fundamental human need, itself predicated upon respect for the person, a positive link in the values–rights relationship. She argues that a renewed commitment to values does not entail ignoring rights (1997, p. 12) and that values and rights are proper partners in the social work project.

So it is possible to identify agreement on three issues. First, there is no dispute that values are central to social work practice. Second, these values are at times contradictory and in themselves do not resolve the dilemmas inherent in the social work task. Third, there have been significant changes since the 1980s, one of which is the increasing importance accorded to law within the education and practice of social workers.

This said, there is almost a note of regret in the writing as if social work has taken a wrong turning. As the law has come to assume a greater importance both in social work education and practice, with increasing accountability to the courts, some would argue that it is this trend which threatens to undermine good practice. How can the social workers get on with the job if they are always having to look over their shoulder? The complaint is that 'defensive practice' is the result of law's new prominence, of the new relationship between the social work profession and the courts. However, this is only one dimension of the law–social work relationship and one that is constantly subject to change; before exploring this further I want to consider some key images of law and the significance of the language of rights.

Images of law

Just as there is debate about the values underpinning social work and how these find expression (or not) in everyday practice, likewise the law is properly characterised by contest and change.

There are a number of ways of seeing the law. The law can be viewed as a means by which the socio-economic status quo is maintained and guaranteed. The machinery of justice can be viewed as a charade or a genuine attempt to grapple with complex issues and arrive, however imperfectly, at a reasoned decision. Judges can be seen as disinterested adjudicators of disputes whose only allegiance is to the law or as biased individuals whose decisions reflect their class interests and preferences. The law can also be seen as a champion of the unprivileged and dispossessed. Within this tradition contests around the law are part of the struggle for social justice, for example for equal treatment. Williams sees law and the language of rights as playing a part in the fight against discrimination:

> For the historically disempowered, the conferring of rights is symbolic of all the denied aspects of their humanity: rights imply a respect that places one in the referential range of self and others, that elevates one's status from human body to social being. (Williams, 1991, p. 153)

This progressive imagery of law is strangely absent from social work. So the law is not just about, for example, the right to property – it also concerns human rights such as the right to liberty and the right to a fair trial. In this sense the law concerns us all, irrespective of our social identity and location. When it comes to discussing the meaning of rights there is no less debate. Positivists argue that the law is simply those rules laid down by the proper law-making procedures. So there is no necessary moral content to the law – in the past different legal regimes have sanctioned slavery, others have emphasised the 'rights of man'. For Utilitarian thinkers like Bentham the question of 'what the law is' is distinct from the question of 'what the law ought to be'. A critique of the law was not to be confused with an accurate account of what was the law. However events in the twentieth century rendered this neat distinction problematic. The state in Nazi Germany had all the trappings of the rule of law (referred to as the 'tinsel of legality') and yet unimaginable horrors were committed. Natural law thinkers like Fuller and Dworkin argued that unless the law satisfied certain criteria in terms of its content and procedures it could not properly be called law. While Fuller (1969) was mainly concerned with procedural questions – for example were the rules of law known to those who were required to obey them, were they comprehensible and was obedience to them possible? – Dworkin addressed the issues of law's content. Dworkin (1980) argued that, in a democracy, individuals require rights and that the interests of the minority cannot be sacrificed to those of the majority. He then argued that such a belief in the importance of rights requires a respect for persons and a commitment to political equality. It is this commitment to an equality of concern and respect which makes rights so important. While Dworkin does concede that there are circumstances in which rights can be overridden, for example because it is necessary in order to uphold another's rights or the costs of not doing so are excessive, it is only if rights are seen as special that there can be said to be any real constraint on the power of government.

This argument is important because it opens up a number of issues, two of which concern us here. First, it alerts us to debates surrounding state power. When the state proposes new legislation in the field of social care it often raises controversial issues concerning, for example, a redistribution of resources or new powers intervening in the private sphere. Second, it serves as a reminder that when we are talking about social work and the law we are also talking about human relationships in which a commitment to an equality of concern and respect is important. However, what also needs to be made explicit is the idea that the public power of the state might be needed in order to correct a past injustice, to prevent discriminatory and oppressive behaviour in the 'here and now' and to practically and symbolically signal that certain forms of behaviour are not acceptable. All legal systems have a value base. The important question about the law is what are the values upon which the laws are built. Some legal regimes have been built on values which were explicitly discriminatory, for example the law in apartheid South Africa or the legal regime in Nazi Germany. In the UK the law, with the passing of the Human Rights Act 1998, has embraced more directly the fundamental freedoms in the European Convention on Human Rights (ECHR). These freedoms are commonly associated with parliamentary democracies, for example the right to a fair trial and the right to family life, both of which are of central concern to social work practice. As a result of s.6 of the Human Rights Act 1998 no public authority can 'act in a way which is incompatible with a Convention right'. In addition in Scotland the Scottish Parliament is not permitted to pass any legislation which is incompatible with the rights contained in the ECHR.

The question of rights

However, according to some, rights talk does not progress the interests of the disadvantaged in our society. The Critical Legal Studies movement argues that rights talk is unable to address structural oppression and often serves to depoliticise social issues (Glendon, 1991). For some feminists the law and the language of rights is suspect. Smart (1989), while recognising the role that rights rhetoric has played in the history of the women's movement, believes that its potential is 'exhausted' – indeed it may even make things worse now. Feminist critiques of rights analysis include the charge that they are abstract, impersonal and atomistic and that they induce conflict. Others suggest that rights talk 'obscures male dominance' while its strategic implementation 'reinforces a patriarchal status quo and, in effect, abandons women to their rights' (Kiss, 1997, p. 2). Perhaps the most sustained arguments against the language of rights come from those who, influenced by the work of Gilligan (1982), 'embrace an ethic of care' with which they seek 'to supplement or even supplant' the ethic of rights. The ethic of care is based on the idea of connectedness and thus focuses on caring as moral action (see further Tronto, 1993 and Hekman, 1995). As such an ethic of care is as concerned with welfare as it is with justice –what is important is the ambiguity and context of the action in question, not simply the application of abstract legal principles. Thus the proper response to dependency and vulnerability is a rethinking of caring relationships. Sevenhuijsen argues for the recognition of vulnerability to be 'incorporated into the concept of a "normal" subject in politics' (1998, p. 146). However she observes:

> Clearer ideas about what constitutes necessary care can be gained by granting those who are the 'object' of care cognitive authority over their needs and giving them the opportunity to express these in a heterogeneous public sphere which allows open and honest debate. (Sevenhuijsen, 1998, p. 146)

Minow and Shanley (1997) agree with feminist critics of rights theory 'that a political theory inattentive to relationships of care and connection between and among people cannot adequately address many themes and issues facing families' (p. 99). Nonetheless they go on to observe that rights-based views require 'public articulation of the kinds of freedoms that deserve protection and the qualities of human dignity that warrant societal support' and that 'rights articulate relationships among people' (ibid.).

There are thus a number of important distinctions to be made about the different ways in which rights are considered. First, at a theoretical level rights can be a source of protection, they allow you to make claims on others, for example for services, and they allow people to change relationships, for example divorce law. Kiss argues that rights can also be seen as being concerned with mutual obligations:

> There is nothing isolating about a right to vote, to form associations, or to receive free childhood immunisations. And while many rights, like political rights and rights to free expression, do enable people to express conflicts, they also create a framework for social co-opera-tion . . . Rights define a moral community; having rights means that my interests, aspirations and vulnerabilities matter enough to impose duties on others. (Kiss, 1997, p. 5)

Kiss (1997, p. 7) argues that the problem is not so much with rights but with 'the tendency to cast the state in the role of exclusive rights violator'; employers, service users and colleagues can all threaten one's rights. What we need to consider is the effect of rights – whether they make a practical and valuable difference to people's lives and the quality of their relationships. Braye and Preston-Shoot, in their discussion of social work and the law in England and Wales, provide the following instance in which it is social work and its organisational and managerial context which is undermining social work values rather than the law. They write:

> Social Workers attending law workshops have recounted experiences of being instructed not to inform service users of their rights, and of users being charged for services which fall outside the legal mandate to charge. (Braye and Preston-Shoot, 1998, p. 58)

It is clear from their discussion that they see part of the social work task as having the skills to challenge unfair or illegal policies and procedures. Good practice at the very least presupposes a respect for service users and their rights.

Conclusion

Social work and law are properly characterised as contested and multi-ple discourses. The value of law and rights resides not in the idea that the law has the answer or that the language of rights makes social conflict disappear – on the contrary the latter is a key part of making it visible. Rights talk is the language in which differently positioned people can articulate their own definitions of their needs and interests.

Thus I would argue that law and the language of rights is a necessary but not sufficient condition for good practice. As Banks argues:

> The law does not tell us what we ought to do, just what we can do ... most decisions in social work involve a complex interaction of ethical, political, technical and legal issues which are all interconnected. (Banks, 1995, p. 11)

The law by itself cannot and does not provide a clear guide to action in a whole host of complex circumstances. To argue that it did would be to misrepresent the importance of law. The law is open-textured and contested and when this is considered alongside the detail of social work decision-making it is clear that the law cannot and does not provide the answer. Rather it provides the frame within which social work knowledge is applied. Nor, it must be conceded, does the law always provide an immediate practical remedy – often, some would say too often, the law lags behind in failing to support anti-oppressive practice. Thus at times the law might deny the legitimacy of a claim, for example proscribe discrimination on the basis of age. At other times, however, it is not the law which fails to provide a remedy, it is the actions of officials working within the authority of the law which deny the remedy, for example police inaction over instances of domestic violence. However, because the law can be seen as among other things an expression of the power of the state to meet certain outcomes and one which can be mobilised to secure a wide range of objectives, it is important not to underestimate its power. Individual decisions of courts, some existing practices of the legal system and indeed some statutory provision might all be vulnerable to criticism when considered in the context of social work's commitment to respect for persons and self-determination. Yet like social work itself the law is the site of contest and debate and the point that must not be lost sight of is that one of the distinctive aspects of modern developments is the deployment of the language of rights by service users and service user organisations.

For social work the relation between social work values and rights need not be seen in negative terms. This is not to deny that there are court decisions which disadvantage the socially marginal or to claim that recourse should always be had to courts and lawyers. It is to recognise that for some service users and professionals the language of rights is the only means by which their perspective can be heard. The language of care might not allow the object of care to break free of their dependent, being-cared-for status; they may not be able to exercise 'cognitive authority over their needs'. The language of rights is also about values – this is not necessarily in the form of a preferred list of 'correct' values but through the recognition of different viewpoints and through the hearing of different and perhaps unfamiliar voices on questions of need and respect.

References

Banks, S. (1995) *Ethics and Values in Social Work*, London, Macmillan – now Palgrave Macmillan.

Braye, S. and Preston-Shoot, M. (1997) *Practising Social Work Law*, London, Macmillan – now Palgrave Macmillan.

Clyde Report (1992) *The Report of the Inquiry into the Removal of Children from Orkney in February 1991*, Edinburgh, HMSO.

Dworkin, R. (1980) *Taking Rights Seriously*, London, Duckworth.

Fuller, L. (1969) *The Morality of Law*, New Haven, Conn., Yale University Press.

Gilligan, C. (1982) *In a Different Voice: Psychological Theory and Women's Development*, Cambridge, Mass., Harvard University Press.

Glendon, M. (1991) *Rights Talk: The Impoverishment of Political Discourse*, New York, Free Press.

Hekman, S. (1995) *Moral Voices, Moral Selves*, Cambridge, Polity Press.

King, M. and Trowell, J. (1992) *Children's Welfare and the Law: The Limits of Legal Intervention*, London, Sage.

Kiss, E. (1997) 'Alchemy or fool's gold? Assessing feminist doubts about rights', in M. Shanley and U. Narayan (eds) *Reconstructing Political Theory: Feminist Perspectives*, Cambridge, Polity Press, pp. 1–24.

Minow, M. and Shanley, M. (1997) 'Revisioning the family: relational rights and responsibilities', in M. Shanley and U. Narayan (eds) *Reconstructing Political Theory: Feminist Perspectives*, Cambridge, Polity Press, pp. 84–108.

Scottish Social Services Council (2002) *Code of Practice for Social Service Workers*, Edinburgh, SSSC.

Sevenhuijsen, S. (1998) *Citizenship and the Ethics of Care: Feminist Considerations on Justice, Morality and Politics*, London, Routledge.

Shardlow, S. (1998) 'Values, ethics and social work', in R. Adams, L. Dominelli and M. Payne (eds) *Social Work: Themes, Issues and Critical Debates*, London, Macmillan – now Palgrave Macmillan, pp. 23–33.

Smart, C. (1989) *Feminism and the Power of Law*, London, Routledge.

Smith, C. (1997) 'Children's rights: have carers abandoned values?', *Children and Society*, vol. 11, pp. 3–15.

Tronto, J. (1993) *Moral Boundaries*, London, Routledge.

Vernon, S., Harris, R. and Ball, C. (1990) *Towards Social Work Law: Legally Competent Professional Practice*, London, CCETSW (CCETSW Paper 4.2).

Williams, P. (1991) *The Alchemy of Race and Rights*, Cambridge, Mass., Harvard University Press.

3

Social Work Practice and the Human Rights Act 1998

KATHRYN CAMERON

This chapter looks at the impact of the European Convention on Human Rights (ECHR) on the practice of social workers and at the ways in which practitioners can try to ensure that their practice is compliant with the Convention. It will not be possible in this chapter to give an exhaustive account of specific ways in which practice will be affected by the Act. Instead, some broad principles will be outlined with some illustrations being given from particular areas of practice.

The Human Rights Act (HRA) 1998 came into force for the whole of the United Kingdom in October 2000 and gave further effect to the European Convention on Human Rights and Fundamental Freedoms. However, it had been in force in Scotland since 1998. The Scotland Act 1998 laid down that all the actions of the Scottish Parliament and the Scottish Executive had to be in compliance with the terms of the HRA. The HRA has profound implications for social work practice. Two sections of the Act in particular will have a major impact. Section 3 of the Act states that primary legislation (statutes) and secondary legislation (statutory instruments) must be read and given effect in a way that is compatible with the Convention rights and s.6 of the Act states that 'it is unlawful for a public authority to act in any way which is incompatible with a Convention right'. This means, in essence, that the actions of social services departments must conform to each of the articles of the ECHR. Failure to conform could result in an authority being found in breach and liable for damages.

Social workers are for the most part employed by local authorities and derive their mandate to practise from statute. Their actions, as agents of a public authority, will, therefore, come under the scrutiny of the Convention. Voluntary organisations are in a more ambiguous position because they are not public authorities although they often perform public functions.

Social work has always had at the core of its concerns a commitment to respect the rights of individuals and groups. As is stated in *Human Rights and Social Work* (1994):

> Human Rights are inseparable from social work theory, values and ethics and practice. (United Nations, 1994, p. 5)

Therefore, it could be argued that all policies and procedures of social services departments should have reflected good social work practice and should have met the requirements of the ECHR even before the passing of the Human Rights Act in 1998. However, there is now an obligation on all social services workers to take account of the ECHR in their work with service users. In addition, social workers in Scotland will have to abide by the new Code of Practice for Social Services Workers (Scottish Social Services Council, 2002) that has been issued by the Scottish Social Services Council. This code describes the standards of professional conduct and practice required of social services workers. The first paragraph of the code states that social services workers must protect the rights and promote the interests of service users. They should do this by treating each person as an individual and supporting the service user's rights to control their lives and make informed choices about the services they receive. They are also required to respect and maintain the dignity and privacy of service users. The requirements of the Code of Conduct mirror in many respects those of the Convention and together they give social workers a very clear blueprint for practice which is both ethically sound and fulfils the demands of the Human Rights Act 1998.

The articles of the Convention are as follows:

Article 2: Everyone's right to life will be protected by law
Article 3: No one shall be subjected to torture or to inhuman or degrading treatment or punishment
Article 4: Prohibition of slavery and forced labour
Article 5: Everyone has a right to liberty and security of person
Article 6: Everyone is entitled to a fair and public hearing
Article 8: Everyone has a right to respect for his [*sic*] private and

family life, his home and his correspondence
Article 7: No punishment without law
Article 9: Everyone has the right to freedom of thought, conscience and religion
Article 10: Everyone has a right to freedom of expression
Article 11: Everyone has a right to freedom of assembly and association
Article 12: Men and women of marriageable age have the right to marry and found a family
Article 14: Prohibition of discrimination

Some of these rights are absolute in that they cannot be balanced against the public interest. Article 2, the right to life, and Article 3, which prohibits torture, fall into this category. Others are limited in that rights may be restricted under explicit circumstances. An example of this is Article 5 which limits the right to liberty in certain defined ways. Others are qualified (Articles 8–11) in that interference is permissible only if it is in accordance with the law and is necessary in a democratic society. In other words, a balance has to be struck between the interests of the individual and those of society.

The principle of proportionality is an important one for workers to understand. This principle allows for actions to be taken which are, on the face of it, contrary to the demands of the ECHR. Proportionality allows a public authority to interfere with the rights of others so long as the actions taken are in accordance with the law and if the objective is to protect others. However, the action taken has to be proportionate to the aim to be achieved. For example, Article 8 lays down that there is a right to privacy and family life. That right may be interfered with if children are seen to be at risk and, in order to protect them, a decision is made to remove them from their carers. A decision has to be made which balances the right of the child to be protected from harm against the rights of the parents to have the privacy of their family life respected. Workers may have to ask themselves if the child could be protected by another kind of action being taken, for example by putting appropriate amounts of support into the home and working closely with the parents to help them with their parenting role. If this has been tried and has not worked and the child remains at risk, then it could be argued that the response to remove the child is proportionate to the aim of protecting the child.

An example of the principle of proportionality can be found in the case of *P, C and S* v. *UK* [2002] 2FLR 631. This involved a case where a child was at birth removed from her mother who had been diagnosed with Munchausen syndrome by proxy in relation to an older child who now resided with his father. Among other things, the court noted that the local authority had a legitimate cause for concern about the child but thought that the removal of a child from her mother at birth required exceptional justification. The court also questioned if the child might have been able to spend time in hospital with her mother under supervision. The court concluded that the draconian step had not been supported by relevant and sufficient reasons and it could not have been regarded as having been necessary in a democratic society for the purpose of safeguarding the child. The court, therefore, found that there had been a breach of the parents' rights under Article 8.

Before October 2000 when the HRA came into force, individuals who were unhappy with the decisions made about them by social services departments and who had used the procedures available to them within the system to challenge these decisions (for example, a couple whose application to adopt a child was turned down by the Adoption Panel), but where there was no legal remedy, had the option to use the process of judicial review. This process is still available but it is somewhat cumbersome and has to be pursued through the Court of Session. The applicants have to base their case on the grounds that the decision taken was illegal, procedurally unfair or irrational. The petition of Arthur McGregor (2000), who sought a judicial review of the decision of South Lanarkshire Council to delay the provision of a place for him in a nursing home, illustrates the procedure. Mr McGregor, aged 90, was assessed in terms of s.12A of the Social Work (Scotland) Act 1968 and a care plan identified the need for a secure environment as the best way of meeting his needs. However, he was not offered a place immediately and was placed on a waiting list. In this case the Outer House of the Court of Session found in favour of Mr McGregor and required the local authority to make provision of appropriate nursing care. The HRA 1998 has extended the options open to individuals. They can now go to court to determine whether or not their human rights have been breached and they can seek redress for this breach including being awarded damages. The case just described could now also be challenged in court on the basis that there had been a breach of Mr McGregor's human rights, in particular Article 3, that he had suffered inhuman and degrading treatment. In addition, the Act provides for individuals to allege that their rights have been breached in any legal proceedings in which they are involved. For example, in an adoption hearing, birth parents might argue that they had not been fully involved in the decision-making prior to the adoption and that the social services department had not given them a fair hearing in terms of Article 6.

As noted earlier, s.3 of the HRA 1998 requires UK courts to interpret statutes in accordance with the Convention and this includes those passed before the date on which the Act came into force. A consequence of this is that the actions of social workers in the present and future could be scrutinised in the light of the articles of the ECHR. Further, where there are ongoing legal proceedings, actions by the local authority predating the HRA 1998 may also be scrutinised. It could be argued that if decisions were made fairly, and needs were balanced one against the other and all parties were consulted and involved in the decision-making, then the decisions should stand up to scrutiny. In other words, if the values were sound and good practice was in evidence throughout, there is nothing to be feared.

At present, it would appear that many practitioners and their managers are unsure of the demands which the Act places on them. Many abrogate the responsibility to their legal departments in the fond hope that the local authority's lawyers will keep them abreast of whatever they need to know to ensure that their practice reflects the requirements of the Convention. However, it is not enough to shrug off personal accountability. Each worker has a responsibility to service users to ensure that their practice is sound and they will have to ask themselves if their practice reflects social work values and the requirements of the Code of Practice and is also compliant with the ECHR. What social workers should not do, however, is develop defensive practice which is about Convention-proofing their work. If they uphold the social work values of respect, partnership and anti-discriminatory practice then it should follow that their practice will, *ipso facto*, be compliant with the ECHR.

The *Core Guidance for Public Authorities* (Home Office, 2000) makes some suggestions about the kind of questions which practitioners need to ask themselves about aspects of their practice which may help them to identify those areas of intervention which might require some thought about the impact of the Act. They include:

- Does my work involve me in making decisions which impinge on someone's private rights?
- Does my work affect a person's physical or mental well-being?
- Does my work affect a person's private or family life?

- Does my work involve me in drawing up procedures which will be used in the determination of cases?

If the answer is 'yes' to any of these questions, then the Human Rights Act 1998 applies and consideration must be given to whether or not practice is compatible with the articles of the ECHR.

One useful way of examining the practice of social work might be to look at it, not in terms of work with specific groups of service users, but rather as a process which goes through a series of well-defined stages. These stages could be broadly identified as assessment, action and evaluation. This description should not be taken as a definitive theoretical position but rather as a device which allows for an examination of practice in terms of the possible ways in which the ECHR might impact but not from the perspective of the knowledge and skills which would be exercised.

Assessment

Assessment is a critical part of the whole social work task. Coulshed and Orme provide a clear definition of assessment:

> Assessment is an ongoing process, in which the client participates, whose purpose is to understand people in relation to their environments; it is a basis for planning what needs to be done to maintain, improve or bring about change in the person, the environment or both. (Coulshed and Orme, 1998, p. 21)

This description addresses the centrality of the participation of the service user which is pivotal to human rights-based practice. The client's views must be properly considered in the assessment process and social workers will need to develop ways of ensuring that service users can participate fully in the process in which they are involved. This will ensure that the service user's right to a fair hearing in terms of Article 6 will be upheld. The department might also be in breach of Article 6 if everyone who should be involved in the assessment process has not been given an opportunity to be heard. Article 14 may also have relevance in that failure to involve someone may be construed as discrimination.

The position of unmarried fathers is particularly relevant here. Unmarried fathers in terms of the Children (Scotland) Act 1995 do not have parental rights unless they have entered into an s.4 agreement with the mother of the child or have been awarded parental rights and responsibilities by a court in terms of s.11. It could be argued that the fact that they do not constitutes a breach of Article 8 (respect for private and family life) together with Article 14 which prohibits discrimination. Nonetheless, as the ECHR is a 'living instrument', in other words it should be interpreted in the light of present-day conditions, social workers should give careful consideration to any decision not to involve unmarried fathers in decisions affecting their children.

Assessment forms will need to be scrutinised to ensure that they are drafted in a way that allows clients sufficient scope to provide full information about their situation. The assessment process should always be meticulously recorded. While this will enable social workers to address possible allegations that they have breached an individual's rights, it will also enable service users to have access to the information on which decisions were based. This would meet the Convention requirement of Equality of Arms which lays down the need for fairness in proceedings and this extends to the requirement that individuals should have access to reports concerning them. Workers will also have to ensure that every assessment has been carried out in a way which is sensitive and respectful. If it has not, there could be a breach of Article 8. Respect for family life does not just mean in relation to that part of the assessment which takes place in the family home. It covers all stages of the process – in a hospital ward, in the local office or in a residential home. Privacy also extends to confidentiality of records. Consideration will have to be given to the way in which information is sought from and given to third parties. This will extend to inter-professional discussions and case conferences which are part of the assessment process.

Action

Action can be further divided into decision-making and intervention.

Decision-making

Evidence of decision-making as a consequence of assessment will be very important. Decisions must be made in a way that ensures that there is no breach of Articles 6, 8 and 14. Questions such as who is involved in decision-making and how these decisions are recorded should be addressed. All decision-making by local authorities may be examined and assessed to see if it is in accord with the principles of the ECHR; any decision that involves the use of discretion could be especially open to challenge. Transparency is crucial. The issue of values is of particular significance whenever social workers are involved in situations in which they have to use discretion. All social workers must be aware of the value base which underpins their practice and which is congruent with the Articles of the Convention. Connections with Articles 6, 8 and 14 are particularly strong and highlight the complementarity of the expectations placed on social workers by the Code of Practice and the ECHR.

One of the areas which might be particularly vulnerable to scrutiny and where discretion is a significant feature is the decision-making in relation to community care. In such cases, social workers undertake assessments for community care services and often have to make difficult decisions in relation to balancing need against the availability of resources. Social services departments will have established eligibility criteria against which individuals are being assessed. They will have to ensure that there is fairness in the decision reached and that individuals have had the opportunity to be heard and to make an input to the decision in terms of the requirements of Article 6. This might involve the use of representatives or advocates and there will have to be care that there is no discrimination in the decision which is reached. In addition, if there are carers involved in providing substantial amounts of care, their needs will have to be assessed and their views taken into account to ensure compliance with Articles 6 and 8. Taking account of the need to respect family privacy is also a significant feature of community care assessments.

The question will have to be asked about how appropriate it is to deny services on the basis of eligibility criteria because this denial might breach Article 3. The denial of services could mean that someone is left to suffer cruel and inhuman treatment because, for example, a place is not made available for them in a residential facility. It may be that departmental policies, which are designed to cover a range of situations, are no longer appropriate. Convention rights are in essence personal rights and so they reinforce the need for assessments to be individually tailored. This will have particular significance for assessments undertaken in terms of s.12A of the Social Work (Scotland) Act 1968. Schwehr (2001) thinks that the balance of decision-making may have to shift 'away from generally applicable policies to a closer consideration of individual cases and wishes rather than just meeting the local authority criteria for "needs" ' (p. 78).

If the assessment being undertaken relates to children and their family, care must be taken to ensure that the parents and/or relevant persons have been give appropriate opportunities to be involved in the decision-making process. If they have not, the authority may be in breach of Article 6. Just inviting them to a case conference or to a looked-after child review might not be sufficient. If, for example, parents have learning disabilities, they may need the services of an advocate to help them to put over their case. Reasonable arrangements will, therefore, have to be made to ensure that they have a fair hearing. Courts are now being asked to consider cases where parents allege that there has been a breach of their human rights, in particular Article 6, because they were not advised of plans for their children and were not adequately involved in the decision-making processes.

Intervention

Various forms of intervention may arise as a consequence of the decision-making process following assessment. One of the questions which the practitioner needs to ask is the degree to which the planned intervention affects someone's private or family life. There are a number of decisions which could fall into this category such as a decision to remove a child from their home; the removal of an elderly person from their home into residential care; putting services into a home either to support parents' care for their children or to enable someone with physical or mental disabilities to remain in their own home. Such decisions would have to be made with the provisions of Article 8 in mind. Any one of these activities interferes with an individual's right to privacy, but the question which social workers need to ask themselves is if the 'interference' is in accordance with the law, in respect of a legitimate aim and proportionate in respect of that aim. In other words, in the case of the removal of an elderly, frail individual to residential care because of concerns for their safety and that of others, is this move a proportionate response or could the concerns be addressed in other ways such as putting in an package of care which allows for a high level of monitoring at different hours of the day and night, if necessary? If a decision is made to keep someone in hospital pending a bed becoming available in a suitable residential facility, this could constitute a breach of Article 3 because it represents cruel and inhuman treatment but also might breach Article 5 because it is tantamount to restricting that person's liberty.

Often social workers are involved in making decisions which have to balance the rights of individuals to autonomy against a need to protect them. This balancing act may involve making decisions which are potentially in breach of Convention rights. For example, doors may be locked in a residential home for older people to prevent individual residents from wandering away and electronic tagging may be considered as a way of monitoring the whereabouts of people with dementia. These actions could be interpreted as being examples of cruel and inhuman treatment, but it might also be argued that the legitimate aim is to protect the individual and that the action is, therefore, proportionate to that aim.

The use of secure accommodation amounts to a restriction of liberty in terms of Article 5 and so requires to be justified under one of the exceptions to that article. The only one applying to children is Article 5(1)(d) which states that detention is only allowed for the purposes of education. The term 'education' has been given broad interpretation (*'W' Borough Council* v. *K & Ors* (Court of Appeal (Civil Division)), 15 November 2000) and can encompass the general development of a child's physical, intellectual, emotional and social abilities, and so the use of secure accommodation as part of a supervision requirement (in terms of s.70 of the Children (Scotland) Act 1995) would seem to be justified. However, Norrie (2001, p. 153) has described this situation as 'one of the most significant shortcomings in Scots law'. The children's hearing merely authorises the use of secure accommodation. Decisions to actually place a child in secure accommodation are made by the head of the establishment and the chief social worker and there is no provision for the child and their representative to be heard. Such decisions may, therefore, be open to challenge because they are in breach of the right to a fair trial (Article 6).

In exercising their powers under the Adults with Incapacity (Scotland) Act 2001, practitioners may be involved in making decisions which will have the potential to affect the freedom and civil liberties of individuals. In a situation where someone is under a guardianship order, returning that person to residential care so that medication can be given could be seen as a breach of Articles 3, 5 and 8. Social services workers in this field will frequently face dilemmas in relation to the assessment and management of risk in which they have to balance the right to protection against the deprivation of civil liberties.

However, it is important for social services workers to be aware that failure to act also contravenes the requirements of the Convention. The decision of the European Court of Human Rights in *Z and others* v. *UK*

[2000] 2FLR 612 makes this clear. The case involved children who had sued Bedfordshire County Council because of its failure to take care proceedings. As a result of this failure, the children had suffered abuse and neglect at the hands of their parents. Although the House of Lords found that the local authority should not be liable, the European Court of Human Rights came to a different conclusion. It found that there had been a breach of Article 3 in that the neglect suffered by the children had reached the threshold of inhuman and degrading treatment and that the local authority had failed in its duty to protect individuals from such treatment. The European Court thus specified that there was a duty on local authorities to act and stated that failure to act could in itself constitute a breach of the Convention. It is crucial, therefore, that workers examine the decisions they make even when they decide that no action at all should be taken.

It is not within the remit of this chapter to explore the possible breaches of Convention rights which may be present within the criminal justice system, such as whether or not electronic tagging of offenders might constitute cruel and inhuman treatment and also interfere with the right to respect for private and family life. However, there are aspects of social work within that setting which could be open to scrutiny. If, for example, an offender is on a probation order and the supervising officer makes a decision to initiate breach proceedings, before he or she is reported to the court every endeavour will have to be made to ensure that the offender has been given a fair hearing in terms of Article 6. The offender could also argue that he or she is being punished for actions which were not criminal, contrary to Article 7 (no punishment without law). However, breach proceedings are in accordance with the law and the appropriate penalty for a breach is made by a court acting as an independent and impartial tribunal.

Evaluation

> Professionals must seek to ensure that their interventions are not only carried out with due competence and in good faith, but are effective in the sense that they lead to the desired outcomes. (Clark, 2000, p. 56)

Practice needs to be evaluated not only in terms of effectiveness and accountability, but also now from the perspective of whether it failed in any of its aspects to address issues of human rights. The questions which were posed in the guidance to local authorities (Home Office, 2000) will need to be revisited to check if practice was compliant with the ECHR. If it was not, then practitioners will need to consider if the non-compliance was as a result of their failure to consider rights. However, practitioners may conclude that their practice was sound but that they had to operate within the constraints of policies or procedures, which in themselves failed to meet the requirements of the Convention. If the latter situation pertains, then practitioners will have to challenge their managers. As Schwehr suggests, the Human Rights Act 'can provide a bulwark against the worst excesses of managerialism run wild' (2001, p. 80).

Conclusion

While the Human Rights Act might be seen as adding another layer to the increasingly complex task faced by social services workers and creating another pitfall which they have to avoid, this is a very negative approach. The Act should not be seen as a threat, but rather as something which provides positive benefits for both workers and service users. Social work practice has always been concerned with trying to uphold and defend the rights of individuals and groups while attempting to meet their needs. It has been concerned with balancing rights in situations of conflict and weighing up risk against protection and the need for autonomy. The ECHR should be seen as a benchmark against which practice is measured. It is an instrument that should promote good practice and enable social services workers to empower service users and help them to challenge authorities who jeopardise their rights.

References

Clark, C. (2000) *Social Work Ethics*, Basingstoke, Palgrave Macmillan.

Coulshed, V. and Orme, J. (1998) *Social Work Practice*, 3rd edn, London, Macmillan – now Palgrave Macmillan.

Home Office (2000) *Human Rights Act: Core Guidance for Public Authorities: A New Era of Rights and Responsibilities*, London, Home Office Communication Directorate.

Norrie, K. (2001) 'A child's right to care and protection', in A. Cleland and Sutherland (eds) *Children's Rights in Scotland*, 2nd edn, Edinburgh, W. Green/Sweet & Maxwell.

Schwehr, B. (2001) 'Human rights and social services', in L. Cull and J. Roche (eds) *The Law and Social Work: Contemporary Issues for Practice*, Basingstoke, Palgrave Macmillan.

Scottish Social Services Council (2002) *Code of Conduct for Social Services Workers*, Dundee, Scottish Social Services Council.

United Nations (1994) *Human Rights and Social Work: A Manual for Schools of Social Work and the Social Work Profession*, Geneva, Centre for Human Rights.

4

Safeguarding and Promoting the Welfare of Children

KATHLEEN MARSHALL

The background to the Children (Scotland) Act 1995

In the late 1980s, there was general agreement about the need for change in Scottish child law to take account of:

- the changing structure of families;
- shifts in conceptualisation of the parent–child relationship;
- increasing knowledge about the prevalence of child abuse; and
- greater sensitivity to the rights and duties of all parties.

Children were affected by both 'private' and 'public' law. Private law addressed the relationship of parents, children and guardians in all families, irrespective of the existence of state support or intervention. It regulated the content and possession of parental rights in relation to children; what those rights were; who held them; and how they could be reallocated. This law was set out in a number of Acts of Parliament, but also in ancient principles found in the 'common law' developed by legal thinkers and courts over the centuries. Public law dealt with state intervention and support. It also straddled a number of pieces of legislation, but its core was to be found in the Social Work (Scotland) Act 1968 – one of whose main claims to fame was the establishment of the children's hearings system.

Consultation on law reform developed along two parallel paths. The private law consultation was undertaken by the Scottish Law

41

Commission, with a view to the ultimate inclusion of the reformed child law in a 'Scottish code of child and family law'. The public law consultation started off with the work of the Child Care Law Review Group, appointed by the Secretary of State in 1988. The aim at that time was to formulate appropriate amendments to the Social Work (Scotland) Act 1968. It had already become clear, for example, that the place of safety order provided by that Act was neither flexible enough to regulate significant matters such as contact and medical examination and treatment of a child removed on the authority of the order, nor rigorous enough to provide adequate protection for the rights of all parties involved. Before the recommendations of the Review Group could be evaluated and implemented, events in Orkney, involving the removal of nine children on the authority of a place of safety order, brought the issues into the public domain in a very dramatic way. The subsequent public inquiry chaired by Lord Clyde recommended a more radical reform of the law, based upon the principles of the European Convention on Human Rights (ECHR) and the UN Convention on the Rights of the Child (UNCRC). The UNCRC had been ratified by the UK in December 1991, during the period between the removal of the children (in February 1991) and the publication of Lord Clyde's report (in October 1992). Other reports, including Sheriff Kearney's report of the Fife Inquiry and Angus Skinner's *Review of Residential Child Care*, also fed into the movement towards a more substantial and principled reform. However, there was a reluctance to make the reform too radical. Many felt, for example, that it would be unhelpful to include a radical reassessment of the children's hearings system. In large part, this was because the system was seen to be working well, with shortcomings being due largely to lack of resources. There was also arguably a fear that the then current political climate would be less sympathetic to the welfare approach of the children's hearings than the era which produced it. Therefore, exposing that system to the winds of reform might result in it being undermined.

Scottish commentators were also taking account of developments in England and Wales. There, the Children Act 1989 had brought together the private law and public law relating to children into one Act, so that the focus was on the child. Many felt this would also be helpful in Scotland. Various groups started lobbying for a Children Act for Scotland.

In August 1993, the Scottish Office published the White Paper *Scotland's Children: Proposals for Child Care Policy and Law* which paved the way for a Children Act for Scotland, bringing together private and public law, and based upon the principles of the ECHR and UNCRC.

The basic principles of the Act

Both the private and public law dimensions of the Act reflect a commitment to safeguarding and promoting the welfare of children. For private law, this is one of the parental responsibilities set out in s.1. For public law, the obligation of local authorities is set out in s.22 and focused upon a group of children 'in need', as defined in s.93.

This commitment is supported by the three basic principles which *more or less* permeate the Act. This statement is qualified because there are exceptions to their application and they are formulated in different ways for different provisions. The principles are:

1. The welfare of the child is the paramount consideration.
2. No formal order should be made by a court or children's hearing unless this would be better for the child than not making an order.
3. Children should be given an opportunity to express their views on matters affecting them, and these views should be taken into account when decisions are made, and given due weight according to the age and maturity of the child. Some formulations of this principle are linked with a presumption that a child of 12 or more has the ability to form a view. This is not intended to exclude under-12s; the principle applies to *all* children, whatever their age. It means that serious questions will be asked if a child aged 12 or over is *not* consulted. With under-12s there is more emphasis on assessing the situation as regards the child's actual competence.

Principle 1 is clearly focused on safeguarding and promoting the welfare of children, which is given the highest priority. Principle 2 seeks to avoid the habit or temptation to make an order as a result of a perceived need to do something about a difficult situation. If children's welfare is to be safeguarded and promoted, the onus is on anyone advocating an order to show how this will actually help the child. Principle 3 is crucial and related to the insight that one cannot truly promote a child's welfare if the child has views on the matter under consideration and the decision-makers do not know what those views are.

At various points, the Act also stresses the need to take account of any religious, racial, cultural or linguistic factors affecting a child (ss.17(4)(c), 22(2) and 95).

The shape of the Act

The main body of the Children (Scotland) Act 1995 is divided into four parts. Of these, Part II is subdivided into four chapters. There are also five 'schedules' attached, which are part of the law and contain detail on: the appointment of children's panels; amendments to adoption legislation; issues about the transition from the old law to the new; and amendment and repeal of other laws effected by the Act. However, we will concentrate here on the four parts.

It is important to understand the structure of the Act for a number of reasons:

- it helps to locate appropriate provisions;
- it assists in the correct understanding of definitions. For example, there are different definitions of 'child' for the different parts and chapters of the Act, extending up to either 16 or 18 (see s.93(2));
- it helps to identify the basic principles of the Act, which are formulated in slightly different terms for its different parts (see in particular ss.6, 11, 16, 17, 25, 95, 96).

Table 4.1 *Structure of the Children (Scotland) Act 1995*

Part	Chapter	Sections	Main Issues
I		1–15	'Private' law Defines parental responsibilities and rights Says who has these responsibilities and rights (the starting point) Sets out how this starting point can be changed, through agreements, court orders, etc. Defines 'child', 'parent' and other terms for the purposes of Part I **This Part defines and regulates parental responsibilities and rights.**
II	1	16–38	Sections 16 and 17 set out principles for the whole of Part II. (Section 25(5) has a supplementary provision about the child's views in relation to the provision of accommodation)

Table 4.1   *(cont.)*

Part	Chapter	Sections	Main Issues
			Local authority plans for services for children
			Support for children 'in need' and their families, including children affected by disability
			The provision of accommodation for children, on the basis that parents can generally demand their return (therefore it is *largely* voluntary)
			The provision of day care and out-of-school care as a supportive measure
			The provision of aftercare for young people who have been 'looked after' by the local authority
			Various provisions about the welfare of children living away from home (e.g. in children's homes, schools or hospitals)
			The provision of short-term refuges for children at risk of harm who request this facility
			In this chapter, parents retain all their parental responsibilities and rights, although the local authority will have some practical responsibilities with legal effect where children are accommodated.
	2	39–51	This is largely about the infrastructure of the children's hearings system, which is oriented towards *compulsory* measure of supervision. It includes provisions about rights and obligations to attend, and appeals against decisions of the children's hearing or Sheriff
			This chapter is largely procedural, but there are implications for parental rights where parents are temporarily excluded from a children's hearing in terms of s.46.
	3	52–85	This is the core of the measures for compulsory intervention in the life of a child. It includes:
			• grounds for referral to the children's hearing;
			• the principles and procedures surrounding the exercise of discretion by the children's Reporter about whether to refer the case to a hearing;
			• child assessment orders (from a Sheriff);
			• child protection orders (from a Sheriff) and subsequent procedures;

Table 4.1   *(cont.)*

Part	Chapter	Sections	Main Issues
			• emergency protection measures (authorised by a Justice of the Peace or implemented independently by the police) when it is not practicable to apply for a child protection order; • children's hearings and associated court procedures; • imposition of a supervision requirement by a children's hearing, its review and termination; • exclusion orders (from the Sheriff) – excluding a named and suspected, or feared, abuser from the child's home; and • recovery of fugitive children and the offence of 'harbouring' **In this chapter, there is no general transfer of parental responsibilities or rights from parents to local authority or other agency. In order to see the impact on parental responsibilities and rights, one would have to look at the actual terms of any order, warrant or requirement, which might regulate contact, residence, medical consent, etc.**
	4	86–93	Parental responsibilities orders – from the Sheriff **This transfers the whole package of parental responsibilities and rights from the parent to the local authority. The only substantive right that remains with the parent is the right to consent or refuse consent to an adoption or freeing for adoption.**
III		94–8	Amendments to Adoption (Scotland) Act 1978 **Adoption is the most radical intervention, locating a child entirely within a new family. The 1995 Act merely amends the Act of 1978, which remains the primary Act.**
IV		99–105	Miscellaneous matters about registration of births, inquiries, panels of curators *ad litem* and safeguarders, and technical matters relating to the implementation of the Act **No relevance to parental responsibilities and rights.**

Table 4.1 sets out the structure of the main body of the Act, which proceeds roughly in the order of increasing intervention in the life of a child or family. The general impact of each part or chapter on parental responsibilities and rights is highlighted in bold text at the end of the relevant section.

Reading the Act

The fact that the substance of the Act originated from different sources is reflected in its style and ease of comprehension. It is arguably easier to read and understand Part I than the rest of the Act. This is because the Scottish Law Commission had not only consulted on the content of that part, but set out a first draft of the legal provisions in its written report. There was plenty of time and expertise available to allow careful wording. The history of the rest of the Act was quite different. As indicated above, there had been a number of reports setting out recommendations at the level of policy. However, the associated legal provisions had not been drafted by the authors (understandably given their origin and context). It was not possible to engage parliamentary draftsmen until it was certain that a Bill would be being presented to parliament. The parliamentary timetable for 1994–95 had not originally included space for a Children (Scotland) Bill, which was only found, so it is said, as a consequence of the setting aside of proposals for Post Office privatisation. The childcare and protection provisions therefore had to be drafted in a very short space of time to take advantage of the parliamentary 'window of opportunity'.

Consequently, they are less elegant and more prone to 'legal jargon' than Part I of the Children (Scotland) Act or even than the comparable provisions of the English and Welsh Children Act 1989 which had a longer gestation period. The point of mentioning this is that one should not be discouraged by any difficulty in understanding the language and cross-references of the public law provisions of the 1995 Act. It is essential that practitioners feel able to consult the Act directly, but it is also very helpful to have the assistance of a good commentary on it.

Evaluating the impact of the Act

The rest of this chapter will explore some principles, concepts and issues, and make some attempt at evaluating the impact of the Act, focusing on the public law. More research, however, has been under-taken on Part I than on the rest of the Act, therefore much of what is said derives from the author's personal experience of teaching about, and advising on, the legislation.

Principles

The paramountcy of the welfare of the child was not an innovation, but existed in the prior law. Some commentators have questioned whether this is compatible with the ECHR which was incorporated into UK law by the Human Rights Act 1998. However, so far this has not been challenged; and indeed, the European Court of Human Rights has made no adverse comment on the paramountcy principle where this has been operative in cases before it.[1] There is a danger of viewing the ECHR as a 'parents' charter'; it must be remembered that children too are entitled to benefit from all of the rights set out in it.

The requirement to have regard to the views of the child already existed in the Social Work (Scotland) Act 1968 as regards children in care and the children's hearings system. However, the explicit commit-ment to the UNCRC and the higher profile given by the 1995 Act to the need to take account of children's views have very likely heightened this emphasis. Nevertheless, issues remain about the extent to which the procedures devised for adults to facilitate the expression of views by children in fact support that expression.[2]

The 'no order' principle was an innovation in public law, although it might be regarded as implicit in some of the earlier provisions about review and termination of a children's hearing supervision requirement. However, there can be tensions between the principle and actual practice. In terms of the principle, it is inappropriate to seek a children's hearing supervision requirement as a means of commanding access to scarce resources; nevertheless, this appears to remain a temptation. Further, the Act itself promotes transgression of the principle in its identification of the thresholds for receipt of aftercare. Sections 29 and 30 apply only if the young person was being looked after by the local authority on or after reaching school-leaving age. This consideration might persuade some to recommend continuation of a supervision requirement in order to meet this threshold condition when they might otherwise recommend its termi-nation.

Concepts

The Scottish Office guidance on the Act stresses the *corporate* nature of local authority responsibilities towards children.[3] This is designed to avoid the impression that the responsibilities lie only with the social work department. For example, housing and leisure and recreation departments also have responsibilities towards children in need. Education departments, as part of the local authority, also have responsibility to implement children's hearing decisions in accordance with s.71 of the Act. Some authorities have moved structurally towards a more corporate approach by combining social work with other services, such as education or housing, in one department. Nevertheless, the success of the corporate approach appears to be patchy. Where difficulties are encountered, it would be appropriate to raise these in the context of the planning for children's services required by s.19.

Section 21 also aims to promote joint working by requiring *cooperation* between local authorities and other agencies, specifically health agencies, where that would help the requesting local authority to carry out its functions under Part II of the Act. This could be useful, for example, where one local authority has a specialist facility which is required by a child resident in another authority area. The local authority that is asked for help is obliged to accede to any lawful request, unless such compliance would hinder them from exercising their own statutory functions. As far as health agencies are concerned, issues sometimes arise about the sharing of confidential information where health professionals are reluctant to expose it to a large group where some attending might not be subject to the same strict culture of confidentiality. These matters need sensitive handling and the development of trusting relationships.

Despite what was said above about the inelegance of some of the public law provisions, there was some attempt to avoid jargon and to use words that were more readily comprehensible. The problem with this is that it can blind readers to the fact that these words have a technical meaning in the Act; they are *defined*, and practitioners need to know these definitions if they are to use the Act properly. The definitions are sometimes set out in particular sections, for limited purposes. However, there are also some major sections of the Act to which one can look for definitions. For Part I, this is s.15, and for Part II it is s.93. It would be worth taking time to read through these sections, not so much to learn the definitions as to take note of what terms are defined, for future reference. In particular, within s.93:

- 'In need' is defined in wider terms than those of the Children Act 1989 as, apart from the more general parts of the definition set out in sub-paragraphs (i) and (ii), it includes both children who are disabled *and* those adversely affected by the disability of a member of their family.
- 'Family' is defined.
- As indicated above, 'child' is defined in different ways for different provisions.
- 'Relevant person' is a very important term for the purposes of the children's hearings system and its definition should be studied carefully.
- 'Looked after' is listed in s.93, where reference is made to the substantive definition in s.17(6). It should be noted here that 'looked after' is an umbrella term for children subject to a number of possible legal provisions. It is not a 'free-standing' concept. Children can become 'looked after' through any of the means listed in s.17(6). When that is the case the local authority, in addition to any other responsibilities associated with their particular legal status, has to all of them the obligations set out in s.17.

Important terms that are *not* defined include 'significant harm', the threshold criterion for some of the child protection measures, and 'practicable', the criterion applied in s.61 to identify whether it is appropriate to pursue emergency protection measures falling short of a child protection order on the basis of the impracticability of applying for or obtaining the latter. Interpretation of these terms needs to be worked out in practice, taking into account the case law and the guidance given by some authors on the subject.[4]

Specific issues

Child protection orders and associated conditions and directions can authorise a number of protective measures including the child's removal from home, or prevention of removal from some place (often a hospital). It is difficult to assess their impact, due to a lack of research. However, it would seem that there are local variations both in the procedures for application and in the numbers sought and granted.[5] One of the most common mistakes made in connection with these orders is the assumption that the local authority can use only the route set out in s.57(2) of the Act and not that in s.57(1), on the basis that the latter refers to 'any person'. This misapprehension is promoted by the unfortunate wording of the headings in the form for application prescribed by the Rules of

Court. Practitioners need to be aware that s.57(2) is a very specific route whose criteria will be fulfilled in only a limited number of cases. The Scottish Office guidance makes it clear that the 'any person' referred to in s.57(1) includes a local authority.[6]

Child assessment orders are a non-emergency measure designed to allow assessment of the state of the child's health or development or the way the child has been treated. These appear to have been little used in practice. This may be because, as suggested in the Scottish Office guidance, the act of explaining the availability and effect of the order 'may help parents agree to voluntary measures for assessment'.[7] However, the usefulness of the order was apparent in a case in which it authorised an assessment to disprove the claim of parents that their two children suffered from autism. On the basis of their belief, the parents had removed the children from mainstream school and placed them in a facility for children with severe disabilities. The assessment order paved the way for a referral to the children's hearing on the basis of the ground of lack of parental care.[8]

Exclusion orders are designed to allow the local authority to apply for exclusion of an alleged abuser from the children's home, as an alternative to removal of the child. The provision set out in s.76 of the Act is modelled on that contained in the Matrimonial Homes (Family Protection) (Scotland) Act 1981, which allows a spouse or cohabitee with occupancy rights to apply for the exclusion of their partner. However, there is one significant difference, which was the subject of heated debate in the parliamentary process. The 1981 Act allows for an interim order to be made pending a full hearing. However, even an interim order cannot be granted without giving formal notice to the person to be excluded, who must be given an opportunity to be heard. If this had been replicated in the Children (Scotland) Act, the exclusion order would not have succeeded in avoiding the initial and potentially harmful removal of the child. The child would have to have been removed while the interim order process was completed, which would have taken at the very least 48 hours. Parliament was eventually persuaded that the welfare of the child justified a departure from the 1981 Act procedure. The result is that the Children (Scotland) Act interim exclusion order can be made without the excluded person being given an opportunity to be heard. The Rules of Court then require that a hearing be held within three working days.

Short-term refuges for children are permitted by s.38 of the Act. It should be noted that entry to such a facility must be 'at the child's request': that is, it cannot be used as a way for the local authority to avoid the ordinary child protection procedures. The criterion for entry is that it appears to the person in charge that the child is 'at risk of harm': note the omission of the word 'significant'. This is a lower standard of risk than that required for the child protection measures. The reason is that this takes account of the need for children to feel safe before they enter into detail about what is troubling them. The provisions of the Act are fleshed out by the Refuges for Children (Scotland) Regulations 1996, which set out a procedure for the local authority to designate residential establishments and foster households as refuges. This clearly envisages *prior* designation. However, there are indications that some local authorities are doing this on an ad hoc basis. It seems that practice is moving ahead of the law on the basis of perceived need, thus indicating a possible need to review the legal provisions.

General assessment

While some of the above comments might seem to indicate some issues that need to be addressed, these should be set within the context of a broad approval of the Children (Scotland) Act. It could be better-written and more consistent about application of principles, but must be regarded as more satisfactory than what it replaced. Its principles clearly aim to safeguard and promote the welfare of children, so far as possible within their family settings. Practitioners must judge for themselves whether this ideal is adequately translated into practice.

Notes

1. See for example, *Keegan* v. *Ireland*, 26 May 1994, A 290; 18 EHRR 342, para. 54; and *K.S.* v. *United Kingdom*, 25 September 2001, No. 45035/98.
2. See K. Marshall, E.M. Tisdall and A. Cleland (2002) *'Voice of the Child' Under the Children (Scotland) Act 1995: Volume 1 – Mapping Paper*, Edinburgh, The Stationery Office, for the Scottish Executive Central Research Unit.
3. Scottish Office, *Scotland's Children: The Children (Scotland) Act 1995 Regulations and Guidance*, Vol. 1, p. viii.
4. See, for example, Kenneth Norrie's annotated version of the Children (Scotland) Act 1995, (2nd edn 1998) published by W. Green/Sweet & Maxwell.

5.   Some research on the first two years of operation of the Act was conducted by Joe Francis and Janice McGhee of Edinburgh University's Department of Social Work.

6.   Scottish Office, *Guidance*, Vol. 1, p. 60, para. 37.

7.   Scottish Office, *Guidance*, Vol. 1, p. 55, para. 19.

8.   The case ended up in the Court of Session where it was reported as *B.R. and A.R + J.N. and A.N.* v. *Evelyn Grant*, 13 January 2000, Lord Prosser (Scottish Courts website).

5

Social Work Practice and Accountability

KATHRYN CAMERON

This chapter will look at accountability in relation to social work practice in Scotland. It will examine what is meant by the concept of accountability and then explore what this actually means in practice situations. Forms of accountability are present in all areas of service delivery but one area of practice, namely community care, will be used to illustrate some of the aspects of accountability of which workers should be aware in relation to their practice with service users. While there is a seductive simplicity in drawing lines of accountability which give a clear picture of the ways in which it is possible to hold someone to account, this belies the complexity of the tensions which exist. Some of these tensions will also be explored.

What do we mean by the term 'accountability'? Broadly, being accountable means being obliged to give an explanation or being held to account for one's actions or inaction. Is it the same as responsibility? It has been said (Clark with Asquith, 1985, p. 41) that the two are synonymous in conventional usage, but Coulshed (1990) argued that there is a difference between the two concepts. She saw responsibility as a personal entity which arises out of being a citizen and a human being and therefore being responsible for one's own actions. Accountability, on the other hand, is an organisational entity and derives from holding a particular position.

Shardlow (1995, p. 67) defines accountability as arising 'where social workers give an explanation and justification for their actions to somebody else who might reasonably expect to be given such an explanation'. The concept, therefore, encapsulates what Braye and Preston-Shoot

(2001, p. 43) have described as 'the twin concepts of "accountability to" – to those on whose authority professionals act – and "accountability for" – the range of activity that is open to scrutiny'.

Why is an awareness of accountability important in social work practice? Social workers interact most frequently with the most vulnerable in society. Their clients are often those who, for a number of reasons, do not have a voice or who cannot make their voice heard. They are disadvantaged and frequently experience discrimination. They are oppressed and at risk of being overlooked and denied services. Many of the clients of social workers are the members of society who are least likely to hold the providers of services to account. Social work values of openness, partnership and empowerment are crucial factors in ensuring accountability to service users, as is an awareness of the inequality of power within the relationship between service users and service providers. The rights discourse which emerged strongly in the 1990s, culminating in the passing of the Human Rights Act in 1998, has contributed to the increasing significance of accountability in all the public services. If individuals have rights, then there needs to be a clear understanding of how these rights will be guaranteed, and a discernible system which can deal with infringements and breaches of these rights. Such a system requires that there be transparency at all levels. Only when there is such transparency can there be identification of possible areas where things have gone wrong and, consequently, the opportunity for challenge to take place.

Accountability within social work is complex. It involves the social worker being accountable to a number of individuals, groups, agencies and institutions. It encompasses public accountability to the state and to society. It embraces legal accountability in terms of the mandate to practise and the duties imposed by statute. It also requires accountability to professional bodies. There can often be tensions between the different demands made by all of these and it behoves social workers to be clear about where and to whom the accountability for their practice lies. The complexity of the task faced by workers is evident in the fact that workers can find themselves faced with a range of different responsibilities which may, at times, conflict with one another. Workers often find themselves working within families or other groups where there are conflicts of interest and opinions. Being clear to whom one owes allegiance can be problematic and the role of the worker can appear to be somewhat ambiguous. Social workers could, therefore, find themselves having to manage the tension between their duties to their agency and to their personal and professional values.

The different forms of accountability will be explored in some detail using the device of a fictional case study to highlight the different lines of accountability. Although a community care case is used, the issues raised are applicable to other areas of practice as well.

Mrs J is an 85-year-old woman who was widowed ten years ago. She has one son aged 60 who lives thirty miles away in another town and who himself has health problems but who has tried to visit as often as he can to help his mother. Mrs J has lived on her own since her husband's death and has made her wishes clear to everyone that she wishes to remain independent. She has recently had a fall and had to be admitted to hospital. While there she began to show signs of forgetfulness and disorientation. A social worker was asked to do a community care assessment to determine what resources and supports Mrs J might need if she were to be returned home.

The worker involved in dealing with this case would be accountable in the following ways.

To the employer: the policies and procedures of the local authority which is her employer bind the social worker undertaking the assessment. Failure to work within these policy guidelines could leave the social worker open to disciplinary action and even personal liability for her actions. In undertaking their work, social workers act as agents for their employer, be that a statutory or voluntary agency. They are accountable to their employers for the work undertaken in their name and so must abide by the conditions of their employment and the policies of the agency. This, therefore, represents an unequal balance of power between the employer and the worker and could place the worker who speaks up against policies or practices in a vulnerable situation. Whistle-blowers have often been represented at worst as villains or at the very least as deluded. The passing of the Public Interest Disclosure Act in 1999 has set out a clear framework for raising concerns about malpractice and provides protection against victimisation for those workers who do raise concerns.

To other agencies: in line with joint working as envisaged in the Joint Future Agenda (Report of the Joint Future Group, 2000), the social worker in the above case would be involved in a single shared assessment and may be making recommendations which will involve health and other professionals. Collaborative working of this kind requires that there are adequate arrangements for accountability and this is often achieved through the application of inter-agency agreements and protocols. Lines of accountability need to be transparent because in situations of collaborative practice there can sometimes be a lack of a clear hierarchical structure with no easy way of establishing who is responsible for particular aspects of the case and for what they are accountable. It can then be difficult for service users to hold anyone to account for a failure to provide services. The mixed welfare economy has contributed to a blurring of lines of accountability. In many cases there is no one person of whom it could be said 'the buck stops here'. This can lead to confusion not only for service users but also for all agencies involved because the responsibility for decision-making is not clearly understood. Many service users find themselves in touch with a bewildering array of professionals whose roles and responsibilities are dimly understood, if at all. In such situations, there is little transparency and so the ability to hold individual professionals accountable is diminished. One way to address this could be the use of case conferences. These can be a useful mechanism for demonstrating accountability to service users by ensuring their presence and providing them with copies of relevant reports and action plans detailing the work of various agencies and clarifying the roles and responsibilities of all involved.

Legal accountability: local authorities derive their mandate to deliver services from statutory duties and responsibilities and these in turn are delegated to their employees. The social worker undertaking this community care assessment will, therefore, need to work within the appropriate legislative framework and may be held accountable for a failure to carry out duties. In this case there will be duties under s.12A of the Social Work (Scotland) Act 1968 to undertake an assessment of needs. Failure to carry out duties could lead to legal challenge by the service user. This could be by way of a judicial review which is a process which can be pursued through the Court of Session and can be raised where there are allegations that a decision taken was illegal, procedurally unfair or irrational. Alternatively, under s.6 of the Human Rights Act the service user could allege that her Convention rights have been breached.

Public accountability: public scrutiny of social work practice is now much more rigorous. The provision of social work services in the area of community care as in other areas will now be monitored through a national system of monitoring and inspection. The establishment of the

National Care Standards will ensure that the provision of services will meet identified standards and will enable the public to know what those standards are. The public can, therefore, hold authorities to account if they fall below the required standards in any way. The Scottish Council for the Regulation of Care, which was set up by the Regulation of Care (Scotland) Act 2001 and is now known as the Care Commission, has a responsibility for the registration and inspection of care provision. If Mrs J was admitted to residential care or offered a package of care to sustain her in her own home, then not only will the standards for her care be established but there will be regular inspection to ensure that these standards are met. If they are not, then the agency will be held to account for its failure. In addition, there is now a Public Services Ombudsman in Scotland. The Scottish Public Services Ombudsman Act 2002 established a one-stop shop to deal with complaints which relate to the public sector. While a full list of such authorities is set out in Schedule 2 to the Act, those which would have relevance to social work in particular include all Scottish public authorities, health boards, the Scottish Council for the Regulation of Care and the Scottish Social Services Council. Mrs J, or her son as her authorised representative, could make a complaint about any maladministration in respect of her case to the ombudsman. She could also complain to the Care Commission which has a procedure whereby a person or someone acting on a person's behalf might make a complaint in relation to a care service. The description of what constitutes a care service is widely defined and covers almost all local authority services to children, support and day care, residential care, fostering and adoption.

To service users: the ethos of empowerment which underpins social work practice has resulted in a significant move towards accountability to service users. The idea of the service user as consumer rather than as the passive recipient of services has been crucial in this development. However, there is a tension here for social workers who formerly had a role in advocating for their clients where these same social workers are now gatekeepers to scarce resources and are also constrained by statutory powers. For some service users, negotiating their way through the labyrinth of services and agencies is a major problem. They have to understand different systems and structures as well as the jargon used by professionals, which is often baffling. Service users can also feel that they are isolated and fear that if they complain services might be withdrawn. For these reasons, the increasing number of pressure groups and user-led services now have an important role to play in holding service providers to account. Service users could use the complaints procedures which have been set up by social services departments. Each local authority is bound to set up and publish details of a complaints procedure (s.5B(1) of the Social Work (Scotland) Act 1968). This allows an individual to make representations concerning the discharge of local authority functions under the 1968 Act and other designated statutes such as Part 2 of the Children (Scotland) Act, the Chronically Sick and Disabled Persons Act 1970, the Adoption (Scotland) Act 1978 and the Mental Health (Scotland) Act 1984. However, this limits the range of individuals who can raise a complaint in law, namely those to whom the local authority owes a duty under the Act. Local authorities are required to designate officers who will receive and investigate representations made. Authorities are expected to assist people to make complaints and direct them to sources of independent advice. Each formal complaint must be investigated by an independent officer of the local authority and responded to within a specified period of time. If the complainant is still dissatisfied he or she can refer the matter to a review committee with an independent chair. The decision of the review is not binding on the local authority though it does need to have regard to the recommendations. The review committee is of course not really independent from the local authority that was responsible for the decision in the first place and so the decision could be challenged either by way of a judicial review or under the Human Rights Act 1998. It could be argued that the process might be a breach of someone's rights to a fair hearing by an independent and impartial tribunal under Article 6. Service users can always hold local authorities to account by using the procedures available to them within the legislation to challenge decisions which have been made. In addition it should not be forgotten that service users can take action against any public authority on the grounds that their rights under the ECHR have been breached.

Professional accountability: there are aspects of this which link with public accountability. Social service professionals in Scotland now have to adhere to the Code of Practice for Social Service Workers drawn up by the Scottish Social Services Council, which set out the standards of professional conduct and practice required of them. The Scottish Social Services Council was set up by the Regulation of Care (Scotland) Act 2001. It has three objectives:

- to strengthen and support the workforce;
- to raise standards of practice;
- to protect those who use services.

To fulfil these objectives to protect service users and their carers, the SSSC has responsibility for key areas:

- to establish registers of key groups of social services staff;
- to publish codes of practice for social services employees and employers;
- to regulate the training and education of the workforce.

Among the other standards, social services workers must be 'accountable for the quality of their work and take responsibility for maintaining and improving their knowledge and skills'. Social services workers will also require to be registered by the Scottish Social Services Council and they may be disciplined or deregistered for misconduct. It will be a condition of employment that workers are registered with the Council. This ensures that social services workers will be held personally accountable for any failure to carry out their professional role.

In addition, the British Association of Social Workers has a Code of Ethics which outlines the values and principles which are integral to social work. These codes of practice and ethics, together, do convey a message that workers are accountable at a personal and professional level for the services which are offered. *The Framework for Social Work Education in Scotland* (Scottish Executive, 2003, p. 19) asserts that 'social work is a moral activity' and goes on to say that social workers 'should be able to understand moral reasoning and make decisions in difficult ethical situations, especially where there are conflicting moral obligations'.

The tensions between accountability to one's employer, to service users and to professional values could be illustrated by returning to our fictional case study. Let us imagine that the worker has undertaken the assessment. She has been influenced by the ethos of community care and her assessment has been needs- rather than resource-led. In her meetings with Mrs J, the latter has been very distressed at the idea that she might be placed in residential care. She is also worried about her son's health and does not want to make unreasonable demands on him. The social worker has identified a package of care for Mrs J. However, her line manager has stated that it is not possible to meet all the expenses which would be incurred because the budget is already over-stretched. He suggests that Mrs J's son will just have to do more for his mother and that the worker should put in place a much reduced care package. The worker feels that Mrs J and her son will be so pleased to get any kind of package which allows her home that they will accept what is offered, but she fears that they will both suffer in the long term. The worker is torn between the professional value of protecting the rights and promoting the interests of Mrs J and her son. She is also accountable to them for the assessment which has been made and the plan for the kind of care which will be offered. Should she explain to them what has happened and what their rights are to challenge the decision which has been made? There is also her accountability to her employer to abide by agency policies. The social worker has a difficult task in finding an accommodation between these conflicting accountabilities.

The way ahead

One of the guiding principles highlighted in the introduction to *The Framework for Social Work Education in Scotland* (Scottish Executive, 2003, p. 18) states that social workers must 'maintain public trust and confidence in social services'. The new structures for accountability which have been put into place by the Scottish Executive may help to reinforce this trust and confidence.

The Scottish Social Services Council (SSSC) has now published the procedures for registration. Registration of the estimated 100,000 workforce began in April 2003. The Council is also responsible for the training and education of the workforce and proposals for the reform in social work education. Accountability forms one of the Standards in Social Work Education (SiSWE), namely to 'manage and be accountable, with supervision and support, for their own social work practice within their organisation'.

The Care Commission has begun its work and a Public Services Ombudsman has been appointed. In addition at the time of writing there is a Bill before the Scottish Parliament to appoint a children's commissioner. However, all of these structures will only work if there is openness towards all the stakeholders who have an interest in the delivery of social services, and, in particular, there is real commitment towards ensuring that accountability to service users is not in the final analysis empty rhetoric.

References

Braye, S. and Preston-Shoot, M. (2001) 'Social work practice and accountability', in L.-A. Cull and J. Roche (eds) *The Law and Social Work*, Basingstoke, Palgrave Macmillan.

Clark, C.L with Asquith, S. (1985) *Social Work and Social Philosophy*, London, Tavistock.

Coulshed, V. (1990) *Management in Social Work*, London, Macmillan – now Palgrave Macmillan.

Report of the Joint Future Group, *Joint Future Agenda*, November 2000.

Shardlow, S. (1995) 'Confidentiality accountability and the boundaries of client–worker relationships', in R. Hugman and D. Smith (eds) *Ethical Issues in Social Work*, London, Routledge.

Scottish Executive (2003) *The Framework for Social Work Education in Scotland*, Edinburgh, HMSO.

Part II

Overviews of Key Areas of Law and Practice

6

Mental Health and Social Work

IAIN FERGUSON

Introduction

On 16 September 2002, the Mental Health (Scotland) Bill was laid before the Scottish Parliament in Edinburgh. The Bill, when passed, will lead to the repeal of the Mental Health (Scotland) Act 1984 and will result in the biggest changes to mental health law in Scotland for more than forty years. This chapter will focus on the changes which the new legislation will bring about and some of the implications for social workers.

The main argument for a new Act is that the nature and provision of mental health services have changed fundamentally since the mid-1980s. The central focus of the 1984 Act was on detention within a hospital setting. Since that time, however, the shift in policy towards mental health care in the community has meant a substantial decline in the level of in-patient hospital provision, with many more people with mental health problems living in the community (Rogers and Pilgrim, 1996; Loudon and Coia, 2002). In that sense, the 1984 Act is seen as failing to address the realities of current mental health care.

Two other factors, however, have also driven the demand for new mental health legislation, both north and south of the border. The first is what might be called the *public safety* agenda. Following a number of widely publicised homicides in England in the 1990s involving individuals with a mental health problem, there has been a growing equation in the public mind (driven in large part by the tabloid media and by some politicians) of mental illness and dangerousness – the 'mad axeman' stereotype (Philo, 1996). Since 1997, public safety, rather than care and treatment, has been the political priority of the UK government in relation to mental health policy (Dobson, 1998; Pilgrim, 2001). In particular, people with a diagnosis of schizophrenia and people with a diagnosis of personality disorder have often been seen as representing a particular threat (in respect of the latter group, for example, see DoH/Home Office, 1999).

While the public safety agenda has been more muted in Scottish political debate, it would be wrong to conclude that that it is necessarily less influential north of the border. The very first Act to be passed by the new Scottish Parliament, for example, the Mental Health (Public Safety and Appeals) (Scotland) Act 1999, was an emergency piece of legislation which changed the definition of mental disorder to include the category of personality disorder and for the first time introduced a 'public safety' test to ensure that people with a mental disorder could be compulsorily detained even where no effective treatment was available, if they were seen to constitute a threat to public safety. This followed a case in which a Sheriff ruled that a patient in the State Hospital at Carstairs who was no longer suffering from a mental illness but only from a personality disorder which was not amenable to treatment could not be detained under the 1984 legislation (for a critical discussion of the *Ruddle* case and this legislation, see Millan, 2001).

As a number of major studies have demonstrated, there has *not* been an increase in the number of such homicides and people with a mental health problem are much more likely to harm themselves than others (Taylor and Gunn, 1999). Nevertheless, the public safety agenda has been an important one through the 1990s and into the first decade of the twenty-first century both north and south of the border and has influenced the proposed mental health legislation in ways which we shall discuss later in the chapter (Atkinson and Patterson, 2001).

The second discourse which has shaped the proposed new legislation comes from a very different quarter. The 1990s saw the emergence, in Scotland and elsewhere, of a new voice in mental health discussion and debate – the voice of people who use or have used mental health services. The emergence of a *user involvement* discourse is due in part to the prominence given to consumerist approaches in the late 1980s and early 1990s (as reflected in the 1990 NHS and Community Care Act), in part to the growth of a mental health users' movement, influenced by the larger disability movement (Lindow, 1995). While it is still the case that mental health user involvement in Scotland as elsewhere is often tokenistic and patchy (it is, for example, much stronger in the voluntary sector than in the local authority sector), nevertheless the *legitimacy* of the user voice – in the preparation of individual care plans, in the development of new mental health services and in the management and development of existing services – is recognised to a much greater extent than was the case in the 1980s (Scottish Office, 1997). As one activist has noted, no service users were involved in the preparation of the mental health legislation in the early 1980s (Campbell, 1996). By contrast, there has been considerable service user involvement in the preparation of the Millan Committee Report, which laid the basis for the Bill currently going through the Scottish Parliament (Rosengard and Laing, 2001). The new Mental Health (Scotland) Bill, then, can be seen as reflecting to a greater or lesser extent these two, very different, agendas.

The Mental Health (Scotland) Bill

The Bill has drawn a mixed response from mental health organisations in Scotland. Positively, both its tone and its provisions are seen as more service user-friendly and less obsessed with public safety than the parallel proposed legislation for England and Wales (which has succeeded in uniting the entire mental health community in opposition to it (Freedland, 2002; Strong, 2002)). In addition, specific provisions have been welcomed (albeit with qualifications, to be discussed below). These include the introduction of mental health tribunals to replace the Sheriff Court when people are being compulsorily detained; the inclusion of independent advocacy services; and the provision for the making of advance statements by service users. The Bill will also involve a wide range of new duties for social workers in their role as Mental Health Officers (MHOs), as does the Adults with Incapacity (Scotland) Act 2000. The role of the MHO under both the 1984 legislation and these newer pieces of legislation is discussed elsewhere in this text.

However, while welcoming the positive elements, there has been sufficient concern about some aspects of the Bill for a 'Let's Get it Right' campaign to have been set up, coordinated by the Scottish Association for Mental Health and involving more than fifty Scottish mental health organisations (www.samh.org.uk/mentalhealthbillcampaign). These concerns will be considered below in the context of a discussion of the Bill's main provisions.

The Bill is a long and complex one (19 parts, 231 sections). In this chapter, therefore, it will be possible to focus only on the main changes which the Bill proposes. Where I make reference to specific sections of the Bill, it is important to note that these may be changed by the time the Bill completes its passage through the Scottish Parliament.

Underpinning principles

According to the Executive Summary which accompanied the Bill, the Bill would incorporate the vast majority of the recommendations of the Millan Committee, which was set up to review the workings of the 1984 Act. In addition to the specific proposals it put forward, that committee argued that any new mental health legislation should be underpinned by ten clear principles: non-discrimination; equality; respect for diversity; reciprocity (that is, where society imposes an obligation on an individual to comply with a programme of treatment of care, it should impose a parallel obligation on the health and social care authorities to provide safe and appropriate services, including ongoing care following discharge from compulsion); informal care; participation; respect for carers; least restrictive alternative; benefit (that is, 'any intervention under the Act should be likely to produce for the service user a benefit that cannot reasonably be achieved other than by the intervention'); and child welfare ('the welfare of a child with mental disorder should be paramount in any interventions imposed on the child under the Act') (Millan, 2001). In fact, while the ten principles may inform the spirit of the Bill as well as some of its specific provisions (though even this is debatable), they are nowhere clearly set out within the Bill itself (in contrast, for example, to the Children (Scotland) Act 1995 or the Adults with Incapacity (Scotland) Act 2000 where the overarching principles are clearly stated). A key demand of campaigners is that these principles be clearly stated within the new Act.

Definition of mental disorder

Three categories are included within the Bill's definition of mental disorder: mental illness; learning disability; and personality disorder (s.227). Personality disorder was not part of the definition of mental disorder under the 1984 Act. Instead, it referred to a 'persistent disorder manifested only by abnormally aggressive or seriously irresponsible conduct' which must be susceptible to treatment (1984 Act, s.17) (what the English legislation refers to as 'psychopathy'). The definition was changed to include personality disorder following the *Ruddle* case, discussed above. There has been considerable debate amongst mental health professionals and service users over whether or not the term 'personality disorder' should be included in the new legislation. Opponents of inclusion argue that the diagnosis is inherently stigmatising and of doubtful validity (for a review of the debates around personality disorder, see Tyrer, 2000 and Pilgrim, 2001). However, a recognition on the one hand that people with this diagnosis have mental health needs and need to be able to access mental health services and, more importantly, the influence of the 'public safety' agenda on the other have been the main factors outweighing these objections.

The 1984 Act excluded a number of conditions from the definition of mental disorder, including promiscuity, sexual deviancy or dependence on alcohol or drugs. Initially the new Bill contained no such list of exclusions but has been amended in its passage through Parliament. As a result, the new Act is likely to state that no person should be considered to be mentally disordered by reason only of:

- sexual orientation
- sexual deviancy
- transsexualism
- transvestitism
- dependence on, or use of, alcohol or drugs
- behaviour that causes, or is likely to cause, harassment, alarm or distress to any other person
- acting as no prudent person would act.

The Mental Health Tribunal

A new Mental Health Tribunal will replace the Sheriff Court as the main forum for decision-making (s.18). The tribunal will act as a judicial body and will authorise compulsory treatment orders, short-term detention, compulsion orders and other mental health disposals affecting mentally disordered offenders. The qualifications, training and experience of tribunal members is to be prescribed in regulations but it seems there may be scope for at least one member of the tribunal to be a service user or carer if they are seen to have the relevant qualifications or experience. The introduction of tribunals has been welcomed both by mental health voluntary organisations and by service users' groups as they are seen as less intimidating than Sheriff Courts and more appropriate to the needs of people with mental health problems.

New duties on local authorities

Part IV of the Bill proposes the introduction of a range of new duties for local authorities to promote the health and well-being of people with mental health problems living in the community. These go further than the duty to provide aftercare imposed by s.8 of the 1984 Act and have been welcomed by mental health professionals, users and carers. Section 8 was notable by its non-implementation. As McKay and Patrick noted:

> This is a very important duty. It is a clear duty of the social work department. It is not subject to any limitations or qualifications. Its existence is one of the best kept secrets around. (McKay and Patrick, 1995, p. 25)

Whether these new duties will fare differently depends primarily on the willingness of the Executive to make funds available to develop appropriate services (especially given the absence of a stated 'right to reciprocity', one of Millan's ten principles, within the Bill).

Emergency and short-term detention

The Bill retains the basic framework of the 1984 Act, with emergency detention of up to 72 hours, short-term detention of up to 28 days and longer-term detention which requires to be authorised by a judicial body (Parts V–VII). However, in contrast to the 1984 Act, it will now be possible for an individual to be admitted directly to short-term detention. The reasoning behind this seems to be that there is no right of appeal under emergency detention and that, in general, the safeguards for people are greater under short-term detention. However, some bodies, such as the Scottish Association for Mental Health (SAMH), have expressed concern that the end result could be more people being detained for longer periods of time. SAMH has also expressed concern that there will now be two routes to compulsory detention – the new Mental Health Act and the Adults with Incapacity (Scotland) Act 2000 (www.samh.org.uk). Given that both the grounds for compulsory detention and also the procedural safeguards are different under these two pieces of legislation, there is scope for confusion here as well as a potential for infringement of people's rights, since the safeguards under the new legislation are stronger than those contained in the Incapacity Act.

Compulsory treatment orders

The Bill proposes the introduction of new powers to compulsorily treat patients while they are living in the community (Part VII). This will involve an application for a long-term compulsory treatment order (CTO) being made to the new tribunal by a Mental Health Officer (MHO), supported by two medical recommendations and including a detailed plan of care. The patient and the patient's named person (not necessarily the nearest relative, as was the case under the 1984 Act) are entitled to challenge this recommendation. If the tribunal is satisfied that the grounds are met, it may make a CTO which can either be community-based or hospital-based. There is no right of appeal, although after three months the patient or the named person can apply to have the order varied or revoked (s.41). While forms of community compulsion already exist in the form of leave of absence (LoA) and community care orders (CCOs), these only apply where someone had already been subject to a long-term hospital order (s.18 under the 1984 Act) and are seen as measures which facilitate rehabilitation. By contrast, CTOs will be available to the Mental Health Tribunal as an alternative to detention (McDougall, 2002).

Community-based CTOS can impose some or all of the following conditions on the patient (s.54):

- To attend at specified places on specified dates or at specified intervals, or in accordance with the direction of the responsible medical officer (RMO) to receive treatment
- To reside at a specified address
- To allow monitoring of the patient in the patient's home or visits there by persons responsible for providing care and treatment
- To obtain approval of the MHO to any change of address.

The proposal to introduce CTOs has been by far the most contentious aspect of the new legislation. Supporters of CTOs argue that these would apply to only a relatively small group of people who are at risk, who respond to medication but refuse to take it, and who are in danger of relapsing without treatment (Dyer, 2002). Opponents of CTOs, both north and south of the border, however, argue against them on several grounds (Mind, 2001; Barcus, 2002; McDougall, 2002). First, it is argued, the conditions stated above would represent a serious restriction on personal freedom. Second, while the number of hospital beds available acted as a ceiling on the number of compulsory detentions under the 1984 Act (despite which s.18 orders had increased by 284 per cent since that time), there is no such ceiling to the number of compulsory orders that can be made in the community. Third, the 'treatment' that is likely to be on offer in the community will usually be medication, rather than 'talking treatments' for example, despite the well-documented fact that many service users find such medication unhelpful or find the side-effects distressing. Fourth, there are concerns about the implications of introducing a coercive element into the relationships between community mental health workers, including social workers acting as MHOs, and service users, since these relationships are dependent on a high degree of trust. Fifth, it is argued, there is research evidence to suggest that given the right kind of services, compulsion is unnecessary since people will use services anyway (Barcus, 2002).

Medical treatment

Under the new Bill, electroconvulsive therapy (ECT) should not be given to a patient who has the capacity to consent and who does not agree to the treatment (by contrast, under the 1984 Act, ECT could be given where a patient had capacity but refused treatment if there was the support of a second medical opinion). However, ECT can still be administered where a person does not have the capacity to consent if the decision is supported by a second medical opinion (ss.165–7). Given the controversial nature of this treatment, campaigning bodies such as SAMH have argued that ECT should never be given without consent, except in emergency situations. Perhaps in response to the concerns of the 'Let's Get it Right' campaign, the Executive has now accepted that neurosurgery cannot take place if the patient objects or resists, even in situations where the person is seen as lacking capacity (s.162 (2)). Again, however, there is concern that the different criteria for capacity contained in Part 5 of the Adults with Incapacity (Scotland) Act 2000 could mean that (with the exception of neurosurgery) these safeguards regarding ECT and other treatments might not always apply, depending on which legislation is employed.

Protection and rights of people with mental disorders

Sections 177–81 of the Bill replace the 'nearest relative' section of the 1984 Act and allow the patient to nominate someone to act on their behalf as the 'named person' (where they fail to do so, the 'primary carer' will take on this role and, in their absence, the 'nearest relative'). Under s.180 they can also specify someone whom they would *not* wish to be the named person.

In relation to advocacy, the Bill proposes that a duty be placed on each local authority and health board to ensure the provision of independent advocacy services to people with mental disorder within their area (s.182). While the inclusion of advocacy provision within the Bill has been welcomed, what is proposed falls far short of the Millan Committee's recommendation that all mental health service users should have a *right* to independent advocacy services and this perceived 'watering down' of Millan has caused dismay amongst campaigning bodies. As the experience of s.8 of the 1984 Act shows, the extent to which 'duties' placed on local authorities are actually carried out will vary considerably, depending on factors such as their financial resources and the ability of interest groups to force them to meet their statutory obligations. Also unclear is the extent to which *collective* advocacy, a key development in the mental health field in the 1990s, will be supported under the new legislation.

'Advance statements' allow the service user to give information while he or she is well about the kind or treatment they would like to receive when they are unwell. The need for such statements has been a demand of the mental health service users' movement for many years and provision for advance statements in the Bill (ss.187–8) has been welcomed. Again, however, there is concern that the status of these statements has been undermined by the provision that the responsible medical officer (RMO) can override these, as long as he or she sets down in writing their reason for doing so. Campaigners have argued that the tribunal, rather than the RMO, should be the only body able to override advance statements, with opportunities for the service user or the named person to make their objections known, as this is more in keeping with the principle of participation (samh.org.uk).

Adults with Incapacity (Scotland) Act 2000

This chapter has focused on the Bill which will become the major governing legislation in the area of mental health. However, it is important to note that another piece of recent legislation which has been referred to above – the Adults with Incapacity (Scotland) Act 2000 – also has implications for social workers in this area, particularly in respect of older people and people with learning disabilities. While space will permit here only a very brief discussion of the provisions of the 2000 Act, social workers need to be aware of the main duties which it places on local authority social work departments. This Act was passed by the Scottish Parliament in 2000 and implemented between 2001 and 2002. Its purpose is to provide for decisions to be made on behalf of adults who lack the legal capacity to do so themselves because of mental disorder or inability to communicate. As noted earlier, the Act is based on a clear set of principles, the essence of which is that all decisions made on behalf of an adult with impaired capacity must:

- benefit the adult;
- take account of the adult's wishes, if these can be ascertained;
- take account of the views of relevant others, as far as it is reasonable and practical to do so;
- restrict the adult's freedom as little as possible while still achieving the desired benefit;
- encourage the adult to use existing skills or develop new skills.

The Act repealed those sections of the 1984 Act relating to guardianship and some of the implications for social workers in their role as Mental Health Officers are discussed elsewhere in this text. In general the Act has been widely welcomed but, as noted above, SAMH and other bodies have raised concerns that confusion (and possible infringement of rights) could be created by the fact that there now exist two sets of criteria for compulsory measures of care and treatment for people with mental disorders, with less stringent safeguards in the Incapacity Act than in the new Bill.

Conclusions

In his history of mental health social work in Scotland, Martin expressed the hope that the 1984 Mental Health (Scotland) Act would lead to the development of a higher status for social work in this area (Martin, 1984). For a variety of reasons, including the growing dominance of child protection social work during the 1980s on the one hand and the Thatcherite attack on local authority spending on the other, that hope was not to be realised. Despite the limitations discussed above, the new Mental Health (Scotland) Bill (alongside the Adults with Incapacity (Scotland) Act) can also to some extent be seen as providing social workers with an opportunity to develop a genuinely anti-oppressive mental health social work, based on a social model of health: in the scope for advocacy, for example; in the provision for advance statements; and in the role of social workers in developing care plans. In addition, encouragingly, the Scottish Executive does appear to be committed to challenging the stigma associated with mental health, through public awareness campaigns for example (www.seemescotland.org). All of these things are to be welcomed. However, the real test of the Executive's commitment to mental health will be its willingness to fund the future development of a framework of community mental health services (including crisis services) which reflect the needs of users and carers. Without such services, the concern must be that it is the more coercive aspects of the new legislation which will dominate.

References

Atkinson, J. and Patterson, L.E. (2001) *Review of Literature Relating to Mental Health Legislation*, Edinburgh, Scottish Executive Central Research Unit.

Barcus, S. (2002) 'Setting the scene', in P. Atkinson and M. Havergal (eds) *The Mental Health Bill: The Three Rs of Implementing Millan – Reciprocity, Representation and Resource*, Report of a conference organised by Holyrood Conferences and Events in conjunction with SAMH, Penumbra, the NSF (Scotland) and the Royal College of Psychiatrists.

Campbell, P. (1996) 'The history of the user movement in the United Kingdom', in T. Heller, J. Reynolds, R. Gomm, R. Muston and S. Pattison (eds) *Mental Health Matters: A Reader*, London, Macmillan – new Palgrave Macmillan.

Dobson, F. (1998) 'Frank Dobson outlines Third Way for mental health', press release, 29 July, London, Department of Health.

DoH/Home Office (1999) *Managing Dangerous People with Severe Personality Disorder*, London, Department of Health/Home Office.

Dyer, J. (2002) 'The Mental Health Bill – a new deal?', in P. Atkinson and M. Havergal (eds) *The Mental Health Bill: The Three Rs of Implementing Millan – Reciprocity, Representation and Resource*, Report of a conference organised by Holyrood Conferences and Events in conjunction with SAMH, Penumbra, the NSF (Scotland) and the Royal College of Psychiatrists.

Freedland, J. (2002) 'Stop this Madness', *Guardian*, 23 October.

Lindow, V. (1995) 'Power and Rights: the psychiatric system survivor movement', in R. Jack, R. (ed.) *Empowerment in Community Care*, London, Chapman & Hall.

Loudon, J. and Coia, D. (2002) 'The Scottish scene', *Psychiatric Bulletin*, vol. 26, pp. 84–6.

McDougall, S. (2002) 'Compulsion and mental health – where do we draw the line?', *SCOLAG Journal*, September, pp. 161–2.

McKay, C. and Patrick, H. (1995) *The Care Maze: The Law and Your Rights to Community Care in Scotland*, Glasgow, ENABLE.

Martin, F.M. (1984) *Between the Acts: Community Mental Health Services 1959–1983*, London, Nuffield Provincial Hospitals Trust.

Millan (2001) *New Directions: Report of the Review of the Mental Health (Scotland) Act 1984* (The Millan Report), Edinburgh, Scottish Executive.

Mind (2001) '10 questions about compulsory treatment in the community', http://www.mind.org.uk.

Philo, G. (ed.) (1996) *Media and Mental Distress*, London, Longman.

Pilgrim, D. (2001) 'Disordered personalities and disordered concepts', *Journal of Mental Health*, vol. 10, No. 3, pp. 253–65.

Rogers, A. and Pilgrim, D. (1996) *Mental Health Policy in Britain*, London, Macmillan - now Palgrave Macmillan.

Rosengard, A. and Laing, I. (2001) *User Consultation on the Millan Report*, Edinburgh Scottish Executive Equality Unit.

Scottish Executive (2002) *Joint Futures Report*, http://www.show.scot.nhs.uk/ isd/Joint_futures/.

Scottish Office (1997) *A Framework for Mental Health Services in Scotland*, Edinburgh: Scottish Office.

Strong, S. (2002) 'From despair to where? The Draft Mental Health Bill', *Care and Health*, vol. 21, pp. 6–9.

Taylor, P.J. and Gunn, J. (1999) 'Homicides by people with mental illness: myth and reality', *British Journal of Psychiatry*, vol. 174, pp. 9–14.

Tyrer, P. (2000) *Personality Disorders: Diagnosis, Management and Course*, Oxford, Butterworth/Heinemann.

7

Confidentiality, Access to Information, Human Rights and Data Protection

DEBORAH BAILLIE

Professionals and organisations are focusing more and more on the issue of confidentiality and access to information. This chapter aims to look at the link between confidentiality and access to information, the right to respect for private life under the European Convention on Human Rights (enforceable against public authorities under the Human Rights Act 1998) and the Data Protection Act 1998.

The law on confidentiality is relatively underdeveloped in Scotland and most professionals work under some kind of professional code. Some codes, such as those of doctors and nurses, carry professional sanctions if they are unjustifiably breached whereas others have no sanctions other than the possibility of disciplinary action by an employer. Some professions do not have a code at all. The general law states that everyone has a basic right to confidentiality, including those under the age of 16. The fact that certain groups are seen as potentially more vulnerable does not diminish their right to confidentiality.

Before examining some of the professional codes, I shall look at two areas of law which have a direct impact on confidentiality and access to information – the Human Rights Act 1998 and The Data Protection Act 1998.

The legislation

The Human Rights Act 1998 came into effect in October 2000 and incorporates most of the Convention into national law. This means that a victim of a human rights breach can bring a case to a national court, rather than the European Court of Human Rights in Strasbourg, and legal aid is available. The Act makes it unlawful for a public authority to act, or to fail to act, in a manner inconsistent with the Convention rights.

Article 8 states that:

1. Everyone has the right to respect for his private and family life, his home and his correspondence.
2. There shall be no interference by a public authority with the exercise of this right except such as is in accordance with the law and is necessary in a democratic society in the interests of national security, public safety or the economic well-being of the country, for the prevention of disorder or crime, for the protection of health or morals, or for the protection of the rights and freedoms of others.

Therefore, any professional working for a public authority must consider Article 8 when considering a breach of confidentiality. The definition of public authority in the Human Rights Act 1998 is very wide and may include voluntary organisations which are funded by other public authorities. In simple terms, when considering a breach of confidentiality the professional must:

- have proper regard to the terms of their code and the general law on confidentiality, including Article 8;
- show that they are pursuing a legitimate aim (for example, protection from significant harm);
- have sufficient and relevant reasons to justify their interference with the right to respect for private life;
- show that they have acted proportionately.

This last concept requires some explanation. It may be described by imagining a set of old-fashioned scales with two sides. On one side, the individual's right to respect for private life weighs down the scales. On the other side, the reasons for breaching confidentiality need to be sufficient to outweigh that right and if they are not, the professional may have acted disproportionately. This balancing of competing rights is reflected in the social work core values which require social workers to promote people's rights to choice, privacy, confidentiality and protection, while recognising and addressing the complexities of competing rights and demands.

Many professionals have not had adequate training on the Human Rights Act 1998 and so are unaware that as well as consulting their code, they should also be consulting a human rights checklist to justify a proposed breach of confidentiality. The British Institute of Human Rights reports that people working in the public sector have little understanding of the Act and what their responsibilities are under the Act. These responsibilities include a positive duty to promote and uphold legal rights (www.bihr.org). It is also worth bearing in mind that a victim of an alleged breach has up to one year from the date of the alleged breach to raise a case against a public authority. It goes without saying, therefore, that proper recording is essential when confidentiality is breached.

We can see that the picture is already quite complicated. However, this is now further exacerbated by the Data Protection Act 1998. Many people think that this Act is only about the right to have access to information held about you, but the Act, which has gradually come into force since 1998, sets out the following principles about the processing of manual and computerised data:

1. Personal data shall be obtained and processed fairly and lawfully.
2. Data may only be held for one or more specified and lawful purposes.
3. Data must be adequate, relevant and not excessive for the purpose.
4. Data must be accurate, and if not, must be amended and kept up to date.
5. Data must not be kept for longer than necessary.
6. Personal data must be processed in accordance with the rights of the data subject.
7. Data must be secure and there must be no unauthorised access, alteration, disclosure to third parties or accidental loss.
8. Transfer of data outside the European Economic Area is restricted.

Principle 7 is the one that is relevant to confidentiality. Unlawful disclosure of personal data under the Act is a criminal offence which carries a maximum penalty of a fine of £5,000. Both the individual who makes the disclosure and the organisation are liable to have proceedings taken against them. Unlawful disclosure effectively means without the consent of the client and without authority from any other legislation or court order. Despite this fact, many organisations do not currently have an up-to-date data protection policy or, if a policy does exist, staff and volunteers have not been made aware of it. There is little point in having policies for issues such as data protection and confidentiality if staff and volunteers are not made aware of them. Policies which were written for the Data Protection Act 1984 may now be inadequate, since the old Act only applied to computer records, whereas the new Act applies to manual files as well. There is evidence from some organisations that policies exist, but staff are told to ask for a copy of the policy 'if they think they need it'. It seems to me that by the time you 'think you need it', it may already be too late!

Unlawful disclosure often takes place without the organisation realising what is happening. For example, it is fairly common for some organisations providing care for adults with learning disability to allow parents to see the client's file. The justification for this is usually that the organisation 'has to work with the parents'. Whilst one understands the need to have a working relationship with the family, it cannot be overlooked that the resident has rights under the Data Protection Act 1998 and that consent should be sought before family members are allowed to see the file. If the resident is unable to give such consent, then the organisation should check whether anyone has been legally appointed to act for the resident. If not, the organisation should decide on an individual basis whether it is appropriate for family members to see the resident's file and, if so, how much information should be shared. Adults with learning disability have the same rights to confidentiality and privacy as everyone else and if they have sufficient understanding, they should be given information about their rights and when information may have to be shared. However, they may also need someone to protect and help to enforce their rights. *The National Care Standards for Care Homes for People With Learning Disabilities* (Scottish Executive, 2002) reinforces these points by stating:

- Confidential information about you is only shared with others if you give permission, unless the law requires otherwise.
- If any information cannot be kept confidential you will be told why not and who has a right to see it.
- You can see for yourself that your records are kept confidential and that access to them is only allowed in controlled circumstances.

Unlawful disclosure can be the result of poor security, for example not storing files in locked cabinets or taking files home where other people may be able to read them. Any employee or volunteer who needs to keep files at home should be provided with a lockable container. Unlawful disclosure can also be the result of leaving computers logged in when they are unattended.

Unlawful disclosure may also be the result of ignorance in relation to young people's rights or an unwillingness to upset parents. In recent training sessions with GP practices, it came to light that although the practices had a strong commitment to confidentiality and knew that under-16s had the same right to confidentiality as adults, it was fairly common for results of tests to be given to parents without the consent of the young person being sought. It has now been acknowledged that this practice cannot continue and that procedures need to be put in place to seek consent from the young person to release results to someone else. Some staff said that it was hard to explain to parents why they might not be entitled to know their child's results. Interestingly, the same sort of statement was made by care workers in residential establishments for people with learning disability. Whilst one can sympathise with staff who have to deal with people who do not understand the law and may become aggressive when confronted with it, staff need to take responsibility for protecting the rights of those clients who may be unable to protect their own rights or may not even know what their rights are.

Principle 6 deals with the client's right to have access to information held about them. There are exceptions to this right in relation to social work files held by local authorities. These are set out in the Data Protection (Subject Access Modification) (Social Work) Order 2000 which states that access to some information may be withheld if it would be likely to prejudice the carrying out of social work by causing serious harm to the physical or mental health or condition of the data subject or another person. Information that identifies third parties may also be withheld, unless that third party consents or is an employee of the local authority. It is worth noting that a child in Scotland is entitled to request access to their file at any age, if they have a general understanding of what it means to make that request (s.66 of the 1998 Act). The exemptions require social workers to exercise discretion in deciding whether to allow a client to have access to all information held about them. This discretion must be exercised objectively and based on the individual circumstances of each case. Blanket policies denying access to under-16s or anyone who has had mental health problems would be open to legal challenge, no matter how well-intentioned, and would be clearly contrary to anti-discriminatory practice. In the case of *Gaskin* v. *United*

Kingdom ([1990] 1 FLR 167) the European Court of Human Rights held that a refusal to allow a client to have access to his file without any independent means of establishing whether the refusal was reasonable was a breach of human rights.

Principle 1 requires personal data to be processed fairly and lawfully. A key element of fair and lawful processing is the requirement to obtain informed consent to the processing and sharing of data. Scottish Executive guidance on single shared assessment for community care services states that informed consent to information-sharing should be sought from the client (in writing) as part of the assessment process. Where it is not possible to obtain informed consent, every effort should be made to obtain the past views and wishes of the client and the client's interests should be safeguarded through the involvement of a legal representative, specialist worker, carer or advocate (Scottish Executive, 2001). This clearly and accurately represents the legal position.

Having mentioned above that people often do not know what their rights are in relation to confidentiality, I shall now turn to the very current issue of young people not seeking help from health services in relation to contraception, pregnancy and sexually transmitted diseases. Young people do not know what their rights are in relation to confidentiality. Research carried out by the British Medical Association in 1994 found that almost 75 per cent of patients under 16 and 50 per cent of patients between 16 and 19 feared that their GP would not or could not preserve confidentiality in relation to requests for contraceptive services (BMA, 1994).

The BMA stated back in 1994 that a primary task must therefore be to educate young people about the confidentiality they can expect from their doctor. It stressed that the duty of confidentiality owed to a person under 16 is as great as that owed to any other person. Regardless of whether or not the requested treatment is given, the confidentiality of the consultation should still be respected, unless there are convincing reasons to the contrary (BMA, 1994). This last point is very important, since one might assume that if a child does not have sufficient maturity to consent, that child also loses the right to confidentiality.

However, in 2002 training sessions have highlighted that some GP practices do not have specific information about young people's rights to offer to patients and that schools do not make this sort of basic information available. Recent statistics show that over 9,000 teenagers become pregnant in Scotland every year and half of those pregnancies end in termination. In addition, since the late 1990s, diagnoses of chlamydia have risen by 75 per cent, but three-quarters of 16–25-year-olds have never heard of it (Scottish Executive, 2000). It would seem that one of the keys to dealing with these issues is easily accessible information about young people's rights to access health services in confidence.

Professional codes

Nurses and midwives have a very well-defined professional code which carries professional sanctions if breached. The code states that registered nurses and midwives must protect confidential information and use it only for the purpose for which it was given. Patients and clients must be made aware that information may have to be shared and their consent should be sought about such information sharing. Confidentiality may only be breached in the public interest or if required by law (Nursing and Midwifery Council, 2000).

Doctors also have a well-defined professional code which states that doctors should:
- seek patients' consent to disclosure of information wherever possible;
- anonymise data where unidentifiable data will serve the purpose;
- keep disclosures to the minimum necessary;
- be prepared to justify decisions in accordance with the guidance. (General Medical Council, 2000)

Teachers, although members of the General Teaching Council for Scotland, do not have the same sort of professional code as health professionals and the Council makes no reference to confidentiality. Many teachers believe that it is their duty to pass information to parents or carers, since they see themselves as being *in loco parentis*. It is also very rare to find a school which has a confidentiality policy.

Since September 2002, social workers do have a set of professional rules enforceable by a professional body – the Scottish Social Services Council (SSSC). The Code of Practice for Social Service Workers is a list of statements outlining the standards of professional conduct and practice required of social service workers. The code states that the SSSC may take action if the code is breached, but does not specify what this action might be.

One might criticise the code's rather superficial reference to confidentiality:

2. As a social service worker you must strive to establish and maintain the trust and confidence of service users and carers. This
   includes:
   2.3 Respecting confidential information and clearly explaining
       agency policies about confidentiality to services users and
       carers. (SSSC, 2002a, p. 5)

The consultation document issued in early 2002 suggested the following
more detailed wording in relation to confidentiality:

As a social care worker you must respect the independence of service
users and protect them, as far as possible, from danger or harm. This
includes:

- respecting confidential information and gaining permission from
  those it concerns to share it for specific reasons e.g. consultation
  with managers or other members of the care team. Disclosures of
  confidential information without consent should only be made
  where they can be justified in the public interest (usually where
  disclosure is essential to protect the service user or someone else
  from risk of death or serious harm) or, where disclosure is required
  by law or order of a court. (SSSC, 2002b)

Social workers and other employees and volunteers in voluntary
organisations will also be working under the code set up by their organisation. For example, Advocacy Service Aberdeen (ASA) has produced
a code that states that:

- Information is confidential within ASA and no client will be discussed
  with someone outside ASA without the client's consent. However, If
  ASA thinks that the client or another person is at serious risk of harm
  this may have to be shared with other people, but ASA would
  normally consult with the client before doing this and would provide
  reasons in writing.
- Any records or documents will be kept for five years from the last
  contact and will be kept in a locked cabinet. Files will be reviewed
  annually and inaccurate or irrelevant information removed.
- In order to protect client confidentiality, advocates will not acknowledge clients outside the office unless the client acknowledges the
  advocate first. (ASA, 2002)

Having looked at these various codes, it is worth pausing to look at the differences. Although they all focus on the fact that risk of significant harm is the trigger for a breach of confidentiality, some of the codes are much more thorough and make the professional responsible for their actions. It is also worth noting that the example given from the voluntary organisation is addressed to the client, rather than the professional. It is quite often the case that clients and patients are not clear about what their rights to confidentiality are and in what circumstances confidentiality might be breached. This seems to be an unacceptable situation if client rights are really important.

This chapter has shown the link between confidentiality and access to information, the right to respect for private life and data protection. The law has changed significantly in this area since 1998. Individuals and organisations should take the opportunity to reflect on existing policies or to develop policies if they do not have them. Directors of organisations should note that they may be held personally liable for breaches of the Data Protection Act 1998. However, a policy is not enough to evidence a real commitment to these issues. A real commitment to confidentiality and privacy is evidenced by an understanding of what the issues are about and a recognition that clients and patients need to be informed of their rights and need help to enforce them.

References

ASA (Advocacy Service Aberdeen) (2002) *Code of Confidentiality,* Aberdeen, ASA (http://www.advocacy.org.uk/artman/publish/article_12.shtml).

BMA (British Medical Association) (1994) *Confidentiality and People Under 16,* London, BMA (http://www.bma.org.uk).

General Medical Council (2000) Confidentiality: Protecting and Providing Information, London, GMC (http://www.gmc-uk.org/standards/default.htm).

Nursing and Midwifery Council (2000) *Code of Professional Conduct,* London, NMC (http://www.nmc-uk.org/cms/content/Advice/Confidentiality%202.asp).

Scottish Executive (2000) News Release: SE2920/2000 (http://www.scotland. gov.uk/news/2000/11/se2920.asp).

Scottish Executive (2001) *Guidance on Single Shared Assessment of Community Care Needs* (CCD8/2001) Edinburgh, Scottish Executive (http://www.scotland. gov.uk/health/jointfutureunit/ssa%20guidance.pdf).

Scottish Executive (2002) *The National Care Standards for Care Homes for People With Learning Disabilities,* Edinburgh, Scottish Executive (http://www.carecommission.com/sitepix/downloads/publications/learning_disabilities.pdf).

SSSC (Scottish Social Services Council) (2002a) *Code of Practice for Social Care Workers,* Dundee, SSSC (http://www.sssc.uk.com/news/code_of_practice.html).

SSSC (Scottish Social Services Council) (2002b) *Draft Code of Conduct for Social Care Workers,* Dundee, SSSC.

8

The Social Work Role in the Children's Hearings System

JANICE McGHEE

The children's hearings tribunal system has remained the central forum for childcare and youth justice decision-making in Scotland since 1971. The philosophy, principles and procedures of the system have remained relatively unchanged in this period although there has been some concern about the effectiveness of the hearings in dealing with persistent offenders.

The report of the Kilbrandon Committee (1964) and the proposals to establish children's hearings represented a radical shift in juvenile justice policy and practice. Previously children who committed offences had been dealt with in the courts although specialised juvenile courts were underdeveloped in Scotland (Cowperthwaite, 1988). Kilbrandon (1964) regarded the juvenile court as an inappropriate forum for dealing with child offenders.

The children's hearings are distinctive in that children who offend and those in need of care and protection are dealt with in the same system. This integration reflects the welfare philosophy of the hearings, which emphasises the 'needs' of the child rather than their 'deeds' in decision-making and intervention. The Kilbrandon Committee (1964) found the legal distinction between juvenile offenders and children in need of care and attention was of 'little practical significance' when the underlying needs and circumstances of the children were examined (para. 13, p. 12). The basis for intervention is whether the child may need compulsory measures of supervision. The lay panel who meet together with the child and his or her family are responsible for this decision. There is a clear emphasis on participation by the child and family in the hearing and on the right of the child to have account taken of his or her views.

The function of establishing the facts of a case is clearly separated from deciding whether compulsory measures are required in the child's best interests. The courts are only involved where these facts are disputed, in appeals and in dealing with serious offences. The Scottish courts also retain decision-making where long-term or permanent changes in status are being sought, such as adoption, freeing for adoption or parental responsibilities orders; and in applications for child protection measures (child protection and exclusion orders).

Social work practitioners have to be able to operate effectively within this system, which places a range of demands upon practice skills, policy and legal knowledge. They must gather information for the Reporter and the hearing, providing social background reports and an assessment of any difficulties the child and family may be facing. Clear recommendations regarding the need for compulsory measures of supervision or whether voluntary support is a more suitable alternative are required. The Reporter is the initial gatekeeper in the hearings system and therefore regular discussion and liaison with him or her about potential new referrals and ongoing cases is an important aspect of practice.

Practitioners must also supervise a child where a formal requirement has been made, coordinating and in many cases directly providing a service to address the needs of the child and the family. This may involve working with children and their families where the main concerns are related to the care or protection of the child and in others where offending is a central feature. It is therefore vital for workers to have a sound understanding of the legal basis, procedures and underlying philosophy of this distinctive system.

National statistical patterns

National annual statistics are published by the Scottish Children's Reporter Administration (SCRA) and provide information on referrals and decisions within the hearings system. The most recent Statistical Bulletin (SCRA, 2002) provides comparisons between 1990 and 2000/01 (the year from 1 April 2000 to 31 March 2001) on a range of measures. Referrals to the Reporter increased by 50 per cent in this period and the number of children involved in referrals to the Reporter also increased by 35.3 per cent (SCRA, 2002, p. 8) (see Table 8.1). The number of children subject to a supervision requirement increased by 11.3 per cent in the same period (SCRA, 2002, p. 8) (see Table 8.1). Responding to these increasing demands has presented a major challenge to the children's hearings system and social work services.

The pattern of referrals has also changed with a lesser proportion of children referred for offending. In 2000/01 the rate of referral per 1,000 population under 16 years was 13.5 per cent for offence referrals, compared to a rate of 22.1 per cent for non-offence referrals (SCRA, 2002, p. 7). A substantial increase in the number of care and protection referrals (69 per cent, SCRA: 2002) over the period 1990 to 2000/01 has brought often complex cases of child abuse into the domain of the children's hearings system.[1]

Children in the hearings

Until recently there was limited knowledge about the backgrounds of children involved in the hearings. Waterhouse *et al.* (2000), in a study of 1,155 children referred to the hearings in 1995, found that many of the children came from families where there was social and economic disadvantage. This was especially likely for those children under supervision (Waterhouse and McGhee, 2002a). Common factors in the children's backgrounds were lone parenting (46 per cent of children's families) and dependence on state benefits (55 per cent of children's families), with the majority of the children's families living in local authority housing (72 per cent). These patterns of social disadvantage are similar to those

Table 8.1 *Children's hearings statistics: comparisons between 1990 and 2000/01*

	1990	*2000/01*	*% Increase*
Number of referrals	37,252	56,003[*]	40
Number of children referred	24,331	32,938	35.3
Children under supervision at 30 June	9,771	10,878	11.3

[*] This was a decrease from the previous year (1999/00) when 63,857 referrals were dealt with.

Source: SCRA, 2002.

found in the background of children admitted to public care (Bebbington and Miles, 1989; Packman and Hall, 1998).

An argument is not being made that poverty and disadvantage caused the children's difficulties, or the need for compulsory measures of supervision; other problems were also present including, for example, parental drug and alcohol misuse, health and/or behavioural difficulties and general concerns about the child's care and upbringing. However it does point to the importance in practice of recognising the impact social disadvantage may have on the lives of children and their families which in turn may give rise to a need for additional support (McGhee and Waterhouse, 2002). There are links between child poverty and educational attainment (Quilgars, 2001) and Gregg *et al.* (1999) have shown poor outcomes in relation to earnings or employment for children in disadvantaged families (defined as in poverty, lone parenthood, having an unemployed father or experience of public care).

Clearly the resources allocated to areas outwith the direct remit of social work such as social security are relevant but supporting parents in accessing wider educational, health, housing and child welfare services is important to practice as these services can have a positive impact on a child's life chances (Waterhouse and McGhee, 2002a).

Assessment and reports

Providing social background reports and recommendations to the Reporter and the hearing is a key aspect of the social work role. Central to good practice is the need to be open and honest about the assessment and reasons for the recommendation being made; this allows the child or family to counter this view within the hearing. Hallett *et al.* (1998), in a study of decision-making in the hearings system, found that in most cases (84 per cent) the hearing's decision was in line with the social worker's recommendation. This can at times lead to some children and families feeling that a decision has been made prior to the hearing (Hallett *et al.*, 1998; Waterhouse *et al.*, 2000).

Relevant persons[2] (broadly parents or carers) since 1996 have had the legal right to receive a copy of all reports sent to the hearing members. The law was changed following the decision of the European Court of Human Rights in the case of *McMichael* v. *United Kingdom* [1995] 20 EHHR 205, when the UK was criticised for failing to give parents the right to see any written reports provided by professionals. It remains good practice for reports to be discussed with the child to the extent appropriate and the family in advance of a hearing.

Access to reports can raise issues of confidentiality for children and their families. A child looked after away from home may wish to write their own report to the hearing, perhaps indicating they do not want to return home. This may be against the wishes of a parent or carer and the child may fear to upset or anger them. As the child's report is part of the hearings papers a copy would be given to the parent or carer, thus potentially inhibiting the child's ability to convey their views. In other situations divorced spouses who have little contact will receive reports which may contain personal information that one partner does not wish revealed to the other. This brings to the fore some of the complexity of report-writing in this context.

Children are not legally entitled to receive copies of reports although practice is changing in light of the case *S* v. *Principal Reporter and Lord Advocate* 2001 (discussed below). Prior to this case being heard the Principal Reporter indicated that children, subject to some protective measures, would be given copies of reports on request. It is clear that some young people do wish to have access to reports (Scottish Office, 1992; Gallagher, 1998; Hallett *et al.*, 1998), although taking account of age and literacy levels practitioners will need to continue discussing their report with the child prior to the hearing.

Confidentiality issues are raised for report writers: a child, for example, may be unaware of a parent's life-threatening illness but this information may be vital for the proper consideration of the case by a hearing. A pilot scheme has been initiated by the Scottish Children's Reporter Administration whereby children aged 12 years or over are automatically given copies of reports and those under 12 years are given access on request. Report writers were asked to indicate and if possible separately append any parts of the report that should not be made available to the child. This places the onus on practitioners to find a sound balance between openness and confidentiality. Further guidance regarding reports will be forthcoming following the outcomes of the pilot study and further consultation.

Working in partnership

Partnership between professionals and parents or carers is a central principle of good childcare practice in the UK. Whilst the Children

(Scotland) Act 1995 does not specifically include the term, government guidance makes clear that local authorities should work in partnership with families when providing services to promote the welfare of children (Scottish Office, 1997, p. 5). Working in partnership means including parents or carers and where possible the child in decision-making and planning, providing real choice to families and clear information about procedures, progress and reasons for decisions (Waterhouse and McGhee, 2002a). Hill (2000) adds that being 'open and honest', working in agreement with parents and avoiding legal action, where possible, and taking into account and respecting 'community and cultural contexts' are also key elements of the partnership model (p. 57). Singh *et al.* (2000), in a survey of some local authorities and representative voluntary agencies, found low numbers of black staff in services for children and families in Scotland (p. 195) and identified a need for more training on issues relating to black and minority ethnic children.

The underlying assumption in the hearings system is that the majority of parents want the best for their child. Partnership with parents or carers therefore has always been an important aspect of the children's hearings. Panel members, parents or carers, children and social work practitioners are all involved in decision-making and planning in the best interests of the child. The increase in care and protection referrals has presented further challenges to panel members, especially in addressing complex child abuse cases where there may be conflicting interests (McGhee *et al.*, 1996). However, this needs to be kept in context; in a study following the progress of 220 child protection cases Thoburn *et al.* (1995) found only a small number of cases where problems were so severe parents could not be involved at all. Moreover better outcomes for children appeared more likely when parents were included.

Professional accountability and power are subject to scrutiny in the hearings, as practitioners are required to account for their work with the child and family. The review system allows all parties to examine earlier decisions, identify where progress has been made or further work is required, and reconsider the need for compulsory measures of supervision. The right of relevant persons (and the child) to seek a review hearing potentially gives them a greater sense of control over the process, providing an environment that supports genuine partnership.

Where there is statutory involvement the power imbalance between the child and family and the social work practitioner needs to be recognised, especially if the child is living away from home by virtue of a supervision requirement. Central to open communication is the necessity for practitioners to be clear about the nature and extent of their powers and their duties within the hearings system.

Communication and information

Many children referred to the hearings for the first time and their families will have little knowledge of the aims and procedures of the system or their rights and responsibilities within it. Practitioners therefore have a crucial role in providing information about the hearings system and the role of the Reporter, panel members and social workers. Waterhouse *et al.* (2000), interviewing a small sample (24 in total) of parents and young people involved in the hearings, found in the majority of cases adequate information was given regarding the differing stages of the process. However, for a small minority the role of the hearings and that of the social work department was not fully clear (p. 109). Hallett *et al.* (1998) interviewed ten parents and ten children or young people involved in a hearing. They noted that most families saw social workers as having a role in preparing them for the hearing and that this was valued (p. 63); families generally wanted to be more aware of the process and operation of the hearings system.

A thorough understanding of the legal and philosophical basis of the system, the role of key personnel and the process of the hearing and a sound awareness of rights and responsibilities are essential to successfully working in partnership in the children's hearings system. Children and their families should be advised of their right to contact the Reporter to discuss the referral and to seek legal advice. In day-to-day practice the social worker in many instances will be a key source of information about the system.

Good communication skills and knowledge of child and adolescent development are central to good practice. Using interpreters where English may not be the child or family's first language and assisted communication if a disability impacts on this aspect are both important.

Participation in the hearing

The original intention of the hearings system was to provide a straightforward procedure with few legal technicalities, encouraging a non-adversarial forum where panel members, children and their families could discuss any difficulties and seek potential solutions. There is a clear onus on the hearing to take account of the child's views (s.16(2) of the Children (Scotland) Act 1995, Rule 15 Children's Hearings (Scotland) Rules 1996, S.I. 1996, No. 3261).

Relevant persons and, following the recommendations of the Orkney Inquiry (Scottish Office, 1992), children have an absolute legal right to attend the hearing. In some circumstances both can be released from the obligation to attend. An example may be where a young person aged 16 is living with a relative under a supervision requirement and has no parental contact. In this case the parent(s) may be permitted not to attend the hearing.

Tensions can arise when child abuse is a central ground for concern and there is a clear conflict between the interests of the child and his or her parent(s) or carer(s). The presence of the alleged abuser at the hearing will often inhibit a child in responding to panel members. At other times conflicting loyalties towards parents or an unwillingness to expose parental difficulties can also make it harder for a child to communicate in the hearing (Griffiths and Kandel, 2000; McGhee, 2000).

There are legal options available that may assist communication, for example the alleged abuser can be excluded from part of the hearing. However this does not give confidentiality to the child as the substance of the discussion between the child and the panel members must be disclosed to the excluded person. In these circumstances children may still be unwilling or unable to give their views. This contrasts with private law applications in relation to parental responsibilities and rights (s.11, Children (Scotland) Act 1995) where the Sheriff can potentially decide to keep the child's views confidential. Allowing some measure of confidentiality to the child may be a way to resolve some of these issues. There is a clear responsibility on practitioners to ensure they listen to and take account of the child's views, although it is important to be honest with children that safeguarding their interests is the primary responsibility.

There have been a small number of studies exploring the participation of parents and children in the hearings system. Petch (1988), interviewing 100 families, found that 58 per cent were satisfied with their level of participation, although a minority retained a more negative view. Martin *et al.* (1981), reporting on interviews with 105 young people aged between 12 and 15 referred to a hearing on offence grounds found the majority were satisfied with their level of participation. A minority of young people (from one-fifth to approaching one-quarter of cases) had less favourable views: some interviewees felt they had not been listened to and that a decision had been made before the hearing began.

More recently Hallett *et al.* (1998), as part of their decision-making study, observed 60 hearings and interviewed 20 family members. They found that participation by children and families in hearings was limited, with many reporting apprehension or nervousness. Children and young people have identified difficulties in communicating with panel members and ensuring their views are heard (Freeman *et al.*, 1994; Triseliotis *et al.*, 1995; Griffiths and Kandel, 2000; McGhee, 2000). Children and families are aware of the importance of ensuring their views are put forward in the hearing and are more satisfied if they have the opportunity to do so (Hallett *et al.*, 1998).

Preparation of children and families prior to hearings and the development of sound communication skills by panel members and professionals are clearly central to ensuring effective communication within a hearing. Other suggestions for change have included: children and families meeting panel members beforehand; reducing the number of people who attend the hearing; ensuring that initial panel members also attend review hearings to ensure continuity (Hallett *et al.*, 1998); more preparation and information for children prior to a hearing; and making language, especially the legal aspects, more readily accessible (Griffiths and Kandel, 2000). The provision of information and preparation for the hearing are a key aspect of the social work role.

Rights and representation in the hearings

Although the intention behind the hearings is to provide a relatively informal forum there are explicit legal aspects that must be undertaken in order to protect children's and families' rights. This inevitably leads to some formality in the process. Reasons must be given for hearings decisions and rights of appeal and review must all be intimated to the child and family. Hallett *et al.* (1998), observing 60 hearings, found these rights were not always fully articulated; the right to appeal the hearing's decision was indicated in 98 per cent of cases but the right to call for a review was explained in only 72 per cent, with time limits sometimes incorrectly given.

The child and the relevant person both have the right to challenge the grounds of referral. It is important that they are aware of this fundamental right, especially for children and young people who commit an offence. Acceptance of the offence ground (or if it is proved in the Sheriff Court) is deemed a conviction for the purposes of the Rehabilitation of Offenders Act 1974. This Act allows certain offences to be deemed as 'spent' after a period of time.

Relevant persons and children do have a right to bring a representative and this can include a friend, relative, a solicitor or a children's rights officer (Rule 11, Children's Hearings Rules 1996). Few solicitors attend hearings, partly as civil legal aid has not been available at that stage. In the recent case *S* v. *Principal Reporter and Lord Advocate* 2001 SLT 531 (and *S* v. *Miller* (No. 2) 2001 SLT 1304) the overall framework of the hearings system was seen to be in line with the European Convention on Human Rights. However the unavailability of legally aided representation for the child at a hearing was not seen as compliant with Article 6(1) of the Convention (the right to a fair and public hearing). The Scottish Executive has indicated they will consult on a long-term solution to this matter. At present legally qualified safeguarders and curators *ad litem* may be appointed to represent children at hearings in certain circumstances: where a residential supervision requirement may be necessary and the child fits the criteria for secure accommodation; or where representation is needed to allow the child to participate effectively (Rule 3, The Children's Hearings (Legal Representation) (Scotland) Rules 2002, S.S.I. 2002 No. 63). It is most likely that the first category (secure care) will generate the greatest demand on legally aided representation. It is unclear if legal aid will become available to relevant persons at the hearings stage.

The potential increasing involvement of legal representatives could conceivably undermine the fundamental aim of creating a non-adversarial hearing. Moreover if social workers, each relevant person and the child, for example, attended with their own solicitor the increased numbers are likely to inhibit open communication. The majority of solicitors are liable to have little experience of children as clients or training in communicating with children (Edwards, 2002), both important skills for practice. Children's and families' rights do require to be upheld in the system to ensure natural justice and fairness. It remains to be seen how representation will develop in practice and what impact it may ultimately have on the operation of the hearings system.

Resources

Hearings do not have direct control over resources; the local authority has the responsibility to implement the supervision requirement. Although this is a corporate responsibility it is the social work service which inevitably takes the main role. The majority of children under supervision remain living at home with a parent, guardian, relative or friend (70 per cent of boys and 70 per cent of girls under supervision at 30 June 2000, Table 16, p. 25, SCRA, 2002). Direct work with children and their families in the context of a partnership approach therefore remains the cornerstone of day-to-day practice in the children's hearings. Developing good links with other services, especially in health and education, are vital to promoting the well-being of the children involved. A recent study by Murray *et al.* (2002) found that panel members, teachers, reporters and social workers identified more social work time as the key factor which would improve the supervision of children at home. They also noted that social work staff shortages in some areas were severely affecting the service provided.

Hallett *et al.* (1998) found that a lack of resources was a significant problem identified by panel members and professionals. Moreover panel members saw cases referred for voluntary measures of supervision as having a lower priority in social work departments with less time allotted; both panel members and social work practitioners saw resources as more likely to be available if compulsory measures were in place. McGhee and Waterhouse (2002), have suggested that hearings' decisions regarding the imposition of a supervision requirement could ultimately be affected by this awareness. They discuss whether a factor in the decision to impose compulsory measures of supervision is the potential to gain access to otherwise limited resources. Although the intention would be to benefit the child and family by making resources available this could infringe children's rights when individual freedom and autonomy are restricted.

Young people who offend

Whilst a child under 16 years of age can be prosecuted in the adult court with the permission of the Lord Advocate this is rare unless it is a serious offence. Kilbrandon (1964) saw juvenile delinquency as only one aspect of a child's life experience, the aim of the new hearings system being to assist and support families without invoking punitive measures such as fines.

Diversion from formal involvement in the hearings system for young offenders is a key part of the system. Children often grow out of criminal activity, and many offences committed up to age 17 are of a minor nature (Whyte, 1998). Early intervention to prevent offending by the most troubled young people is important, especially as for the majority of young offenders at age 16 there is a clear move away from the welfare-based system of the hearings into the traditional adult criminal justice system.

It is often when addressing the needs of young people who offend that the tension between welfare and justice approaches is most apparent. The welfare approach emphasises the need to address underlying difficulties in the child's social and personal circumstances. The justice approach places an emphasis on 'just deserts', proportionality in sentencing and a focus on rights within the system. There is a need to directly address the offending behaviour of some young people, and a balance needs to be struck between these aspects in practice.

Professionals and panel members have expressed concerns about the ability of the hearings system to deal with persistent young offenders (Hallett *et al.*, 1998). It may be that social work intervention does not systematically address offending behaviour. A recent report by Audit Scotland (2002) found that the lack of specialist services and social workers was a factor and that qualified social workers required better training in working with young offenders. There also may be an expectation amongst social workers and panel members that young people should be discharged from supervision at 16 years (Pickles, 1992). Waterhouse *et al.* (2000) found that supervision requirements made on the offence ground were often terminated at age 15 (p. 77). Overall a reason for the termination of some supervision requirements was that the child was seen to have 'outgrown the system or the hearings system had nothing to offer the child' (p. 49).

Effective and early intervention is important to practice in working with children and young people who offend. There is a developing body of knowledge practitioners can draw upon which outline successful methods of working with young offenders. Cognitive behavioural and social learning approaches appear to be more effective in reducing offending than traditional non-directive or psycho-dynamic counselling approaches (CJSW Briefing, 2001). Assessment is important in this context as the largest positive results arise where there is a higher risk of reoffending; intensive services are not appropriate for young people who are unlikely to reoffend (CJSW Briefing, 2001).

Working with young and sometimes persistent offenders presents a challenge to social work services. Whyte (1998) argues that combining work with individuals, families and groups is most likely to be effective, and these approaches can allow for the involvement of key family members in the supervision process. Structured community-based programmes have been developed in Scotland such as the Freagarrach Project run by Barnardo's, suggesting further work of this nature needs to be developed.

The Scottish Executive (2002a) has an action programme to reduce youth crime, which includes investment to develop and improve community-based programmes for persistent offenders. Multi-agency groups have been established in all local authorities with a key role in strategic planning to reduce youth crime and to promote integrated childcare and youth justice provision (Scottish Executive, 2002a). They are also expected to have close links with youth justice practice and operational teams. Restorative justice approaches which allow the victim a role are also being explored, although confidentiality for the child and the family is an issue as personal family matters are often discussed in the hearing.

The Ad-Hoc Ministerial Group on Youth Crime recommended a range of actions including the development of national standards for youth justice services. These were published in December 2002 and set out standards for hearings and local authorities on, for example, timescales to reach and implement hearings' decisions, for assessment of offenders and on developing a range of programmes to stop youth offending (Scottish Executive, 2002b). Moreover there will be a feasibility project to explore the development of youth courts for persistent offenders aged 16/17 but which could also include some 15-year-olds, and a pilot to 'fast-track' persistent young offenders in the hearings system will also be undertaken. In England there is a separate Youth Court and there are concerns that a similar development in Scotland could potentially undermine the role of the hearings in this area. The availability of effective programmes to meet the needs and address the offending behaviour of some young people is as important as the specific forum.

These proposals present a major challenge to social work practitioners operating within the children's hearings system and will demand further development of knowledge and skills in working effectively with young people who offend.

Conclusion

Working within the children's hearings system is a central feature of social work practice in Scotland. Some of the issues highlighted above are likely to bring new challenges to practitioners but the essential components of openness, honesty and respect in working with children, young people and their families remain fundamental to good practice.

Notes

1. The Scottish Children's Reporter Administration now includes the ground set out in s.52(2)(a) in the definition of a care and protection referral.
2. Defined in s.93(2)(b), Children (Scotland) Act 1995 Act. Those fitting this definition and the genetic father of the child if he is living with the genetic mother are entitled to receive a copy of all reports and other documents sent to panel members (Rules 5(3), 12, Children's Hearings (Scotland) Rules 1996, S.I. 1996 No. 3261).

References

Audit Scotland (2002) *Dealing with Offending by Young People*, Edinburgh, Auditor General/Accounts Commission.

Bebbington, A. and Miles, J. (1989) 'The background of children who enter local authority care', *British Journal of Social Work*, vol. 19, no. 5, pp. 349–68.

CJSW Briefing (2001) *CJSW Briefing, Paper 1: December 2001. Responding to Youth and Adult Crime: Future Directions,* Edinburgh, Criminal Justice Social Work Development Centre for Scotland (www.cjsw.ac.uk).

Cowperthwaite, D.J. (1988) *The Emergence of the Scottish Children's Hearings System: An Administrative/Political Study of the Establishment of Novel Arrangements in Scotland for Dealing with Juvenile Offenders*, Southampton, University of Southampton.

Edwards (2002) 'Legal representation arrives at the Children's Hearing – but at what cost?, *Green's Family Law Bulletin*, Issue 57, pp. 2–5.

Freeman, I., Morrison, A., Lockhart, F. Swanson, M. and Duffy, C. (1994) *An Account of a Pilot Consultation Exercise with Young People*, Glasgow, Strathclyde Regional Council.

Gallagher, R. (1998) *Children and Young People's Voice on the Law, Legal Services and System in Scotland*, Glasgow, Scottish Child Law Centre.

Gregg, P., Harkness, S. and Machin, S. (1999*) Child Development and Family Income*, York, YPS.

Griffiths, A. and Kandel, R.F. (2000) 'Hearing children in children's hearings', *Child and Family Law Quarterly*, vol. 12, no. 3, pp. 283–99.

Hallett, C. and Murray, C., with Jamieson, J. and Veitch, B. (1998) *The Evaluation of Children's Hearings in Scotland. Vol. 1 Deciding in Children's Interests,* Edinburgh, Scottish Office Central Research Unit.

Hill, M. (2000) 'Partnership reviewed: Words of caution, words of encouragement', *Adoption and Fostering*, vol. 24, no. 3, pp. 56–68.

Kilbrandon, L. (1964) *Children and Young Persons, Scotland*, Cmnd 2306, Edinburgh, Scottish Office, HMSO.

McGhee, J. (2000) 'Young people's views of the children's hearings system in Scotland', unpublished report to NCH-Scotland.

McGhee, J. and Waterhouse, L. (2002) 'Family support and the Scottish children's hearings system', *Child and Family Social Work*, vol. 7, Issue 4, pp. 273–83.

McGhee, J., Waterhouse, L. and Whyte, W. (1996) 'Children's hearings and children in trouble', in S. Asquith (ed.) *Children and Young People in Conflict with the Law*, Research Highlights in Social Work 30, London, Jessica Kingsley.

Martin, F.M., Fox, S. J. and Murray, K. (1981) *Children Out of Court*, Edinburgh, Scottish Academic Press.

Murray, C., Hallett, C., McMillan, M. and Watson, J. (2002) *Children (Scotland) Act 1995, Research Findings No. 4. Home Supervision*, Edinburgh, Scottish Executive.

Packman J. and Hall, C. (1998) *From Care to Accommodation: Support, Protection and Control in Child Care Services*, London, The Stationery Office.

Petch, A. (1988) Answering Back: Parental Perspectives on the Children's Hearing System', *British Journal of Social Work*, vol. 18, pp. 1–24.

Pickles, T. (1992) *Selective Hearings. A Descriptive Study of the Children's Hearing Initiative: Dumbarton Project*, Edinburgh, Save the Children Fund (Scotland).

Quilgars, D. (2001) 'Educational attainment', in J. Bradshaw (ed.) *Poverty: The Outcomes for Children*, London, Family Policy Studies Centre.

Scottish Executive (2002a) *Scotland's Action Programme to Reduce Youth Crime 2002*, Edinburgh, Scottish Executive.

Scottish Executive (2002b) *National Standards for Scotland's Youth Justice Services*, Edinburgh, Scottish Executive.

Scottish Office (1992) *The Report of the Inquiry into the Removal of Children from Orkney in February 1991*, Edinburgh, HMSO.

Scottish Office (1992) *Who's Hearing? A Summary of a One Day Seminar on Children's Hearings in Scotland*, Edinburgh, HMSO.

Scottish Office (1997) *Scotland's Children. The Children (Scotland) Act 1995 Regulations and Guidance. Volume 1: Support and Protection for Children and their Families*, Edinburgh, Stationery Office.

SCRA (2001) *Statistical Bulletin No. 24, Referrals of Children to Reporters and Children's Hearings. 1999/00*, No. SCRA/MJH 2000/24, Stirling, Scottish Children's Reporter Administration.

SCRA (2000) *Statistical Bulletin, Referrals of Children to Reporters and Children's Hearings. 1996/97*, No. SCRA/1999/21, Stirling, Scottish Children's Reporter Administration.

Singh, S., Patel, V.K.P. and Falconer, P. (2000) 'Confusion and perceptions: social work conceptions regarding black children in Scotland', in D. Iwaniec and M. Hill (eds) *Child Welfare Policy and Practice*, London, Jessica Kingsley.

Thoburn, J., Lewis, A. and Shemmings, D. (1995) 'Paternalism or partnership? Family involvement in the child protection process in Department of Health', *Child Protection Messages from Research*, London, HMSO.

Triseliotis, J., Borland, M., Hill, M. and Lambert, L. (1995) *Teenagers and the Social Work Services*, London, HMSO.

Waterhouse, L., McGhee, J., Whyte, W., Loucks, N., Kay, H. and Stewart, R. (2000) *The Evaluation of Children's Hearings in Scotland. Vol. 3: Children in Focus*, Edinburgh, Scottish Executive Central Research Unit.

Waterhouse, L. and McGhee, J. (2002a) 'Social work with children and families', in R. Adams, L. Dominelli and M. Payne (eds) *Social Work. Themes, Issues and Critical Debates*, 2nd edn, Basingstoke, Palgrave Macmillan.

Waterhouse, L. and McGhee, J. (2002b) 'Children's hearings in Scotland: compulsion and disadvantage', *Journal of Social Welfare and Family Law*, vol. 24, no. 3, pp. 279–96.

Whyte, B. (1998) 'Rediscovering juvenile delinquency', in A. Lockyer and F.H. Stone (eds) *Juvenile Justice in Scotland. Twenty-five Years of the Welfare Approach*, Edinburgh, T. & T. Clark.

9

Social Work Practice in the Criminal Justice System

ROBERT MACKAY

Introduction

Since the introduction of *National Objectives and Standards for Social Work in the Criminal Justice System* (1991) social work in this field has undergone a sea change. The advent of firm expectations in protocols of practice, the institution of ring-fenced funding and the dedication of social workers to the criminal justice sector have transformed social work practice. It has raised standards, but it has also created new tensions.

In this chapter I will look at current policy issues affecting practice; the role of the social worker in the criminal and youth justice sectors; issues connected with making sense of offending behaviour; and responses to offending. I conclude with some brief thoughts about the future of criminal and youth justice social work.

A basic assumption within this chapter is that social workers in the criminal and youth justice sector share their professional world with other practitioners: judges, prosecutors, defence agents, police officers and prison staff. All draw upon the same disciplines of criminology and penology. Even if the system is not always a coherent one, and I refer to it as a criminal justice – penal archipelago, they are all bound by the terms of the same professional concepts and debates.

Current policy issues

Risk and fear

Social work is now part of an overarching policy to reduce crime and antisocial behaviour in society. It forms part of the agenda of community safety. This policy is a response to a complex of political, media and real-life agendas about crime, the fear of crime and social disorder, and social nuisance. This agenda embraces everything from 'youths causing annoyance' and noise between neighbours, through to sex offending and terrorism.

The watchword of this policy is risk. The theme of managing risk has much wider ramifications in society (Beck, 1992), affecting other policy areas such as environment, commercial practice, agriculture, food and health. Within social work itself, the management of risk has become a major preoccupation. We need to evaluate the use of this concept in social work practice. However, the emphasis on risk intersects with the phenomenon of fear. Fear of crime is a vexed issue, because the actual risk of victimisation does not correlate with the levels of fear among different groups of the population. There are, therefore, two related policy concerns: managing risk and managing fear. This creates a difficult tightrope for policy-makers and practitioners because, on the one hand, it is so easy to be seen to be minimising the problem while, on the other, talking up risk of crime creates further erosion of social trust.

Implicit in this approach is a concern for victims of crime. This is important for social work because historically we have not dealt routinely with victims of crime, except in the field of child victims of abuse.

Best value

Throughout the public services the consequences of the market philosophy that inspired the Thatcher and Major administrations continue to be felt. Public services are continuously required to justify their utility and their competitiveness. Social work services have been provided on a competitive tendering basis by the independent sector, and sometimes by the statutory sector itself. A major example of this is the competition between independent agencies and local authorities for the social work services to Scottish prisons. Sometimes services are purchased on the basis of a 'preferred bidder'. Whatever the mechanism, the clear expectation is that services are purchased on the basis of 'best value', the most cost-efficient bid set against the standard of service required. Local authorities are now required to account for the use of funds through the discipline of 100 per cent funding of criminal justice services.

A preponderance of public expenditure in relation to criminal justice and penal policy is dedicated to the police and the Scottish Prison

Service. The dominance of the prison in the 'archipelago' of the criminal justice–penal system and the accompanying and often unstated assumption that punishment is the norm for offending form a counterweight to the drive for economic use of resources in penal services. Nevertheless, the question must be posed. How do we know whether any intervention is cost-effective towards the aim of reducing offending? The implication is that those charged with decision-making and resource allocation in individual cases (judges, prosecutors, children's reporters and others) should consider the economic use of resources (Nicholson, 1992).

The shape of criminal justice, youth justice and antisocial behaviour policy

The policy on crime and antisocial behaviour has very clear contours and involves many agencies. Its outline comprises a threefold approach of prevention, minimal intervention and maximum protection. It is a mistake to think that it simply involves the mainstream criminal justice agencies, statutory and voluntary. The policy also involves education, health, the fire service and leisure and social services within the statutory sector, and a whole range of voluntary organisations and businesses in the independent and commercial sectors. The discipline of community planning entails a holistic approach to developing, implementing and delivering services. In the spirit of this legislation, the Scottish Executive's requirement for Youth Justice Strategy Teams, involving senior staff over a wide range of areas to develop a coherent range of services designed to meet prescribed standards, is setting new challenges for all the community-based agencies (Scottish Executive, 2002).

The contours of the policy (prevention, minimal intervention, maximum protection) can be detected in the spectrum of practice.

In the domain of *prevention* there is a concern to design out crime. This has implications for policing, building design and the provision of general services that can reduce the incidence of specific types of offending. This policy thus has two strands: hard and soft. The former relates to such measures as CCTV; the latter to the provision of facilities that assist people to stay out of trouble, such as youth clubs and services for those misusing substances.

In the domain of *minimal intervention* we find that, in the area of antisocial behaviour, community mediation is encouraged before the application of more formal sanctions such as eviction or application for antisocial behaviour orders (Crime and Disorder Act, s.19). The 'no order' principle in relation to decisions about children gives particular emphasis to the capacity of the Children's Reporter to refer a child to the local authority (Children (Scotland) Act 1995). Similarly, with adults, the Procurator Fiscal has the power to refer any case to another agency for assistance with or without conditions, for instance to a social work diversion scheme, or to a mediation scheme. Such measures are collectively categorised as diversion. However, such a term, like that of 'alternative', neglects the perspective that a proper set of criteria should determine whether a case requires prosecution or a custodial outcome. Such terms imply leniency, and, as well as reflecting a bureaucratic rather than a juridical approach, give comfort to those who would portray community sanctions as a soft option.

In the domain of *maximum protection* we find at the community level the use of antisocial behaviour orders (ASBOs) and the use of eviction by local authorities. It should be noted that these measures are civil, although behaviour that might be deemed criminal may have occurred, and a breach of an ASBO is a criminal offence. In Youth Justice, the children's hearings have the long-standing measures of supervision requirements. However, we can see in the Children (Scotland) Act 1995 an internal strain between the principle of welfare and the principle of public safety. For the first time since the 1968 Act, public protection is acknowledged as an objective that can take priority over the best interests of the child (1995 Act, s.16(5)). In the adult courts the whole range of sentences and orders reflects an agenda of public protection. The measures relating to the Sex Offenders Register and the longer periods of supervision for post-custodial elements of sentences for sex offenders, and the assessment of risk associated with parole applications, are clear evidence of an overriding agenda to protect the public (Criminal Procedure (Scotland) Act 1995; Sex Offenders Act (1997), Criminal Justice (Scotland) Bill (2003)).

Human rights

It is important for social workers to recognise that in all aspects of their work they are governed by the principles of human rights legislation. This embraces and takes further the provisions of anti-discriminatory legislation. The implications for the criminal justice system are manifold, but chief amongst them are that the operation of the system itself may provide grounds for actions under human rights and anti-discrimination legislation. Patterns of recommendations or sentencing or the provision of services may all give rise to claims of discrimination. Social workers must, therefore, be acutely aware of the implications of their recommendations and interventions. This must entail attempts to understand properly the circumstances and social factors having a bearing upon all service users, irrespective of sex, ethnicity, religion or disability.

The role of the social worker

Social workers no longer 'advise, assist and befriend': they 'advise, assist and guide'. With this shift of emphasis has come an apparent alteration in the role of the social worker. The social worker is now to be less concerned with meeting welfare needs than with addressing offending behaviour. Dealing with 'crimogenic' need is a means to an end in dealing with the agenda of reducing crime in society. The social worker is responsible for getting offenders to take responsibility for their actions.

It should be noted, too, that just as the management of policy has become multi-agency in focus, so too has the delivery of practice. We find that there is mixing of roles. Police officers may engage with diversion schemes, prison officers may serve as welfare officers. Social workers may play an investigative role in child protection. Social programmes may be delivered in the independent sector by staff who are not social workers. Social workers who are supervising orders may not undertake the main intervention with the service user. As in other areas of social work practice, the social worker effectively becomes a commissioner of services and a supervisor of the offender: a broker between the criminal justice referrer, the client, the local authority and the service provider.[1]

Does this position not represent a fundamental change of stance? Historically, the probation officer played a dual role as officer of the court and social worker to the probationer. Now the promotion of welfare appears to relate only to crimogenic need. The main responsibility is to the court, to assess, to supervise and to report. However, a social worker is bound by *The Values and Principles and Social Work Practice in the Criminal Justice System* by the Association of Directors of Social Work which states:

> The object of social work is to promote social welfare and social justice through helping to alleviate personal and social problems and

seeking to enhance the quality of life of individuals, families and communities. Social work is rooted in the belief that the origins of personal and social problems, including criminal behaviour, may be found not only in the exercise of individual choice but also in factors over which the individual has little or no control. (Association of Directors of Social Work, 1996)

To this extent, the original social work agenda holds primacy still. However, the emphasis on concern for the victim of crime has the effect of balancing this value commitment.

In actuality, although the fundamental elements of the social work role remain similar, there are many operational changes. The practice of social work is governed by the local interpretations of the second edition of *National Objectives and Standards for Social Work in the Criminal Justice System*. The normative and prescriptive requirements for assessment, supervision and reporting (including breach proceedings) provide a structure for practice that did not exist between the demise of the Scottish Probation Service and 1991.

Furthermore, the injunction to implement measures of intervention that are seen to have an impact upon offending behaviour has transformed the culture of practice. The attempt to work in a scientific way with offenders, in the use of methods of assessment and models of practice, also reflects a radical change in culture and a strengthening of the professionalism of the social work role.

Making sense of offending behaviour

Culpability

Social workers in the criminal justice system are required to report on the attitude of the offender to the offence, and to devise action plans that specifically address offending behaviour. This statement appears uncomplicated, but it is far from being so.

The attitude of the offender to the offence, which, historically, was often not addressed in the past by social workers in pre-sentence reports, goes to the heart of the functioning of our criminal justice system. One of the necessary criteria of guilt in most criminal offences is *mens rea*, the 'guilty mind'. This is constituted by the intention and the attitude of the offender at the time of committing the offence, and the level of his or her awareness. The social worker, when undertaking the social inquiry into the offender's background, behaviour and attitude to the offence, plays a critical part in the assessment of culpability. However, the current ethos of assessment lays particular emphasis on the responsibility of offenders for their actions. This is problematic. It has always been difficult to determine culpability. The insights of contemporary science, especially in the fields of genetics and neurochemistry, can make it extremely hard to assess this. Recognition that the concept of *mens rea* may be constructed in ways that are prejudicial to women, as the issue of provocation in cases where a woman has killed a partner after sustained abuse has shown, should give us pause for thought. *Mens rea* assumes that people who are not clinically impaired mentally are to be deemed responsible for their actions. That pre-sentence reports are sometimes used unashamedly by defence agents as their text for the plea in mitigation should also make us cautious.

Age of criminal responsibility
The issue of culpability also has a bearing upon youth justice. There are considerable discrepancies across the world about the age of criminal responsibility. Scotland's formal age of responsibility at eight years is one of the lowest in the world. However, this position is complicated by the existence of the children's hearings system, to which children who offend are mostly referred rather than to the courts. The children's hearing only makes judgements about welfare needs and public protection. This picture is further muddled by the provision that the court may remit a young person between the ages of 16 and 17 to the children's hearings for disposal (Criminal Procedure (Scotland) Act 1995). The rationale for this is that certain children may not be deemed mature enough to face the courts. This reflects a policy view about the need to 'ease the transition' between the children's hearings system and the courts (Scottish Executive, 2002).

Risk

Making sense of offending behaviour also entails that we address the risk of reoffending. This is now laid upon local authorities by the Scottish Executive in respect of youth crime, whereby every young offender must have an approved form of risk assessment provided to the hearing or the court. The National Objectives and Standards refers social workers who are undertaking pre-sentence reports to national standards in risk assessment in providing risk assessments to the courts.

Here we must be careful to distinguish risk of recidivism (frequency of repetition) and risk of harm (serious reoffending). There are debates about the accuracy of prediction measures. Although it is argued that any prediction measure is better than 'clinical judgement', actuarial models do not deliver levels of predictive accuracy that enable us to be entirely comfortable about applying them in practice (Kemshall and Pritchard, 1996).

Thus any measure is going to have a less than 100 per cent accurate prediction rate. It may wrongly predict that some will offend who do not (false positives) or will fail to predict those who will (false negatives). In the one case an injustice is done, in the second case a crime has not been prevented. It is, of course, impossible not to attempt some judgement about future behaviour. The management of risk in the community is essential, unless we are to revert to a purely punitive system of justice. Nevertheless we must be alert to the need to ensure that we do not simply supply formulaic risk assessments to courts without understanding the actuarial assumptions on which they are based, or without drawing these to the attention of judges or other decision bodies such as the Parole Board for Scotland.[2]

How to respond to offending behaviour

Our responses to offending behaviour are dependent on our views about why we have a criminal justice system at all. Historically, crime is an extension of the idea of the violation of the sacred. It then developed into the notion of an affront to the majesty of the king or the state. Wrong actions such as assault, theft and murder acquired criminal status long after they acquired the status of socially unaccepted activities (Mackay, 2002). Similarly, how we respond to crime has evolved. The original response to crime as sacrilege was always punishment. Later, punishment was the norm for offences against the king or the state. There was no particular motive to emend the offender's behaviour, merely to repress it and to discourage the others. Mercy might be shown by the king. A philosophy of rehabilitation can be detected as early as the Middle Ages, when, and perhaps this will not seem a natural example, recantation of heretical ideas gave grounds for less punitive sanctions than burning at the stake. However, by the seventeenth and early eighteenth centuries a distinct ethos of moral reclamation can be detected in the fictitious example of the minister of religion attending Moll Flanders in Defoe's famous account of life in Newgate Prison. Since that time a tension has existing between two main schools of thought: the retributive and the rehabilitative.

The *retributive model of justice* (sometimes also referred to as the justice model or the just deserts model) argues that the offender has to pay for what he or she has done, normally in the coin of punishment. How to calculate the payment is, of course, a complex, and some would argue an impossible, task. The nature of the harm done and the intention of the offender both play a part in the calculation. This approach is widely supported within the community. It was once presented to the author by a retired judge in the following terms: 'Crimes are to be punished for the same reason that a promise is to be kept'.

The *rehabilitative model of justice* (sometimes referred to as the welfare or treatment model) suggests that the offender's behaviour is the product of factors that can be influenced and changed, leading to rehabilitation. This model originally derived from the philanthropically and religiously inspired notions of moral reclamation. However, with the advent of psychological theories of behaviour, particularly psychoanalytic and behavioural theories, the rehabilitative model took on an increasingly medical and deterministic quality. At its heyday, the model prescribed indeterminate sentencing for offenders until such time as they were cured of the condition of criminality. Although this model never completely held sway in the United Kingdom, it was very powerful in the United States of America.

Beyond rehabilitation and retribution – restorative justice

Reaction to rehabilitation had two strands: it was unjust in terms of 'distributiveness' and it often did not work. This reaction led to a revival of the retributive model in the 1970s (the 'just deserts' model), and a counter-reaction, a revisionist rehabilitative school which suggested that some rehabilitative measures do work. This can be seen in the measures which have provided opportunities for life sentences for repeat serious offenders and the development of cognitive behavioural programmes for a whole range of offenders.

At the same time a new approach was gathering strength. This model, now internationally referred to as the *restorative justice model*, suggests that the key focus of criminal justice should not be primarily upon the offenders and their culpability and treatment, but upon the offence: how to repair the harm done to the victim and to the community. This focus on repair also embraces the offender who may not have had the life chances to develop as a well-integrated member of society (Mackay, 2000). This school of thought has influenced developments in criminal justice work internationally. It is now mandatory for jurisdictions to introduce measures relating to 'mediation in penal matters' (EU Framework Decision on the Standing of Victims in Criminal Proceedings, Article 10). The practice of restorative justice primarily involves mediation between the victim and the offender, by direct meeting or by shuttle, leading to the making of amends by the offender to the victim. The outcome will normally have a bearing upon what happens to the offender. A variant of mediation, involving a more structured procedure and other parties such as social service workers, is family group conferencing, known in Scotland as 'restorative justice conferencing'. Mediation mostly occurs at the level of adult diversion and referral by the Children's Reporter. However, it can be applied at all levels of the criminal justice process. SACRO (Scottish Association for the Care and Resettlement of Offenders) is the leading agency offering restorative justice services in Scotland.

The restorative model argues that the criminal justice system needs to hold the offender to account (retributive principle), it needs to provide opportunities for reintegration and healing for the victim, the community and the offender (rehabilitative principle) and it needs to focus on repairing the harm (the reparative principle). Taken together these form the basis for a restorative theory of criminal justice (Mackay, 2000).

Conclusion – for the future

In this chapter there are a number of issues I have not touched on directly, especially issues of discrimination. There are, however, three questions that remain hanging for the future of the criminal justice system. In the resolution of these questions, social work has a central part to play.

Which theory of justice?

As debates continue about what our criminal justice system is supposed to achieve, one of the key points is the role of restorative justice. Is it to be a set of measures on the margin of a system that is primarily a compromise between the old retributive and rehabilitative models? Or will restorative justice provide a new rationale for criminal justice that gives victims a stronger place, and which genuinely looks to restoration of victims, offenders and the community?

What system of justice?

The current archipelago is dominated still by the practice of punishment. A system that looks to developing dialogue between the parties involved in the crime and which looks more to repairing harm would look rather different. Whilst we can never envisage a community that would not need to segregate its more dangerous members, a society that relied on processes of dialogue and practical resolution of conflicts created by crime would look very different from what we have at the start of the twenty-first century. We must question our reliance on the basic assumption of punishment.

Which agency for social work?

There is a continuing debate about where social work in the criminal justice system should be located. There is a certain sterility about this debate, for it tends to reflect bureaucratic considerations both within local authorities and between central and local government. However, the new discipline of community planning raises a much more interesting set of considerations. First, it means that there have to be local partnerships between agencies, whether or not they are local or national. Second, it entails the need for pooling of resources, expertise and ideas. Third, it should help us to define our roles in new ways that enable us to retain distinct professional roles but in a way that is non-competitive. Whatever their institutional base, social workers have a distinct professional role to play.

Notes

1. Social workers must be aware, however, that the sharing of information between agencies about individuals does not necessarily constitute a breach of human rights to privacy.
2. There is a range of specific theories about the origin of crime. A good resume of these is to be found in Braithwaite's *Crime, Shame and Reintegration* (1989).

References

Association of Directors of Social Work [1996] *The Values and Principles and Social Work Practice in the Criminal Justice System*, http://socialwork. ed.ac.uk/EAL/InteractiveEAL/justice_1/02_materials.html (was accessed on 6 June 2003).

Beck, U. (1992) *Risk Society – Towards a New Modernity*, London, Sage.

Braithwaite, J. (1989) *Crime, Shame and Reintegration*, Cambridge, Cambridge University Press.

Kemshall, H. and Pritchard, J. (eds) (1996) *Good Practice in Risk Assessment and Risk Management* London, Jessica Kingsley.

Mackay, R.E. (2002) 'Punishment, guilt and spirit in Restorative Justice: an essay in legal and religious anthropology', in E.G.M. Weitekamp and H.-J. Kerner (eds) *Restorative Justice – Theoretical Foundations*, Cullompton, Willan.

Mackay, R.E. (2000) 'Ethics and good practice in Restorative Justice', in The European Forum for Victim–Offender Mediation and Restorative Justice (ed.) *Victim–Offender Mediation in Europe – Making Restorative Justice Work*, Leuven, University of Leuven Press.

Nicholson, C.G.B. (1992) *Sentencing: Law and Practice in Scotland*, Edinburgh, W. Green.

Scottish Executive (2002) *National Standards for Scotland's Youth Justice Services: A Report on the transforming Effectiveness of the Youth Justice System Working Group*, Edinburgh.

10

Disability and the Law

IAIN NISBET

Introduction

Disabled people have never had so many rights as is the case now. The law in Scotland now recognises and protects the rights of disabled people – principally by making discrimination based on a person's disability unlawful, but in other ways as well. According to the more readily accepted 'social model' of disability, people with impairments (such as a visual impairment or mobility difficulties) are disabled by society's failure to respond adequately to the existence of such impairments. For example, a failure to provide written materials also in Braille or audio format disables someone with a visual impairment – not the impairment itself. The Disability Rights Commission, established in April 2000, has statutory functions to assist disabled people through the provision of information, advice, research, conciliation and legal enforcement.

In legal thinking, disability is defined according to more definite criteria and often has a medical or practical focus. The fact that different definitions are used for different pieces of legislation means that there is a lack of understanding surrounding the term 'disability'. Social workers may be the first point of contact for disabled people seeking to access their legal rights. As such, a good working knowledge of the law in this area is necessary in order to provide the best advice and assistance. Additionally, a local authority's social work department is a service provider and, therefore, is subject to the duties imposed under the Disability Discrimination Act 1995, principally Part 3. The local authority is responsible for the discriminatory actions or omissions of its employees and accordingly this is a matter of concern for every social worker.

Disability Discrimination Act 1995

It is only disabled persons (and those who were formerly disabled) who are protected from discrimination under this Act. A disabled person is:

> a person who has a physical or mental impairment which has a substantial and long-term adverse effect on his ability to carry out normal day-to-day activities.

This definition of disability is somewhat complex and involves consideration of four distinct questions:

1. Does the person have a physical or mental impairment?
2. Does the impairment have an adverse effect on the ability to carry out normal day-to-day activities?
3. Is the adverse effect a substantial one?
4. Is the adverse effect long-term?

Impairment

The term 'impairment' is not defined in the legislation but it covers a wide variety of conditions and circumstances. It is to be widely interpreted and has been held in case law to include things such as: eating disorders; depression; undiagnosed conditions causing adverse effects; heart disease; and so on.

However, where a mental impairment consists of or is caused by a mental illness, then that illness must be clinically well-recognised. If it is not, then there is no impairment and, hence, no disability.

The guidance on the definition of disability suggests that a mental illness will be clinically well-recognised if it is included in the World Health Organisation's official classification of diseases.

Normal day-to-day activities

Assuming there is a physical or mental impairment, the next question is whether or not the impairment has an adverse effect on the person's normal day-to-day activities.

An impairment has an adverse effect on a person's normal day-to-day activities only if it affects one or more of the following:

- mobility;
- manual dexterity;
- physical coordination;
- continence;
- ability to lift, carry or otherwise move everyday objects;
- speech, hearing or eyesight;
- memory or ability to concentrate, learn or understand; or
- perception of the risk of physical danger.

Where an impairment is corrected or controlled or is capable of correction or control by the use of medication, surgery, prostheses, aids and so on, then that correcting or controlling effect must be disregarded in assessing whether there is a substantial adverse effect on a person's normal day-to-day activities. The one exception to that rule is that the effect of spectacles or contact lenses is not disregarded.

It has been suggested[1] that cases involving those with mental health problems are more difficult to fit into the tightly drafted definition of normal day-to-day activities. This leads to problems in accessing protection from discrimination for people with mental health difficulties.

Substantial

Substantial in this context means more than minor or trivial. An impairment which has only a minor or trivial adverse effect on a person's normal day-to-day activities is not sufficient to constitute a disability for these purposes.

Where a person has a progressive condition such as multiple sclerosis, muscular dystrophy, cancer or infection with the human immunodeficiency virus which has a more minor adverse effect, that impairment is taken to have a substantial adverse effect on the person's day-to-day activities if it is likely in time to have such an effect.

Where a person has a severe disfigurement, they are to be taken as having an impairment which has a substantial adverse effect on the person's normal day-to-day activities, even if it does not.

Long-term

An adverse effect is long-term if it has lasted for at least twelve months *or* is likely to last for at least twelve months *or* is likely to last for the remainder of the person's life.

Where a person has a recurring condition, an adverse effect is to be taken as continuing if it is likely to recur.

Structure of the Act

The Disability Discrimination Act 1995 is divided into parts. Part 1 deals with the definition of disability and certain other general matters. Part 2 deals with discrimination in employment; Part 3 deals with discrimination in the provision of goods and services (including the provision of most social work services); and Part 4 deals with discrimination in education. Chapter 1 of Part 4 deals with school education. Chapter 2 of Part 4 covers further and higher education, and also community education and youth work services provided by the local authority.

Social workers may have to advise on any aspect of the Act, but of particular relevance is Part 3 which impacts directly on social work practice and affects the way in which these services require to be delivered.

Part 3 – goods and services

It is unlawful for a service provider (including the local authority in exercising its social work functions) to discriminate against a disabled person:

- in the standard of service offered or provided;
- in the terms on which the service is provided; or
- by refusing or failing to provide a service which is (or may be) provided to the public.

There are two different forms of discrimination: less favourable treatment; and failing to make reasonable adjustments.

Less favourable treatment

It is discrimination if a service provider treats a disabled person less favourably (for a reason relating to their disability) than it treats other people to whom that reason does not apply (or would treat those to whom the reason would not apply) *and* the treatment is not justified.

The topic of justification is dealt with below.

Reasonable adjustments

Service providers (including the social work department) have legal duties to take reasonable steps to:

- change their practices, policies or procedures if these make it impossible or unreasonably difficult for disabled people to make use of their services;
- provide auxiliary aids or services if this would enable disabled people to make use of its services (or make it easier for them to do so); *and*
- provide a reasonable alternative way of accessing services if a physical feature makes it impossible or unreasonably difficult for disabled people to access them.[2]

This is known as the 'reasonable adjustments' duty. A failure to comply with this duty is unlawful discrimination (unless the failure can be justified) if it means that it is impossible or unreasonably difficult for a disabled person to make use of the service in question.

Justification

Less favourable treatment and/or a failure to make reasonable adjustments can, in certain circumstances, be justified. If these can be justified, then the service provider has not acted unlawfully.

Less favourable treatment/failure to make reasonable adjustments will be justified if the service provider reasonably believes that:

- the health and safety of any person would otherwise be at risk;
- the disabled person does not have the necessary legal capacity to enter into the contract in question;
- they would otherwise be unable to provide the service to the public;
- they have acted or failed to act in order to allow them to provide the service to the disabled person or to other people; or
- there is a greater cost in providing a tailor-made or individualised service for the disabled person.

Enforcement

Complaints of discrimination can be brought to the Sheriff Court. Disabled persons claiming discrimination may be seeking a declarator (a statement from the court that there has been discrimination), interdict, order for specific implement or damages.

Part 2 – employment

It is unlawful to discriminate against a disabled person in the field of employment. This includes recruitment, training, remuneration, promotion and benefits. It is also unlawful to discriminate against a disabled employee by dismissing them or subjecting them to any other type of detriment. Again, discrimination means either treating someone less favourably or failing to make reasonable adjustments. Under Part 2 of the Act, the employer may have to make a wider range of adjustments to arrangements at the workplace or the physical features of premises. Such adjustments must be made if a failure to do so would mean that the disabled person is placed at a substantial disadvantage in comparison to non-disabled people, and might include:

- altering hours of work;
- allowing absence during working hours for rehabilitation, assessment or treatment;
- arranging special training for the disabled person;
- acquiring or modifying equipment;
- providing a reader or interpreter;
- providing supervision for the disabled person; etc.

Part 2 duties do not currently apply to small employers, that is, those employing fewer than 15 employees. This exemption is set to be abolished as of October 2004.

Justification

Less favourable treatment or a failure to make reasonable adjustments may be justified (and will not therefore be unlawful) if, and only if, the reason for the treatment or failure is both material to the circumstances of the case and substantial.

Enforcement

Complaints of discrimination can be brought before the employment tribunals, who can make an order for compensation, including compensation for injury to feelings.

Other provisions

Part 2 also makes discrimination on the part of trade organisations unlawful, and makes certain special rules in relation to occupational pension schemes and insurance services.

Part 4 – education

Part 4 applies to education: Chapter 1 to schools and Chapter 2 to 'post-16' education, including adult education and community education.

Discrimination may occur in these fields in one of two ways: less favourable treatment or a failure to make reasonable adjustments. These are similar to the forms of discrimination with the same names outlined in Parts 2 and 3.

The Chapter 1 duties do not require the bodies responsible for schools to make reasonable adjustments which would involve the provision of an auxiliary aid or service, nor those which would involve alterations to physical features. However, the Education (Disability Strategies and Pupils' Educational Records) (Scotland) Act 2002 requires responsible bodies to plan ahead to improve the accessibility of both the curriculum and the physical environment of schools to disabled pupils, and to provide information to pupils in alternative formats.

The Chapter 2 duties do not require responsible bodies to make reasonable adjustments which would involve the provision of auxiliary aids and services until September 2003; nor those which would involve alterations to physical features until September 2005.

Justification

In both chapters, a failure to make reasonable adjustments can be justified only if there is a material and substantial reason for the failure.

In Chapter 1, less favourable treatment can be justified if there is a material and substantial reason, or if the treatment is the result of a permitted form of selection. Independent schools are allowed to restrict admission on the basis of ability without discriminating and there are certain specialist schools in the public sector which, with the approval of the Scottish ministers, can do the same.

In Chapter 2, less favourable treatment can be justified if it is necessary to maintain academic standards (or sporting, musical or artistic standards) in relation to a particular course. It can also be justified if there is a material and substantial reason.

Enforcement

Complaints of discrimination can be brought to the Sheriff Court for determination. Disabled people claiming discrimination may be seeking a declarator, interdict, order for specific implement or compensation. Claims brought under Chapter 1 (schools) cannot seek compensation, as it is specifically excluded as a remedy in these cases.

General provisions

Victimisation

Victimisation is a particular form of discrimination which applies whether or not the victim is disabled. Discrimination occurs if a victim is treated less favourably than other people would be because the victim has:

- brought court or tribunal action under the Act;
- given evidence or information in such legal action;
- done anything else under the Act; or
- made an allegation that someone has acted unlawfully under the Act.

These are all protected under the Act. It is not discrimination to treat someone less favourably if that person has made a false allegation which was not made in good faith.

Liability for employees' and agents' acts

Employers are responsible for anything done by their employees in the course of their employment. The fact that the employer was unaware of the actions of their employees will not avail as a defence. A defence is available if the employer took all reasonably practicable steps to prevent such discrimination. Such steps would almost certainly include staff training and disability awareness policies. Organisations are also responsible for anything done by their agents (or contractors) if done with their authority, whether that authority is express or implied and given before, during or after the discriminatory act or omission in question.

Individual agents, employees or others may, in some circumstances, be found individually liable for having aided an employer, service provider or other responsible body in committing an unlawful act. This means that that individual can be sued on an individual basis by the disabled person who has been discriminated against.[3]

Chronically Sick and Disabled Persons Act 1970 and the Disabled Persons (Services, Consultation and Representation) Act 1986

This is significant legislation in terms of social work practice with regard to disability. However, it uses a different definition of the term 'disabled person' which can be confusing. The definition is, thankfully, much more concise than that in the 1995 Act.

Disabled person

For the purposes of the application of this Act in Scotland, a 'disabled person' is anyone who is chronically sick or disabled or who has a mental disorder.

Under s.4 of the 1986 Act, if a disabled person (including a disabled child) or their carer requests that the local authority carries out an assessment to see whether their needs require the provision of any of the specified services in the 1970 Act, then they must do so. In addition, if the local authority is carrying out a community care assessment under s.12A of the Social Work (Scotland) Act 1968 and identifies the person as disabled, it has a duty to carry out the disabled person's assessment as well.

This assessment (in terms of s.2(1) of the Chronically Sick and Disabled Persons Act 1970) should determine whether the disabled person requires any of the following arrangements to be made in order to meet their needs:

- provision of practical assistance within their home (home help);
- provision or assistance in obtaining radio, television, library or other recreational facilities;
- provision of lectures, games, outings or other recreational facilities outside their home;
- assistance in taking advantage of educational facilities available to them;

- provision of or assistance with transport to and from their home in relation to certain services provided by the local authority;
- provision of or assistance in arranging aids and adaptations in their home in order to improve their safety, comfort or convenience;
- facilitating the disabled person in taking holidays;
- provision of meals (at home or elsewhere); or
- provision of or assistance in obtaining a telephone (including any special equipment needed to allow the disabled person to use it).

If the disabled person is assessed as needing any of these services, then the local authority is under a duty to make the necessary arrangements. The assessment can be (and often is) combined with a community care assessment (s.12A of the Social Work (Scotland) Act 1968) or a disabled child assessment (s.23 of the Children (Scotland) Act 1995).

Summary

There is a range of legislation therefore which imposes duties on the local authority to assess the needs of disabled people and to provide services to meet those needs. The Disability Discrimination Act 1995 provides protection for disabled people from discrimination and provides for financial compensation for unlawful discrimination. Social workers can play an advocacy role in encouraging employers, service providers and education institutions to make reasonable adjustments and otherwise comply with this Act.

Notes

1. See H. Patrick (2002) 'The Disability Discrimination Act: failing people with mental health problems?', *SCOLAG Legal Journal*, June/July.
2. From October 2004, service providers will also have to take reasonable steps to remove, alter or help avoid such physical features as well.
3. This does not apply to cases under Chapter 1 of Part 4 of the Act (schools).

11

Care in the Community

ALISON PETCH

Unlike childcare or formal intervention for mental ill health, those working in the field of community care rarely think of their roles in terms of the law on which their activity is based. Individuals working with older people or individuals with learning or physical disabilities may well forget day to day that they are working within a legally defined framework. Moreover there have been few legal challenges by way of judicial review at the Court of Session, restricting the amount of case law and diluting further day-to-day familiarity with legal implications.

Similarly, community care law is not to be found in a single piece of legislation. Instead there have been various amendments and additions inserted into the Social Work (Scotland) Act 1968 as a result of more recent pieces of legislation on carers and Direct Payments, for example s.2 of the Carers (Recognition and Services) Act 1995 amends s.12A of the 1968 Act to allow an informal carer to request an assessment 'of his ability to provide and to continue to provide the care for the relevant person'. The most recent legislation, the Community Care and Health (Scotland) Act 2002, adds further amendments as well as introducing new elements to promote joint working.

Community care assessments

The assessment process is the most common area of community care activity which rests on a legal basis. Yet because the process of assessment is so central to the day-to-day activity of health and social care workers its status as a legal process is often forgotten. The community care assessment as a legal entity was created by the NHS and

Community Care Act 1990 which inserted s.12A into the Social Work (Scotland) Act 1968, with a duty to assess the needs of any individual who it appears may require community care services that the local authority has a duty or power to provide or secure. This legislation marked the shift from service-led provision, slotting individuals into available services, to a vision of tailoring provision to individual need. Section 12A has been further amended by the 2002 Act to make it a legal requirement that the views of both the person being assessed and any carer are taken into account in deciding what services to provide.

The implementation of needs-led assessment dominated much of the 1990s, at times to the detriment of the other stages of the care management process, including the development of more imaginative care packages and attention to monitoring and review (Petch *et al.*, 1996). Critical of course to the whole assessment process is the interpretation of the concept of need and when 'needs' may merge into 'wants'. Front-line workers play a key role in such interpretation. The case of a young man with learning disabilities who pursued his preference for a specific residential placement to judicial review over two and a half years, eight different homes and two complaints procedures highlights the dilemma whereby more costly provision for one to meet individual preference for specific sporting facilities and related psychological needs may impinge on the resources available for others (*R* v. *Avon County Council ex p Mark Hazell*). More recently, Waterson (1999) has suggested that, in the face of resource constraints, needs assessment is in danger of being transformed into risk assessment.

Single shared assessment

Radical changes are in train for the way in which assessments are carried out. Most particularly, the promotion of the single shared assessment as part of the Joint Future Agenda in Scotland signals a major shift towards partnership working and the delivery of holistic, integrated care. Those undertaking a community care assessment have always been required to notify health or housing if it was thought likely that the person being assessed required their services. Nonetheless, even within a single agency, there has been the danger of multiple assessment, for example by a social worker, an occupational therapist and a homecare organiser. Following Circular CCD 8/2001 (Scottish Executive, 2001c), the single shared assessment applies to social work, housing and health services.

Initially implemented for older people from April 2003, the expectation is that this should be in place for all care groups by April 2004. Although CarenapE has been promoted as the basis for the single shared assessment for older people, local authorities have opted for a range of assessment tools and associated IT. The greater the similarity between tools, the easier it is for an individual worker to adjust to a new area and a new care group; work is therefore ongoing on the identification of a common core Carenap.

The single shared assessment was one of the key recommendations of the Joint Future Group (Scottish Executive, 2000). It has been supplemented by other major initiatives for partnership working enacted through the Community Care and Health (Scotland) Act 2002 which together may well preface significant change for the identities and working methods of the individual professionals. From April 2003 there has been a requirement for joint resourcing and management of services for older people (Scottish Executive, 2001b), with the 2002 Act promoting joint working and flexibility through provision for payments between NHS bodies and local authorities (aligned budgets), and delegation between NHS bodies and local authorities designed to promote pooling of budgets and transferability of staff. A subsequent circular (Scottish Executive, 2002d) has spelt out the detail of these arrangements, with provision for ministerial intervention if agencies fail to deliver. 'At an individual level, a pooled budget will support Single Shared Assessment of needs by ensuring an integrated response is deployed promptly, with the minimum of bureaucracy' (p. 7).

The response to assessment

Assessment is of course the forerunner to the provision of services or other forms of support designed to meet the needs that have been identified. The fact that a person's needs have been assessed does not in itself give a person a right to have that need met. If, however, there is a right to a service because of other legislation, this will be easier to enforce if the need has been established in a community care assessment. The most obvious example is the rights that a 'disabled' person has to certain services under the Chronically Sick and Disabled Persons (Scotland) Act (CSDPA) 1970. For this reason McKay and Patrick (1998) have argued forcefully that when carrying out a community care assessment for an individual qualifying as a 'disabled' person, the disabled person's assessment under the Disabled Person's (Services, Consultation and Representation) Act 1986 should be completed as a route to access this right to services. In fact, s.12A of the Social Work (Scotland) Act 1968 states that when carrying out a community care assessment, the local authority has a duty, if they identify the person as disabled, to carry out the disabled person's assessment as well. In practice, however, this is not routine, a further example of the divergence of day-to-day practice from what should be the legal optimum. Moreover, even if the right to provision under s.2 of the CSDPA has been established, the list of required provision, for example access to recreational or educational facilities, assistance with transport and home adaptations and access to holidays, would ring hollow compared to practice for many service users.

A key issue is whether authorities can take their available resources into account in deciding whether they provide the resources listed at s.2. What has become known as the Gloucestershire Judgment (*R* v. *Gloucestershire County Council and the Secretary of State*) confirmed, following a House of Lords appeal, that local authorities can take their resources into account in deciding what services to arrange. However, a Scottish Office letter circulated in November 1997 (Scottish Office, 1997) emphasised that this did not give authorities 'a licence to take decisions on the basis of resources alone'. All other relevant factors must be taken into account and, once it has been decided that it is necessary to arrange a specific service to meet needs, the authority is under a duty to arrange it; moreover, 'an authority cannot arbitrarily change the services which it is arranging for a disabled person merely because its own resource position has changed'. New eligibility criteria would have to be defined, with reassessment against these criteria. More routinely, however, the challenge is to ensure that those designing care packages in response to identified needs do this with imagination and in partnership with the service user, ensuring an optimal rather than merely adequate solution.

Carers' assessments

Much of the support to individuals within the community is of course provided by informal, unpaid carers – relatives or friends. Recognition that they also might have needs and an associated requirement for assessment was first acknowledged in the Carers (Recognition and

Services) Act 1995. This offered carers over the age of 16 'providing substantial care on a regular basis' the opportunity to have their own needs assessed alongside those of the person they provided support to – although there was no requirement that any needs that were identified had to be met.

Following the report of the Scottish Carers' Legislation Working Group (Scottish Executive, 2001a), Scotland started to diverge from England in terms of how informal carers were conceived. This group had been established in the wake of the *Strategy for Carers in Scotland* (Scottish Executive, 1999) which had as one of its six key priorities the introduction of legislation to allow carers' needs to be met more directly. The group concluded, however, that the carer should be recognised as a partner to the formal sector in providing support rather than a potential service user with needs to be met. Any needs that arise are a product of their caring role and are more appropriately regarded as the needs of the cared-for person. The carer is not a consumer of services but a resource. This has implications not just in terms of role perception and interaction with professionals, but more practically in terms of paying for services – 'we do not envisage carers as direct recipients of services in so far as their caring role goes, and thus we do not see a case for carers being asked to contribute to the cost of services or support' (p. 40). This differs from the situation in England where the Carers and Disabled Children Act 2000 provides for carers to be provided with support services and to be charged for their provision.

Consultation on the recommendations of the Carers' Legislation Working Group indicated strong support for carers having an independent right to an assessment, regardless of whether the person they cared for had agreed to a community care assessment. Situations may arise where an individual being supported by a family member does not agree to be assessed. In the past this would have precluded any carer's assessment but, with the transformation of the recommendation into s.8 of the Community Care and Health (Scotland) Act 2002, 'substantial and regular' carers are given a legal right to a direct assessment of their needs as carers. This right to an independent carer's assessment is also extended to carers of disabled children and to young carers under 16.

Legal rights will have little impact if individuals are unaware of them and there is evidence that the number of carers' assessments following the initial legislation was low. The latest Act, however, places a duty on local authorities to inform eligible carers of their right to an assessment and gives the Scottish Executive the power to require NHS boards to draw up carer information strategies informing people of their rights. Duties to inform can of course be pursued with greater or lesser enthusiasm – a discrete footnote on a lengthy form or a widely distributed poster campaign. Front-line staff are often pivotal in the extent to which high take-up of initiatives is achieved through the dissemination of information and promotion of participation. Detailed guidance on the implementation of ss.8–12 of the 2002 Act, the sections on carers, will be issued following draft guidance circulated for comment at the end of 2002 (Scottish Executive, 2002c). This guidance discusses, *inter alia*, the interpretation of 'substantial and regular', what information to provide to whom and in what form, the requirement to record and aggregate unmet need, the particular considerations that should apply in respect of young carers, and how to manage tensions between the carer and the cared-for person.

With the recognition of carers as care providers, and any support they receive as a resource rather than a service, tensions may arise if the cared-for person does not themself wish to be assessed and receive services that would reduce the burden of caring. The guidance on ss.8–12 outlined above explores the options for such a scenario.

Direct Payments

The emergence of Direct Payments allows for an alternative response following the assessment of needs. Following the Community Care (Direct Payments) Act 1996, local authorities can make a Direct Payment in lieu of the community care services that an individual has been assessed as requiring. Many would argue that Direct Payments have the potential to transform the ways in which support is provided to those that require it. Initially Direct Payments were available on a discretionary basis, with local authorities in Scotland given the power to introduce, should they choose, a scheme of Direct Payments for people with disabilities of age 18 to 64 from April 1997. From July 2000, eligibility was extended to individuals of 65 and over. The Regulation of Care (Scotland) Act 2001 and subsequent amendment regulations extended access to Direct Payments to disabled 16- and 17-year-olds and to the parents of disabled children for the purchase of children's services. Interim guidance has been issued following these amendments (Scottish Executive, 2002b), with further guidance anticipated to cover the provisions below of the 2002 Act.

The Community Care and Health (Scotland) Act 2002 transformed the provision of Direct Payments from a discretionary to a mandatory requirement, with a duty on local authorities to offer Direct Payments to all disabled people from June 2003. Moreover, in a revision to the earlier requirement that those using Direct Payments should be 'willing and able' to manage a Direct Payment 'alone or with assistance', new regulations have been framed that allow attorneys or guardians to receive a payment on behalf of an individual who is unable to give consent. From April 2004 it will additionally become a duty for local authorities to offer Direct Payments to all those assessed as needing care, including non-disabled groups, for example people over 65 who are frail, people receiving rehabilitation after an accident or operation, people fleeing domestic abuse, refugees, homeless people, or people recovering from alcohol or drug dependency. The regulations for Direct Payments currently prohibit them being paid, save in exceptional circumstances, to an individual's partner or to a close relative. Direct Payments cannot be used for the purchase of long-term residential care but can be used for short stays up to four weeks in any twelve months.

People with physical impairments have tended to be the initial users of Direct Payments, often using the payments to employ personal assistants. In this context Direct Payments are seen as promoting choice and empowerment and as a major route for achieving the principles of independent living (Glasby and Littlechild, 2002). Conversely, research showing that few people with mental health problems have been able to access Direct Payments (Ridley and Jones, 2002) suggested that key factors in the low uptake were lack of awareness amongst both users and professionals, lack of adequate support and lack of community care assessments. Social workers have a key role to play here in terms of providing information, exploring the implications of different options, and accessing local support systems for users of Direct Payments, for example payroll services for payment of wages to personal assistants. Indeed from June 2003, local authorities have a duty not just to offer Direct Payments but to inform people of their availability.

Local authorities have been ambivalent towards the development of Direct Payments during the discretionary period and provision has been patchy. One distraction appears to have been a concern that individuals purchasing their own support would threaten the viability of services, for example day support, provided by the local authority. Initially Direct Payments could not be used for the purchase of services provided by the agency offering the Direct Payment; this point has been conceded however and Direct Payments can now be used for the purchase of in-house provision.

The development of Direct Payments and their link to principles of independent living also, however, implies a different approach to the assessment process itself. Exercising choice and control over decisions and opportunities may well start with a process of self-assessment, and a number of Centres for Independent Living provide a self-assessment list to guide individuals through such a process. The professional input to the assessment would then involve discussion with the individual based on the completed self-assessment and agreement of the 'care plan' and costings for the Direct Payment.

An example of the potential of Direct Payments is demonstrated by Fife Council which adopted Direct Payments as a community care service in 1998 and by early 2003 had around 90 people, including over twenty with learning disabilities, using Direct Payments. From the start there has been a specific budget earmarked for Direct Payments, increasing on an annual basis to over £750,000 in 2002/03. The Council also funds a Direct Payments Support Service with a management committee made up of users and carers and representatives from the voluntary sector. This has given confidence in the scheme, ensuring that once the agreement has been reached on funding, the Support Service helps the recipient look for staff and set up bank accounts. It also has a payroll service and will help people with financial monitoring of their payments. Promotion of the scheme amongst social work staff has been very important, encouraging them to see Direct Payments as 'just another community care service'. Three assistant support staff help with the running of the scheme, two employed through the Same As You Project and assisting people with learning disabilities to access Direct Payments, and one employed through free personal care monies. A video with supporting guidance has been produced for wide distribution showing two service users and their families successfully managing Direct Payments. To further assist with the promotion of Direct Payments, the Scottish Executive has provided £530,000 to fund 'Direct Payments Scotland' to provide information, support and training.

Some tensions are introduced by the promotion of Direct Payments at the same time as the legislation for the regulation of care (Regulation of Care (Scotland) Act 2001) comes into force. Whereas people receiving Direct Payments are not required to use services that are regulated by the Care Commission (Scottish Commission for the Regulation of Care), all other care provision, including domiciliary support, is now subject to regulation and inspection by this body against national care standards. Based on a set of six principles – dignity, privacy, choice, safety, realising potential and equality and diversity – there are 19 separate sets of care standards covering the range of service provision from adult placement services through care homes for different care groups to short breaks and respite care.

Free personal care

Of particular significance for the provision of support services in Scotland is the decision to implement free personal care on the basis of assessed need for individuals over 65 (Scottish Executive, 2002a). Regarded by many as one of the first major products of devolution, in January 2001 the Scottish Parliament overturned an earlier decision to follow the lead of England and not implement the recommendation from the Royal Commission on Long Term Care (1999) for free personal care. Following the report of the Care Development Group (2001) and specification of the detail for implementation, free personal and nursing care has been available since July 2002 as a result of the Community Care and Health (Scotland) Act 2002. Personal care has been carefully defined, extending the original definition suggested by the Royal Commission to include counselling and support needs that may result from, for example, dementia. An important consideration for the future is whether such provision should be extended to younger, disabled people. This provides a further example, similar to assessment for carers and Direct Payments, of how legislation, mediated through the actions of individual front-line workers, can have a profound effect on the manner in which individuals with community care needs spend their lives.

References

Care Development Group (2001) *Fair Care for Older People*, Edinburgh, Scottish Executive.

Glasby, J. and Littlechild, R. (2002) *Social Work and Direct Payments,* Bristol, The Policy Press.

McKay, C. and Patrick, H. (1995, revised 1998) *The Care Maze: The Law and Your Rights to Community Care in Scotland*, Glasgow, ENABLE/SAMH.

Petch, A., Cheetham, J., Fuller, R., MacDonald, C., Myers, F. with Hallam, A. and Knapp, M. (1996) *Delivering Community Care: Initial Implementation of Care Management in Scotland,* Edinburgh, HMSO.

Ridley, J. and Jones, L. (2002) *Direct What? A Study of Direct Payments to Mental Health Service Users,* Edinburgh, Scottish Executive.

Royal Commission on Long Term Care (1999) *With Respect to Old Age: Long Term Care – Rights and Responsibilities* (Sutherland Report), London, The Stationery Office.

Scottish Executive (1999) *Strategy for Carers in Scotland,* www.scotland.gov.uk/library2/doc10/carerstrategy.asp

Scottish Executive (2000) *Community Care: A Joint Future,* Edinburgh, Scottish Executive.

Scottish Executive (2001a) *Report of the Scottish Carers' Legislation Working Group,* www.scotland.gov.uk/library2/health/carerslaw/wglthc-00.asp.

Scottish Executive (2001b) *Joint Resourcing and Joint Management of Community Care Services,* Circular No. CCD 7/2001.

Scottish Executive (2001c) *Guidance on Single, Shared Assessment of Community Care Needs,* Circular No. CCD 8/2001.

Scottish Executive (2002a) *Free Personal and Nursing Care in Scotland,* Circular No. CCD 4/2002.

Scottish Executive (2002b) *Social Work (Scotland) Act 1968: Sections 12B and 12C – Direct Payments: Policy and Practice Guidance,* Circular No. CCD 8/2002.

Scottish Executive (2002c) *Community Care and Health (Scotland) Act 2002 – New Statutory Rights for Carers: Draft Guidance,* Circular No. CCD 10/2002.

Scottish Executive (2002d) Implementation of the Provisions of Joint Working in Part 2 of the Community Care and Health (Scotland) Act 2002 and the Community Care (Joint Working etc) Regulations 2002, Circular No. CCD 11/2002

Scottish Office (1997) *Community Care: Implications of Recent Legal Judgements in England and Wales,* Social Work Services Group, 20 November.

Waterson, J. (1999) 'Redefining community care social work: needs or risks led?', *Health and Social Care in the* Community, vol. 7, pp. 276–9.

12

Children Looked After in Residential and Foster Care

ANDREW KENDRICK

Introduction

Children and young people looked after in residential and foster care are some of the most vulnerable in our society. *For Scotland's Children* highlighted the 'continuing failure of many local authorities as "corporate parents" to provide these young people with the care and education they are entitled to by law' (Scottish Executive, 2001a, p. 10). The statutory responsibilities of local authorities and voluntary agencies in Scotland are primarily set out in the Children (Scotland) Act 1995 which came fully into force on 1 April 1997.

The number of children looked after away from home has fallen by about half since 1977 and the balance between foster care and residential care has changed significantly. In 1976, almost twice as many children and young people were in residential care compared to those in foster care. The reverse is true in 2003.

On 31 March 2002, 11,241 children and young people were looked after in Scotland. Over half of these (56 per cent) were looked after at home or in the community with relatives or friends; 3,434 children and young people (30 per cent) were looked after and accommodated with foster carers, prospective adopters or in other community resources; and the remaining 1,595 children and young people (14 per cent) were in residential accommodation – local authority homes, voluntary sector homes, residential schools, secure accommodation or other residential provision (Scottish Executive, 2002a).

General principles in care of children

In the early 1990s, the White Paper which presented the government's proposals for childcare policy and law in Scotland set out eight clear principles to 'incorporate the philosophy of the United Nations Convention on the Rights of the Child' (Scottish Office, 1993, p. 6). These were that:

- Every child should be treated as an individual
- Children have the right to express their views about any issues or decisions affecting or worrying them
- Every effort should be made to preserve the child's family home and contacts
- Parents should normally be responsible for the upbringing and care of their children
- Children, whoever they are and wherever they live, have the right to be protected from all forms of abuse, neglect and exploitation
- Every child has the right to a positive sense of identity
- Any intervention in the life of a child or family should be on formally stated grounds, properly justified, in close consultation with all the relevant parties
- Any intervention in the life of a child, including the provision of supportive services, should be based on collaboration between all the relevant agencies. (Scottish Office, 1993, pp. 6–7)

However, while children's rights are included in many parts of the Children (Scotland) Act, these overarching principles are not included in the Act itself (Tisdall, 1996). It did introduce a new concept of 'parental responsibility' whereby a parent has the responsibility to 'safeguard and promote the child's health, development and welfare'; to provide 'direction' and 'guidance'; and 'to act as the child's legal representative'. Along with these responsibilities, the parent has rights, including 'to have the child living with him [*sic*] or to otherwise regulate the child's residence'; 'to control, direct or guide … the child's upbringing'; and 'to act as the child's legal representative' (Children (Scotland) Act 1995). These parental responsibilities and rights provide an important context for provision of services for children and young people looked after away from home.

Looked-after children

The Children (Scotland) Act 1995 changed the terminology of previous legislation so that children are no long 'in care' but are 'looked after'. Children are 'looked after' if:

- they are 'accommodated' under s.25 of the Act;
- they are subject to a supervision requirement from a children's hearing;
- they are subject to various orders, authorisations or warrants set out in the Act, such as child assessment orders, child protection orders, warrants or authorisations, or parental responsibilities orders; or
- they are subject to orders elsewhere in the UK, which are deemed by the Secretary of State to parallel the orders above.

Hill (2002) summarises the core principles of the Children (Scotland) Act:

1. the *welfare principle* – a child's welfare throughout childhood must be a paramount consideration when decisions are made;
2. the *minimum necessary intervention principle* – compulsory orders should not be made unless less intrusive measures have been considered and are inadequate to safeguard or promote the child's welfare;
3. the *participation principle* – children's views should be heard and taken into consideration, according to their age and understanding;
4. the *sensitivity to identity principle* – decisions should take into account a child's religious persuasion, racial origin and cultural and linguistic background. (Hill, 2002, p. 6; see also Fabb and Guthrie, 1997; Plumtree, 1997)

The Children (Scotland) Act also stresses the importance of interagency working, through the statutory requirement to produce Children's Services Plans. The recent government emphasis on 'joined-up working' recognises that interrelated issues and problems need interrelated assessment, planning and practice for effective solutions. The moral and strategic arguments for collaboration are powerful, especially in relation to the welfare and best interests of children. However, *For Scotland's Children* concluded that 'in many parts of Scotland services are not pulling together. Children and families experience services as having different objectives which are sometimes in conflict' (Scottish

Executive, 2001a, p. 74). It sets out a six-point action plan to better inte-
grate children's services: consider children's services as a single service
system; establish a joint children's services plan; ensure inclusive access
to universal services; coordinate needs assessment; coordinate intervention; and target services.

Children and young people looked after away from home

There has been a marked decrease in the proportion of children looked
after in residential and foster care and there are a number of reasons for
this, including a long-standing preference for children and young people
to be cared for in family settings. In a report linked to the Orkney
Inquiry, the Directors of Social Work in Scotland stated that there was a
'high degree of commonality in core statements of values and principles' (Directors of Social Work in Scotland, 1992, p. 7). Services should
be directed towards supporting and helping the family as a unit to
prevent the need for children to be received into residential or foster
care; if a child is to be received into care a family setting is preferable
unless a comprehensive assessment indicates that this is contrary to the
child's best interests; reception into care should be planned and should
be part of a longer-term plan to return the child home; if a return home
does not prove to be a viable option, the child should be provided with
permanent substitute family care (Directors of Social Work in Scotland,
1992).

The more recent *Child Protection Review* in Scotland reflected on
some of these principles when it reported that, in some instances, children continued to suffer harm at home because, although professionals
recognised the weaknesses of this approach, they had clear reasons for
not removing children from their homes: children had strong attach-
ments to their family; research showed that outcomes for looked-after
children were poor; there was a lack of good-quality foster homes and
residential provision; residential provision would not meet the needs of
the child (Scottish Executive, 2002b). Further, a number of scandals
have highlighted the abuse of children in care, particularly those in residential care, in England (Levy and Kahan, 1991; Brannan *et al.*, 1993,
Kirkwood, 1993), Scotland (Marshall *et al.*, 1999) and Wales
(Waterhouse, 2000). These, in their turn, have led to a number of
government reviews of issues relating to the safety of children in public
care (Utting, 1991; Skinner, 1992; Kent, 1997; Utting, 1997). Driven in

no small part by the scandals and the recommendations made by the inquiries and reviews, there have been major developments in the UK: both directly focused on the 'special protection' of children living away from home; and more general developments which affect all areas of social care for vulnerable people (Kendrick, 1998; Kendrick and Smith, 2002).

Over a number of years, research has highlighted the poor outcomes for children leaving residential and foster care. Most recently in Scotland, a survey of care leavers identified that: the majority of care leavers had poor education outcomes with only 39 per cent having one or more standard grades; over half were unemployed; and many of the young people had experienced mobility and homelessness (Dixon and Stein, 2002). One important aspect of these poor outcomes relates to instability whilst in care, multiple placements and educational disruption (Kendrick, 1995; Triseliotis *et al.*, 1995; Jackson and Thomas, 1999; Dixon and Stein, 2002).

There has been debate about the extent to which the poor outcomes for children leaving care are caused by the care experience itself, or by their experiences prior to entering residential and foster care. Borland *et al.* (1998) state that 'many of those who come into care already have established education problems in terms of non-attendance, behaviour in school and/or attainment' (Borland *et al.*, 1998, p. 34; see also Kendrick, 1995; Triseliotis *et al.*, 1995). Minnis *et al.* (2001) found that, in a sample of children in foster care, 93 per cent had experienced some kind of abuse or neglect; 77 per cent had been sexually abused; and 60 per cent had clinical mental health problems; while van Beinum *et al.* (2002) highlight similar issues in relation to children and young people in residential care. Grant *et al.* (2002) highlight the health disadvantages of children and young people who enter residential childcare.

Jackson and Martin (1998), however, focused on young people in care who had achieved educational success; five or more O levels or GCSEs at grades C or above, or in further or higher education. Only a tiny percentage of these 'high achievers' were unemployed or were homeless; none were in prison. A number of protective factors were identified: stability and continuity; learning to read early and fluently; having a parent or carer who valued education; having friends outside care who did well at school; developing out-of-school interests and hobbies; meeting a significant adult who offered consistent support and encouragement and acted as a mentor and possibly role model; attending school regularly.

Research has consistently shown that the personal qualities of professional helpers are the main criteria by which children and young people judge a service (Hill, 1999). They place great importance on: a genuine willingness to understand the child's perspective and to listen to their point of view; reliability and consistency; respecting confidences; and making an emotional commitment (Hill, 1999; Fletcher, 1993; Triseliotis *et al.*, 1995; Who Cares? Scotland, 1998). The increasing body of writing around 'resilience' (Daniel *et al.*, 1999; Gilligan, 2001; Daniel, 2003) similarly indicates the importance of staff and young people sharing activities across a range of sporting, cultural and leisure pursuits. 'Resilience-led practice not only considers problems and difficulties, but draws on strengths and nurtures positives' (Daniel, 2003).

Hill notes that foster care is 'now dealing with some young people who were formerly thought to require residential care and who tend to be more testing in their behaviour' (Hill, 2002, p. 13). Specialist foster schemes have been developed which, for example, are providing alternatives to secure accommodation (Walker *et al.*, 2002). Similarly, residential care is now providing services for young people who present more serious and challenging behaviours. Research has shown that residential care and foster care tend to have different aims. Most residential placements had the primary aim of either 'education', 'assessment', 'treatment', 'preparation for independence' or short-term 'holding'. Foster placements, on the other hand, mostly had the aim of either 'care and upbringing', 'preparation for long term placement', short-term 'child protection' or 'respite' (Kendrick, 1995).

Assessment, planning, monitoring and review

All looked-after children should have a care plan which addresses the nature of the service to be provided; alternative courses of action; the need to seek a change of the child's legal status; the arrangements for when the child is no longer looked after; and the views of the child. Where the child is looked after away from home, the care plan should also address contact with the child's family; health arrangements; educational needs and continuity of education; and appropriateness of placement (Scottish Office, 1997). However, *Learning with Care* found that in two of the five local authorities inspected, care plans were in place for only a minority of the children. Where care plans were in place they 'did not usually address educational needs and goals in any detail' (Scottish Executive, 2001b, p. 3).

The local authority is required to visit the child looked after within one week of placement and thereafter at intervals of not more than three months in order to: safeguard the child's welfare; monitor the agreed range and standards of service; evaluate the achievement of goals and progress; and provide support to the carers (Scottish Office, 1997).

Local authorities also have a duty to review the cases of looked-after children, and regulations stipulate that where a child is placed away from home, the first review must be held within six weeks of the child being placed, a second review within three months of the first review and subsequently every six months. Research on reviews in Scotland has shown that reviews play an important role in allowing the participation of children and young people, and their parents, in the decision-making process (Kendrick and Mapstone, 1991). Reviews have an important function in monitoring the care plan and placement; contact arrangements; long-term needs and the role of social work staff, carers and other professionals in meeting these needs.

Throughcare and aftercare

The transition to independence is a crucial time for young people who have been in residential and foster care. It is a time when they have 'a right to expect the sort of help that loving parents would provide for their children, help to reach their full potential, and the same chance to make mistakes secure in the knowledge that there is a safety net of support' (Jamieson, 2002, p. 2). However, as we have seen, research has consistently shown that the outcomes for young people leaving care are poor.

Local authorities have a duty to provide advice, guidance and assistance to young people who leave care up to the age of 19, unless the local authority is satisfied that their welfare does not require it. They also have the power to provide advice, guidance and assistance to young people aged 19 but less than 21, if the young person makes an application.

Most recently, research in Scotland showed that although most authorities (77 per cent) offered a planned throughcare programme, less that half (39 per cent) of young people surveyed had received one. There were significant variations in throughcare and aftercare arrangements across Scotland and there was a lack of adequate data collection and processing systems for monitoring and evaluation and identifying the number of young people eligible for services (Dixon and Stein, 2002).

The provisions for throughcare and aftercare have been strengthened by s.73 of the Regulation of Care (Scotland) Act 2001 which includes a duty to carry out an assessment of the needs of young people leaving care and to establish a procedure for considering representations (at the time of writing these have not come into force). Another important change concerns the withdrawal of Department of Work and Pensions benefits to young people aged 16 and 17 who had been looked after and accommodated away from home, and the transfer of these resources to local authorities. However, the Scottish Executive has decided to delay full implementation until 1 April 2004 (Scottish Executive, 2002c).

The Working Group on Throughcare and Aftercare considered that the development of service delivery should be the primary focus and should include the following key features: a nominated key worker or adviser to act as a contact point for advice and assistance; clear written policies accessible to young people on what they could expect from the service; minimum service standards; inter-agency working agreements and partnership agreements with other agencies; accessible resolution/complaints procedures; and a designated senior manager to promote corporate responsibilities to young people leaving care (Scottish Executive, 2002c).

Regulation of care services and the workforce

'The primary function of inspection . . . is serving the public interest by providing an additional safeguard for vulnerable people' (Utting, 1997). This agenda has been taken forward through independent national bodies to regulate care services. In Scotland, the Regulation of Care (Scotland) Act 2001 established the Scottish Commission for the Regulation of Care (Care Commission) from 1 April 2002. The Care Commission will issue a Certificate of Registration to care services which meet the statutory requirements. It takes over the inspection of services from local authorities and NHS boards, taking into account the new National Care Standards. Relevant care standards for looked-after and accommodated children include those for: adoption agencies; care homes for children and young people; foster care and family placement services; and school care accommodation services. As an example, the

National Care Standards for Care Homes for Children and Young People are set out to include:

* beginning your stay (arriving for the first time; first meetings; keeping in touch with people who are important to you; support arrangements; your environment; feeling safe and secure; management and staffing)
* leading your life (exercising rights and responsibilities; making choices; eating well; keeping well – lifestyle; keeping well – medication; learning; private life; daily life; supporting communication)
* moving on (moving on)
* expressing your views (concerns, comments and complaints; and advocacy).

The main principles underpinning the standards are: dignity, privacy, choice, safety, realising potential, equality and diversity. The Care Commission will enforce the standards and when other routine actions have failed to improve the quality of services, it will be able to use legal sanctions which include condition notices, improvement notices and cancellation of a registration.

There has been a long-standing debate in the UK about the need to regulate the social care workforce and on 1 October 2001, the Scottish Social Services Council (SSSC) was established (along with three equivalent councils in England, Wales and Northern Ireland). The Council's tasks are to: set standards of conduct and practice for the workforce and publish codes of practice for social services workers and their employers; establish a register of individuals in specified groups; and regulate education and training and approve courses. In Scotland, phase one of the registration process will include: social workers (those with DipSW or equivalent); registration and inspection staff of the Care Commission; all staff in residential childcare; all heads of residential care homes; and all heads of adult day care services.

Conclusion

Residential and foster care have the potential to make significant differences in the lives of some of the most vulnerable children in Scotland. It is crucial to use the framework of legislation, rights and responsibilities to ensure that children and young people who are looked after and accommodated receive the best of services so that their life outcomes are as positive as possible.

References

Borland, M., Pearson, C., Hill, M., Tisdall, K. and Bloomfield, I. (1998) *Education and Care Away from Home*, Edinburgh, Scottish Council for Research in Education.

Brannan, C., Jones, J.R. and Murch, J.D. (1993) *Castle Hill Report: Practice Guide,* Shropshire County Council.

Daniel, B. (2003) 'The value of resilience as a concept for practice in residential settings', *Scottish Journal of Residential Child Care*, vol. 2, no. 1, pp. 6–16.

Daniel, B.M., Wassell, S. and Gilligan, R. (1999) Child Development for Child Care and Protection Workers, London, Jessica Kingsley.

Directors of Social Work in Scotland (1992) *Child Protection: Policy, Practice and Procedure – An Overview of Child Abuse Issues and Practice in Social Work Departments in Scotland*, Edinburgh, Her Majesty's Stationery Office.

Dixon, J. and Stein, M. (2002) *Still a Bairn? Throughcare and Aftercare Services in Scotland*, http://www.scotland.gov.uk/library5/health/still-abairn.pdf (accessed 20 February 2003).

Fabb, J. and Guthrie, T.G. (1997) *Social Work Law in Scotland*, 2nd edn, Edinburgh, Butterworths.

Fletcher, B. (1993) *Not Just a Name: The Views of Young People in Foster and Residential Care*, London, National Consumer Council.

Gilligan, R. (2001) *Promoting Resilience: A Resource Book on Working with Children in the Care System*, London, British Agencies for Adoption and Fostering.

Grant, A., Ennis, J. and Stuart, F. (2002) 'Looking after health: a joint working approach to improving the health outcomes of looked after and accommodated children and young people', *Scottish Journal of Residential Child Care*, vol. 1, no. 1, pp. 23–9.

Hill, M. (1999) '"What's the problem? Who can help?": the perspective of children and young people on their well-being and on helping professionals', *Journal of Social Work Practice*, vol. 13, no. 2, pp. 135–45.

Hill, M. (2002) 'Introduction: adoption and fostering in Scotland – contexts and trends', in M. Hill (ed.) *Shaping Childcare Practice in Scotland*, London, BAAF.

Jackson, S. and Martin, P.Y. (1998) 'Surviving the care system: education and resilience', *Journal of Adolescence*, vol. 21, no. 5, pp. 569–83.

Jackson, S. and Thomas, N. (1999) *On the Move Again? What Works in Creating Stability for Looked After Children?*, Ilford, Barnardos.

Jamieson, C. (2002) *Forward, Report from the Working Group on the Throughcare and Aftercare of Looked After Children in Scotland*, Edinburgh, Scottish Executive.

Kendrick, A. (1995) *Residential Care in the Integration of Child Care Services*, Edinburgh, The Scottish Office Central Research Unit.

Kendrick, A. (1998) 'In their best interest? Protecting children from abuse in residential and foster care', *International Journal of Child and Family Welfare*, vol. 3, no. 2, pp. 169–85.

Kendrick, A.J. and Mapstone, E. (1991) 'Who decides? Child care reviews in two Scottish social work departments', *Children and Society*, vol. 5, no. 2, pp. 165–81.

Kendrick, A. and Smith, M. (2002) 'Close enough? Professional closeness and safe caring', *Scottish Journal of Residential Child Care,* vol. 1, no. 1, pp. 46–53.

Kent, R. (1997) *Children's Safeguards Review*, Edinburgh, Scottish Office.

Kirkwood, A. (1993) *The Leicestershire Inquiry 1992*, Leicester, Leicestershire County Council.

Levy, A. and Kahan, B. (1991) *The Pindown Experience and the Protection of Children: The Report of the Staffordshire Child Care Inquiry*, Stafford, Staffordshire County Council.

Marshall, K., Jamieson, C. and Finlayson, A. (1999) *Edinburgh's Children: The Report of the Edinburgh Inquiry into the Abuse and Protection of Children in Care*, Edinburgh, City of Edinburgh Council.

Minnis, H., Pelosi, A., Knapp, M. and Dunn, J. (2001) 'Mental health and foster carer training', *Archives of Disease in Childhood*, vol. 84, pp. 302–6.

Plumtree, A. (1997) *Child Care Law: Scotland – A Summary,* London, BAAF.

Scottish Executive (2001a) *For Scotland's Children: Better Integrated Children's Services*, Edinburgh, Scottish Executive.

Scottish Executive (2001b) *Learning With Care: The Education of Children Looked After Away from Home by Local Authorities*, Edinburgh, Scottish Executive.

Scottish Executive (2002a) *Children Looked After 2001–02*, Edinburgh, Scottish Executive National Statistics Publication.

Scottish Executive (2002b) *'It's Everyone's Job to Make Sure I'm Alright': Report of the Child Protection Audit and Review*, Edinburgh, Scottish Executive.

Scottish Executive (2002c) *Report from the Working Group on the Throughcare and Aftercare of Looked After Children in Scotland*, Edinburgh, Scottish Executive.

Scottish Office (1993) *Scotland's Children: Proposals for Child Care Policy and Law*, Edinburgh, HMSO.

Scottish Office (1997) *The Children (Scotland) Act 1995 Regulations and Guidance: Volume 2 – Children Looked After by Local Authorities*, Edinburgh, The Stationery Office.

Skinner, A. (1992) *Another Kind of Home: A Review of Residential Child Care*, Edinburgh, Scottish Office.

Tisdall, K. (1996) 'From the Social Work (Scotland) Act 1968 to the Children (Scotland) Act 1995: pressures for change', in M. Hill and J. Aldgate (eds)

Child Welfare Services: Developments in Law, Policy, Practice and Research, London, Jessica Kingsley.

Triseliotis, J., Borland, M., Hill, M. and Lambert, L. (1995) *Teenagers and Social Work Services*, London, HMSO.

Utting, W. (1991) *Children in the Public Care: A Review of Residential Child Care*, London, HMSO.

Utting, W. (1997) *People Like Us: The Report on the Review of Safeguards for Children Living Away from Home*, London, The Stationery Office.

van Beinum, M., Martin, A. and Bonnett, C. (2002) 'Catching children as they fall: mental health promotion in residential child care in East Dunbartonshire', *Scottish Journal of Residential Child Care*, vol. 1, no. 1, pp. 14–22.

Walker, M., Hill, M. and Triseliotis, J. (2002) *Fostering and Secure Care: An Evaluation of the Community Alternative Placement Scheme (CAPS)*, Edinburgh, Scottish Executive.

Waterhouse, R. (2000) *Lost in Care: Report of the Tribunal of Inquiry into the Abuse of Children in Care in the Former County Council Areas of Gwynedd and Clwyd since 1974*, London, Stationery Office.

Who Cares? Scotland (1998) *Feeling Safe? Report: The Views of Young People*, Who Cares? Scotland, Glasgow.

13

Older People, Abuse and the Law

DEBORAH BAILLIE, LESLEY-ANNE CULL AND
ALAN FERRY

Introduction

The abuse and neglect of older people have only recently been perceived as a social problem. The abuse of older adults was little commented on prior to the 1970s, when isolated incidents of 'elder abuse', labelled 'granny bashing', were reported in the press. McCreadie (1994) has argued that relatively little was written about the abuse of older adults in the UK until 1989. However there is now a growing awareness that the abuse/neglect of older adults is an important social issue. A report by Jenkins *et al.* (2000) on telephone calls to the Action on Elder Abuse's national helpline highlighted the issue of elder abuse, its prevalence and the settings in which it occurred. There is now guidance from the Department of Health (2000) and the National Assembly for Wales (2000) and recommendations for Scotland in the Millan Report (Scottish Executive, 2001). The growth of campaign groups on behalf of older adults has probably played a role in raising awareness of the scale and extent of the problem.

Biggs *et al.* (1995) are of the opinion that effective responses to elder abuse have to take into account and respond to negative attitudes and assumptions of ageism and the marginalisation of older adults. This requires the development of social policy that recognises, rather than colludes with, the ageist assumptions that Biggs *et al.* argue form a backdrop to abuse and neglect (see also Bytheway, 1995). Culturally, it appears that there are predetermined responses to ageing and older

147

adults, and these responses are generally not positive. To be old in many cultures and societies is to be reduced to the margins, and to be regarded as increasingly frail, dependent and lacking in power. Wilson (2000) argues that there are few societies in the world where the majority of older men and women are flourishing and where old age is a time to look forward to. Others such as Kingston and Penhale (1995) note that with powerlessness comes oppression, and the increased likelihood of abuse or neglect. It is also important to note that when we are talking of the abuse of older adults that 'abuse' is not clearly defined. It includes not only personal and sexual violence but also deliberate neglect, emotional abuse and financial abuse.

Knowledge of patterns of elder abuse and neglect amongst minority ethnic groups is also patchy. This may be further complicated by a range of factors such as stereotypical attitudes towards minority groups and the assumption that care of older adults will be offered exclusively by the community. An ignorance of cultural norms, customs and needs may also lead to issues of elder abuse and neglect being ignored. George (1994) suggests it is a myth that minority ethnic groups are universally good to the older adults, who are always protected and cared for by their families. The ageing of the population from minority ethnic groups means that demands will be placed on service providers to meet the particular needs of older adults, and services will be expected to respond in an appropriate manner to enable these needs to be met effectively. George suggests that consultation, especially with carers from minority ethnic communities, is central to the development of effective services that reflect the multicultural society in which we live.

Why does abuse take place?

Why does the abuse and neglect of older adults take place? A number of different reasons have been given in order to account for the incidence of elder abuse. These include the marginal social status of older people, dependency, stress experienced by the carer, poverty and social isolation. Studies undertaken reveal that between 5 and 10 per cent of older adults may have been physically abused, with 7 per cent suffering from verbal abuse (Homer, 1994).

Hughes (1995) suggests that abuse between two people can take place only if a power imbalance exists between them. When one person in a relationship is in a position of power over the other, misuse of that power can have damaging consequences, including where the exercise of it means that necessary action has not been taken. Biggs *et al.* (1995) identify a number of other predisposing factors that are likely to lead to abuse and neglect within domestic settings. These include: intra-individual dynamics such as mental health problems or alcohol and drug abuse (the abuse of alcohol or drugs may prevent the carer from making appropriate decisions regarding care or may lead to the misappropriation of the person's assets); unrealistic expectations about the role of carer and an inability to understand the situation of the person being cared for; being forced to adopt the role of primary carer especially where the carer was originally reluctant to take on this responsibility (the withdrawal by others from the caring role once this occurs may also produce in the carer feelings of stress, isolation or abandonment). However it is not just in the family home that the abuse of older adults takes place. Whilst the vast majority of older adults live in the community, it should not be assumed that the potential for abuse and neglect is not an issue in residential care settings; indeed the risk of abuse in an institution may be much higher than in the community. Glendenning (1999) has argued that by concentrating on family violence as the primary cause of abuse towards older adults, the abuse that occurs in residential settings has been neglected. Clough (1999) suggests that abuse in residential homes is especially ugly and unpalatable because of the fact that people, in moving to a home, expect to be cared for.

Responses to institutional abuse may take a number of forms, although Glendenning (1999) suggests that recognising and preventing abuse can be encapsulated by one word – quality. He suggests that well-trained staff, increased resources, a positive environment and user-friendly management systems are required to improve the quality of services offered to older adults and hence to a reduction of incidences of institutional abuse. Social workers are likely to play a key role in dealing with cases of elder abuse and social services have a number of powers to provide community care services to older adults. Intervention may involve the provision of an appropriate care package, following a needs-led assessment, as the first step to prevent abuse from taking place or to minimise the possibility of an already abused person being subject to further abuse (Brammer, 2001). Further, proper complaints procedures and increased inspection and monitoring of establishments are essential.

Lymbery (1998) observes that work with older adults has been regarded as work of a lower status than, say, working with children and their families. Lymbery suggests that such work was often carried out by unqualified or inexperienced workers with the work being perceived as having a limited scope and challenge, or as requiring only a 'common sense' approach. Thompson (1995) challenges this latter notion, instead recognising the complexity of the tasks involved. He recognises the development of care management, stating that the care manager has a vital role to play in coordinating services and ensuring services are used to optimum effect. Biggs *et al.* (1995) propose a 'social work intervention model' that has as its core a care management approach to working with the complexities that elder abuse and neglect often bring. The introduction of the NHS and Community Care Act 1990 contributed to the development of care management models. The adoption of such an approach should enable an individually tailored, flexible package of care that responds to the needs of the older adult and their carer following any assessment. The allocation of a designated, named worker should enable any issues including abuse or neglect to be identified and, by working within a multi-agency framework, allow the skills, experience and knowledge of workers in several core professions to be utilised.

This said, issues of abuse can be difficult to identify and respond to. However, if abuse or neglect is suspected or confirmed, workers must respond effectively to ensure the individual's needs are met and resources identified to support them. It is in this context that the legal framework is important.

The legislative context

The legal framework for dealing with elder abuse lacks cohesion (Brammer, 2001): vulnerable adults are not protected from abuse to the same extent that children and young people are, since there is no equivalent of the child protection system and the statutory duty to investigate. However if an adult is being physically abused, this is a criminal matter and can be reported to the police. A charge of assault (or, if appropriate, indecent assault) could be brought against the abuser and there are also specific criminal offences provided for in both the Mental Health (Scotland) Act 1984 and the Adults with Incapacity (Scotland) Act 2000:

- Section 105 of the Mental Health (Scotland) Act 1984 deals with ill treatment or wilful neglect of in-patients and outpatients and residents of care homes by staff.

- Section 106 makes it unlawful for a man to have sexual intercourse with a woman to whom he is not married, if that woman suffers from a state of arrested or incomplete development of mind which includes significant impairment of intelligence and social functioning, whether she consents or not.
- Section 107 protects women and men with mental health problems, learning disability, brain injury or dementia whether in-patients or outpatients or living in a care home or under the care or control of another person or receiving services under the Social Work (Scotland) Act 1968 from sexual abuse or exploitation by those in a position of trust.[1]

Further, s.83 of the Adults with Incapacity Act 2000 creates the offence of ill treatment and wilful neglect by a person exercising powers under the Act relating to the personal welfare of an adult.

It must be emphasised, however, that whilst criminal provisions do exist, many adults will not wish to report abuse. Evidential difficulties, including the fact that there will often be no witnesses to the abuse, may influence the decision not to report it. Even if an adult does report the abuse, given that the prosecution must prove guilt beyond reasonable doubt, there may be problems in bringing a prosecution if the capacity and credibility of the victim are likely to be questioned in court. In practical terms, where the alleged abuser is also the primary carer, the arrest of the alleged abuser also creates potential difficulties in relation to the continuing care of the adult.

Civil law provides some protection for vulnerable adults. Under the Adults with Incapacity (Scotland) Act 2000 the local authority has a duty to investigate any circumstances made known to them where the personal welfare of an adult seems to be at risk. In addition, the local authority has a duty to supervise welfare guardians and attorneys and to investigate any complaints made against them (s.10). If there appears to be a need for guardianship and there is no one willing or able to apply, then the local authority has a duty to apply itself, in the case of welfare guardianship, or to arrange for someone else to apply, in the case of financial guardianship. With respect to financial abuse, under s.6, the Public Guardian has a duty to investigate any circumstances made known to them where the property or financial welfare of an adult appear to be at risk and to investigate any complaints relating to those exercising authority in relation to property or financial matters.

With regard to support for carers, under ss.12AA and 12AB of the Social Work (Scotland) Act 1968 Act (as inserted by the Community

Care and Health (Scotland) Act 2002), a carer has a right to request an assessment of his or her ability to continue caring for the person who is receiving a community care assessment and the local authority has a duty to carry out this assessment. Carers are entitled to have an assessment even if the person for whom they care is not being assessed at the same time. There is also a duty to advise carers that they have a right to an assessment. The assessments should highlight any concerns about the level and quality of care being provided by a carer and also any concerns about the carer's ability to cope. It should be emphasised, however, that while 'carer stress' may be a factor in some cases of abuse, it is clear that not all stressed carers abuse (Brammer, 2001).

Under the Human Rights Act 1998 a public authority may be held liable for a failure to protect an adult for whom it has responsibility from inhuman and degrading treatment under Article 3 of the European Convention on Human Rights. Even where treatment is not sufficiently serious to meet the high threshold for Article 3, there may still be a breach of Article 8 – the right to respect for private and family life – since this has been held to cover treatment that affects 'bodily integrity'.

The Matrimonial Homes (Family Protection) (Scotland) Act 1981 offers protection to spouses and, to a more limited extent, partners against domestic violence in the form of exclusion orders and matrimonial interdicts. The Protection from Abuse (Scotland) Act 2001 substantially extended protection against abuse to allow any person applying for or who has an interdict for the purpose of protection against abuse to apply for a power of arrest to be attached to the interdict. Under this Act it is not necessary to show that there is any relationship between the parties and so the protection it offers extends to separated or divorced spouses, co-habiting partners, whether living together or apart, and other victims of abusive behaviour.

Despite these provisions, the reality is that vulnerable adults may either be unaware of their rights and remedies, or would find it very difficult to raise such issues unless they have adequate support from someone they trust and adequate access to legal services.

The social work response to the abuse of older adults

Penhale (1994) argues that whilst effective lessons can be learned from our knowledge of child abuse and domestic violence towards spouses, there remain differences in causation in elder abuse that require unique responses to be developed. Elder abuse cases can present complex and ethical issues for social workers, for example in relation to the right of people to choose to stay living independently in less than perfect relationships and in the tension between the need for protection to ensure safety and the need to respect autonomy and preserve dignity (Brown, 2002). Biggs *et al.* (1995) identify a number of barriers to intervention, for example a dearth of effective intervention strategies, lower expectations by the workers themselves about what can be achieved, and a failure to undertake a sufficiently thorough assessment to determine the severity of the situation. Additionally, workers may be faced by an older adult fearful of the consequences of disclosing to others their experiences of abuse or neglect. Pritchard (2001) recognises, however, that social workers do have a crucial role to play in identifying and investigating abuse, assessing risk and identifying needs as well as working with other agencies to develop protection plans and to monitor and review the situation. For example, older adults are potentially likely to have some degree of contact with several statutory or voluntary agencies and organisations as well as social services, such as health and housing. These organisations and the staff working within them have key roles to play in responding effectively to issues of elder abuse and neglect. Moves to develop and implement joint working practices and procedures should improve the identification of situations of elder abuse and communication of any concerns to the relevant organisation.

Conclusion

Older adults should be no different from younger adults in being able to access legal services and gain the full protection of the law. Age should not be a barrier to individuals receiving appropriate or adequate help. However, accompanying increasing age there can be a diminution in mental capacity or abilities and in such cases it may be difficult for the older adult to articulate their exposure to abuse or neglect. They are less well regarded by society, often being marginalised and subject to discrimination in the form of ageism. The contradiction between the rhetoric around treating older adults as respected citizens and the continuing notion of them as dependent beings highlights problems in developing effective responses to abuse and neglect. However, the emerging understanding of issues around elder abuse highlights the crucial role that social workers have to play in offering support and, where appropriate, protection for older adults who have been abused or are at risk of being abused.

Note

1. These provisions appear in improved and modified form in the Mental Health (Scotland) Bill.

References

Biggs, S., Phillipson C. and Kingston, P. (1995) *Elder Abuse in Perspective*, Buckingham, Open University Press.

Brammer, A. (2001) 'The law, social work practice and elder abuse', in L.-A. Cull and J. Roche (eds), *The Law and Social Work, Contemporary Issues for Practice*, Basingstoke, Palgrave Macmillan.

Brown, H. (2002) *K259 Care, Welfare and Community*, Milton Keynes, Open University.

Bytheway B. (1995) *Ageism*, Buckingham, Open University Press.

Clough, F. (1999) 'The abuse of older people in institutional settings: the role of management and regulation', in N. Stanley, J. Manthorpe and B. Penhale (eds) *Institutional Abuse: Perspectives Across the Life Course*, London, Routledge.

Department of Health (2000) *No Secrets: Guidance on Developing and Implementing Multi-agency Policies and Procedures to Protect Vulnerable Adults from Abuse*, London, The Stationery Office.

George, J. (1994) 'Racial aspects of elder abuse', in M. Eastman (ed) *Old Age Abuse: A New Perspective*, 2nd edn, London, Age Concern/Chapman & Hall.

Glendenning, F. (1999) 'The abuse of old people in institutional settings: an overview', in N. Stanley, J. Manthorpe and B. Penhale (eds) *Institutional Abuse: Perspectives Across the Life Course*, London, Routledge.

Homer, A. (1994) 'Prevalence and prevention of abuse in old age', in M. Eastman (ed.) *Abuse: A New Perspective*, 2nd edn, London, Age Concern/Chapman & Hall.

Hughes, B. (1995) *Older People and Community Care: Critical Theory and Practice*, Buckingham, Open University Press.

Jenkins *et al.* (2000) Listening is Not Enough: An Analysis of Calls to Elder Abuse Response, London, Action on Elder Abuse.

Kingston, P. and Penhale, B. (1995) *Family Violence and the Caring Professions*, London, Macmillan – now Palgrave Macmillan.

Lymbery, M. (1998) 'Care management and pofessional autonomy: the impact of community care legislation on social work with older people', *British Journal of Social Work*, vol. 28, pp. 863–78.

McCreadie, C. (1994) 'The issues, practice and policy', in M. Eastman (ed.) *Old Age Abuse: A New Perspective*, 2nd edn, London, Age Concern/Chapman & Hall.

National Assembly for Wales (2000) *In Safe Hands: Protection of Vulnerable Adults in Wales*, Cardiff, National Assembly for Wales.

Penhale, B. (1994) 'Intervention problems in old age', in M. Eastman (ed.) *Abuse: A New Perspective*, London, Chapman & Hall.

Pritchard, J. (2001) 'Elder abuse', in L.-A. Cull and J. Roche (2001) *The Law and Social Work, Contemporary Issues for Practice*, Basingstoke, Palgrave Macmillan.

Scottish Executive (2001) *New Directions: Report on the Review of the Mental Health (Scotland) Act 1984*, Edinburgh, Scottish Executive.

Thompson, N. (1995) *Age and Dignity: Working with Older People*, Aldershot, Arena Publishing.

Wilson, G. (2000) *Understanding Old Age*, London, Sage Publications.

14

Homelessness and the Law in Scotland

MIKE DAILLY

Introduction

This chapter looks at the law on homelessness in Scotland from a practical perspective: 'how can I get somewhere to sleep tonight?' In practice, many homeless applicants would rather stay with friends or family than accept a damp flat on the fourteenth floor of a dodgy multi-storey. Homeless applicants are often searching for a decent home. Accordingly, this chapter will examine the legal scope for applicants to secure 'decent' housing.

Historically, homelessness law in Britain has never guaranteed decent, permanent, housing. In the House of Lords judgment of *R* v. *London Borough of Brent ex p Awua* [1996] AC 55, Lord Hoffmann held that local authorities were under no duty to provide settled or permanent accommodation. Lord Hoffmann made it clear that the law on homelessness was intended to provide a 'minimum safety net, and nothing more'. A council could discharge its duty by placing a homeless family in bed and breakfast accommodation, or within one of the many tardy 'homeless hotels' in Scotland. The *Awua* decision has now been superseded by the Housing (Scotland) Act 2001 which has improved the rights of homeless applicants in Scotland.

Housing (Scotland) Act 2001

The Housing (Scotland) Act 2001 ('the 2001 Act') amends the principal statute concerned with homelessness in Scotland: the Housing

(Scotland) Act 1987 ('the 1987 Act'). The 2001 Act ensures that home-less applicants (found to be entitled to accommodation) must be provided with permanent accommodation.[1] Importantly, permanent accommodation must be 'reasonable to occupy' and meet 'any special needs' of the applicant.[2] Before this reform took effect on 1 April 2002 homeless applicants could find themselves in a 'revolving door of home-lessness'. This term was coined in the case of *Bradley* v. *Motherwell District Council* 1994 SCLR 160.

In *Bradley* a family who were firebombed by neighbours applied as homeless upon the basis that their home was no longer reasonable to occupy.[3] The local authority offered them accommodation at the other end of their street. The court held that a local authority was under no duty to provide accommodation which was 'reasonable to occupy'. Accordingly, the only option for applicants such as Mr Bradley was to accept the accommodation offered and reapply as homeless: placing themselves in a 'revolving door of homelessness'. As noted, this anom-alous position was removed by the 2001 Act.[4]

Asylum seekers

The provision of accommodation for asylum seekers is dealt with by the Immigration and Asylum Act 1999. The Home Secretary may provide accommodation for an asylum seeker who is 'destitute or likely to become destitute' in terms of s.95 of the Asylum Act 1999. Accommodation is provided through the National Asylum Support Service (NASS) which is a part of the Home Office. Scope for help was restricted by s.55 of the Nationality, Immigration and Asylum Act 2002 which came into force on 8 January 2003. Section 55 provides that asylum seekers will be refused help if their claim for asylum was not made as 'soon as reasonably practicable' after arrival in the UK.

Many commentators have claimed that the Home Office has inter-preted s.55 unreasonably. For example, the Refugee Council has reported that asylum seekers making claims within 24 hours of entry have been refused accommodation and have been left to sleep rough without food. On 19 February 2003 the High Court held that the NASS application of s.55 in practice was wrong, and breached Articles 3 and 8(1) of the ECHR (contained in Schedule 1 of the Human Rights Act 1998).[5] This was because s.55(5) safeguarded asylum seekers' human rights, and the NASS standard rejection letter failed to consider whether claimants would be left destitute. This decision is subject to appellate proceedings.

Qualifying for full help

A homeless person will be entitled to permanent accommodation if the local authority accepts that the applicant is (a) 'homeless' or 'threatened with homelessness',[6] (b) has a 'priority need', and (c) is not 'intentionally homeless'. At this stage of the decision-making process, the local authority may decide to consider whether or not the applicant has a 'local connection'. If there is no local connection, the applicant can be referred to a local authority area where a connection exists. All of these legal concepts are discussed below. However, it is worth noting that local authorities do not have to use the local connection test to refuse help. This test, unlike the other qualifying homelessness tests, is entirely discretionary.

Qualifying for temporary help

If an applicant is accepted by a local authority as homeless but does not have a priority need or is found to be intentionally homeless, that person will only be entitled to temporary accommodation.[7] The duty to such persons is to provide 'accommodation for such a period' as the local authority think will give 'a reasonable opportunity' for the applicant to secure their own accommodation. In practice, this can mean a one-off stay in bed and breakfast or bleak hotel accommodation for days or weeks. Stark as this is, it should be remembered that before 30 September 2002 such applicants were only entitled to 'advice and assistance'. In practice this could be a sheet of A4 paper with a list of private landlords – so the current position represents relative progress.

Inquiries and interim duty to accommodate

When someone applies as homeless it may take a local authority hours, days, or even weeks to carry out all of its statutory inquiries. In terms of s.28(1) of the 1987 Act a local authority 'shall make such inquiries as are necessary to satisfy themselves' whether or not an applicant is homeless. Meantime, if it appears to the local authority that the applicant is homeless,[8] they must provide that person with temporary accommodation pending further inquiries and a formal decision.[9] Where a local authority is satisfied that an applicant is homeless, they must make 'further inquiries necessary to satisfy themselves' as to (a) whether the applicant has a priority need and (b) whether he or she became homeless intentionally. Again, the applicant must be provided with temporary accommodation pending inquiries and a formal decision. Section 4(1) of the 2001 Act extends the interim duty to accommodate to include those persons who are awaiting a review of a homelessness decision.

First hurdle: homeless

Section 24 of the 1987 Act sets out the definition of 'homelessness' and 'threatened with homelessness'. Applicants are 'homeless' if they have no accommodation which they are entitled to occupy or have accommodation but (a) cannot secure entry to it; (b) it is probable that occupation will lead to violence or threats of violence from someone else residing in it; (c) the accommodation is a movable structure and there is nowhere to locate it; (d) the accommodation is overcrowded within the meaning of s.135, 1987 Act and may endanger the health of the occupants; (e) it is not reasonable to continue to occupy the accommodation, and; (f) the accommodation is not permanent (where the local authority has placed the applicant in temporary accommodation in implementation of its homelessness duties). Applicants are 'threatened with homelessness' if it is likely they will become homeless within two months.[10]

In deciding whether or not it is not reasonable for an applicant to continue to occupy accommodation, a local authority can have regard to the general availability of housing in their area. In *McAuley* v. *Dumbarton District Council* 1995 SLT 318 a family was not homeless because the court found that there had been no evidence to demonstrate there was alternative or more suitable accommodation available. In these circumstances it was reasonable for the family to continue to occupy their accommodation.

Where an eviction order has been granted against someone but not implemented, that person should generally be regarded as 'threatened with homelessness' from the date of the order. In *Stewart* v. *Inverness District Council* 1992 SLT 690 Lord Coulsfield held that 'a person who is liable to be removed at any moment does not, in a proper sense, in my view, enjoy permission to remain in occupation'.

Where an applicant claims that accommodation is not reasonably fit for human habitation, and is not reasonable to continue to occupy, they will often have obtained a letter from their GP. A local authority cannot simply dismiss medical evidence. In *R* v. *Medina Borough Council ex p Dee* (1992) 24 HLR 562 an applicant's doctor and health visitor said a house was not safe for the applicant's newborn baby. The council said the accommodation was fine and refused to accept the applicant as homeless. This decision was quashed by the court.[11]

Second hurdle: priority need

Section 25 of the 1987 Act sets out the definition of priority need. A person is in priority need if:

(a) he or she is homeless or threatened with homelessness due to a flood, fire or other disaster;[12]
(b) she is pregnant;
(c) he or she is living or might reasonably be expected to reside with a dependent child;
(d) he or she is vulnerable;
(e) he or she is living or might reasonably be expected to live with someone who is pregnant or vulnerable;
(f) he or she is under 21 and was previously looked after by a local authority at school-leaving age or later.

An applicant may be vulnerable as a result of 'old age, mental illness or handicap or physical disability or other special reason'. In *Wilson* v. *Nithsdale District Council* 1992 SLT 1131 a single woman had been living in transient accommodation and had been subject to a sexual assault. She applied as homeless and was told she had no priority need. The court quashed this decision. Lord Prosser held that vulnerability was to be measured by comparing the position of the applicant in the housing market with others:

The comparison must . . . be with some assumed average or normal or run-of-the-mill homeless person. But if there is a lesser ability to fend for oneself, against that comparison, in a housing context, so that injury or detriment would result when an ordinary homeless person would be able to cope without harmful effects, then in my opinion, vulnerability for special reason is established for the purposes of the Act; and nothing more special (far less anything odd or exceptional) is required.[13]

Where a child resides with a separated partner on a part-time basis this should be sufficient to obtain priority need. This is because s.25 is concerned with 'dependence' and 'residence', as opposed to 'wholly and exclusive dependence and residence'. In *R* v. *Lambeth London Borough Council ex p Vaglivello* (1990) 22 HLR 392 Mr Vaglivello looked after his son for three and a half days each week. The Court of Appeal held that he had a priority need.

Third hurdle: intentional homelessness

Where an applicant is found to be 'intentionally homelessness' they will be ineligible for permanent accommodation. Applicants are intentionally homeless in terms of s.26 of the 1987 Act where they have deliberately done or failed to do something which results in them ceasing to occupy accommodation (a) which was available for occupation and (b) where it was reasonable for that accommodation to be occupied. Section 26 provides that any act or omission made in good faith by an applicant who was unaware of a relevant fact must be ignored and must not be counted as 'deliberate'.

In determining whether an act or omission is deliberate a local authority must investigate and consider the facts and circumstances in each case. In *Wincentzen* v. *Monklands District Council* 1988 SLT 259 and 847 a homeless teenager resided with her father. She wanted to stay with her mother during college time; however, her father said she would not be allowed back to his house if she did so. She was deemed intentionally homeless by the Council. However the Inner House of the Court of Session accepted that Ms Wincentzen genuinely did not think her father was serious and held that her action was taken in genuine ignorance of her father's intent and was not a 'deliberate act'.[14]

In *Speck* v. *Kyle and Carrick District Council* 1994 SLT 1007 a resident hotel manager was dismissed for misconduct and lost his accommodation. The local authority deemed Mr Speck intentionally homeless as he had been sacked. Lord Prosser quashed this decision and ordered the council to make proper inquiries, applying the proper legal test – in other words, whether Mr Speck's loss of accommodation was due to 'any deliberate act or omission'.

When someone loses their accommodation in consequence of multiple debt it should not be assumed they are necessarily intentionally homeless. For example, in *R* v. *Tower Hamlets London Borough Council ex p Mahmood*[15] a council tenant was evicted for arrears. She was found to have become homeless intentionally. Sir Louis Blom-Cooper QC quashed the council's decision as it failed to indicate whether the council had found that Ms Mahmood deliberately failed to pay her rent – as opposed to being in multiple debt and unable to pay.[16]

Final hurdle: local connection

Section 27 of the 1987 Act sets out the definition of 'local connection'. As previously noted this final hurdle is discretionary. A person can have a local connection with a local authority area because of normal residence, employment, family associations,[17] or special circumstances. A local authority may refer a homeless applicant to another council if an applicant (a) has no local connection with the referring authority; (b) does have a connection with another local authority; and (c) is not at risk of domestic violence in the other local authority area.

The House of Lords held in *R* v. *Eastleigh Borough Council ex parte Betts* [1983] 2 AC 613 and (1983) 10 HLR 97 that the onus of establishing a local connection rests on the applicant.

Code of Guidance on Homelessness

In order to facilitate the uniform treatment of homeless people across Scotland the 1987 Act makes provision for formal guidance to be given to local authorities. Section 37 of the 1987 Act provides that local authorities must have 'regard' to this guidance when exercising its duties towards homeless applicants. The current Code of Guidance on Homelessness came into effect on 1 December 1997 and runs to 14 chapters.[18]

While the Code of Guidance advocates best practice it is possible for a local authority to have regard to it and then effectively ignore it. In *Mazzaccherini* v. *Argyll and Bute Council* 1987 SCLR 475 Lord

Jauncey observed that 'if a housing authority considers that in a particular case the circumstances do not merit the rigid application of a part of the Code I do not consider they could be faulted at law or said to have acted unreasonably'.[19] That said, if a local authority fails to have proper regard to the Code of Guidance (or completely fails to consider it), its homelessness decision may be rendered unlawful and subject to challenge.[20]

Making a homeless application

In making a homeless application a person will generally attend the appropriate office of a local authority to be interviewed. A dependent child cannot make a homeless application under the 1987 Act.[21] The purpose of the interview is to ingather information in order for a decision to be made as to whether the applicant is homeless or threatened with homelessness. If the homelessness officer is satisfied that the applicant is homeless, a decision must then be made as to whether the applicant (a) is in priority need, (b) is intentionally homeless and (c) has a local connection.[22] In most cases, the interview will throw up issues that require further investigation. For example, if an applicant says they were ejected from the family home, the homelessness officer will probably want to check this assertion with a member of the applicant's family and ascertain the reasons for this.

The onus of undertaking inquiries is upon the local authority.[23] While inquiries need not be to a 'CID' standard, they must be independent, fair and sufficient.[24] The local authority has a legal duty to issue its decision to the applicant in writing in terms of s.30 of the 1987 Act. Where an applicant is found to be ineligible for help the decision or determination letter should set out the reasons for this conclusion.[25]

Where the applicant appears to be homeless and the local authority requires more time to reach its decision, it must provide the applicant with temporary accommodation meantime. In practice, local authorities have been known to sidestep this duty on occasion by failing to treat the applicant's request as a homeless application. The applicant must be clear that they wish to apply as 'homeless'. This application need not necessarily be in writing. However, if the applicant comes away from a local authority office without a decision letter or temporary accommodation for that night, it is more than likely that they have been 'sidestepped'.

The solution here is for the applicant to go back and insist upon a decision letter. If the applicant does not secure somewhere to sleep, they should at least have a decision letter which can be reviewed. Temporary accommodation must be provided while a review is carried out.[26] If the review is undertaken quickly and the applicant is rejected again, the decision should be examined, as described below, to see whether a judicial review ground of challenge exists.[27]

Right to request review of decision

Where a homeless applicant is unhappy about a decision letter, they may request a review of that decision in terms of s.35A of the 1987 Act. A review should be requested within 21 days of being notified of the local authority's decision. No prescribed form is required to request a review. It can be requested orally or by letter. As noted, a homeless applicant must be provided with temporary accommodation pending a review decision.[28] The review must be undertaken by a senior housing officer who has had no prior involvement in the application.[29] The review decision must be intimated to the applicant in writing, and where the applicant has been unsuccessful, reasons must be given for the conclusions reached.[30] A review can be requested with respect to a decision deeming the applicant (a) not homeless or threatened with homelessness; (b) not in priority need; or (c) intentionally homeless. A review can also be requested against a decision related to a local connection referral and whether permanent accommodation offered discharges the local authority's statutory duty.

Can unsuitable accommodation be refused?

An applicant should never simply reject an offer of homeless accommodation. To do so may discharge the local authority's duty towards the applicant and leave the applicant ineligible for any help.[31] The proper course of action for an applicant is to request a review of the decision offering the accommodation in terms of s.35A of the 1987 Act.[32] If the applicant is unsuccessful on review they still have the offer of accommodation to accept.

Grounds for review would include arguments that the offer of accommodation (a) was unreasonable to occupy or (b) would not meet any special needs of the applicant or a member of his or her family.[33] 'Special needs' is not defined by the 2001 Act. It is suggested that the term will include a wide range of educational and health needs. For example, if an applicant suffers from mental health problems and is offered a damp flat on the top floor of a run-down tower block, it will be arguable whether this accommodation will be conducive to good mental health.[34]

Challenging decisions generally

Where an applicant is unsuccessful on review under s.35A of the 1987 Act (or has been refused a late review) it may still be possible to challenge the decision by way of judicial review proceedings in the Court of Session. Judicial review is a legal procedure where the applicant (known as the 'petitioner') seeks to quash a decision, so that the decision-maker has to reconsider the matter afresh. Judicial review is not concerned with the merits of a decision, rather it examines the fairness and propriety of how a decision was reached.[35]

Homelessness etc. (Scotland) Bill

The Homelessness etc. (Scotland) Bill was passed by the Scottish Parliament on 5 March 2003. The Bill provides an ambitious framework designed to eliminate homelessness by 2012. Key reforms to be introduced over time include:

- phasing out the distinction between 'priority' and 'non-priority' applications for local authority help, with a view to ensuring that everyone assessed as unintentionally homeless is entitled to permanent accommodation by 2012;
- providing 'probationary' tenancies to intentionally homeless applicants; and
- enabling the test of 'local connection' to be suspended.

Notes

1. Section 3(3) of the 2001 Act, which amends s.31 of the 1987 Act. Permanent accommodation includes accommodation secured by a

Scottish secure tenancy, an assured tenancy, or, for certain applicants with a history of antisocial behaviour, a short Scottish secure tenancy: see Schedule 6 to the 2001 Act.

2.   Section 3(1)(a), 3(1)(c), 3(4)(b) and s.4 came into force on 1 April 2002 (The Housing (Scotland) Act 2001 (Commencement No. 4, Transitional Provisions and Savings) Order 2002, SSI 2002/168(c.9)), while the remainder of s.3 and ss.5–6 came into force on 30 September 2002 (The Housing (Scotland) Act 2001 (Commencement No. 5, Transitional Provisions and Savings) Order 2002, SSI 2002/321(c.16)).

3.   Section 24(2A), 1987 Act.

4.   Section 3(4)(b)(ii), 2001 Act.

5.   *R(Q) and others* v. *Secretary of State for the Home Department*, Mr Justice Mills, Queens Bench Division 19 February 2003 (http://www.refugeecouncil.org.uk/downloads/news/s55judgment.pdf).

6.   The term 'homeless' will be used in this text to include 'threatened with homelessness'.

7.   In terms of s.31(3), 1987 Act (which is amended by s.3(3) of the 2001 Act).

8.   The interim duty to accommodate does not apply to those 'threatened with homelessness'.

9.   Before 30 September 2002, the interim duty to accommodation only applied to those who appeared to be homeless *and* had an apparent priority need. The duty was widened by s.3(2) of the 2001 Act (which amends s.29, 1987 Act).

10. Section 24(3)(e), 1987 Act. The former period of 28 days was increased to two months from 30 September 2002.

11. See also *R* v. *Wycombe DC ex p Homes* (1990) 22 HLR 150.

12. The English Court of Appeal has held that the expression 'any other disaster' means disasters of a similar nature to fire or flood only. Thus an impending demolition was held not to be a qualifying disaster: *Noble* v. *South Herefordshire District Council* (1983) 17 HLR 80.

13. See also: *Kelly* v. *Monklands District Council* 1985 SLT 165; *Hoolaghan* v. *Motherwell District Council* 1994 GWD 31-1871; and *R* v. *Waveney DC ex p Bowers* [1982] 3 All ER 727; (1982) 4 HLR 118.

14. See also *Robson* v. *Kyle and Carrick District Council* 1994 SLT 259.

15. March 1993, *Legal Action* 12, Queen's Bench Division.

16. See also *R* v. *Tower Hamlets London Borough Council ex p Ullah* (1992) 24 HLR 680 (a case where an owner-occupier in multiple debt sold his house to repay debts: insufficient inquiries were made into the necessity of this course of action and a decision of intentional homelessness was quashed).

17. See *McMillan* v. *Kyle and Carrick District Council* 1996 SLT 1149.
18. It can found online at: http://www.scotland.gov.uk/homelessness/cog-00.asp.
19. This approach was also taken in *De Falco* v. *Crawley Borough Council* [1980] QB 460.
20. *Kelly* v. *Monklands District Council* 1986 SLT 169; *R* v. *Wyre Borough Council ex p Joyce* (1984) 11 HLR 73; and *R* v. *West Dorset District Council ex p Phillips* (1984) 17 HLR 336.
21. *R* v. *Oldham MBC ex p Garlick* [1993] AC 509 and (1993) 25 HLR 319. A local authority may have a duty to provide accommodation to a child under 18 'in need' in terms of ss.17, 22, 25 and 26 of the Children (Scotland) Act 1995; see also the Arrangements to Look After Children Regulations 1996. Of course, a non-dependent child aged 16 and over can apply under the 1987 Act.
22 Section 28, 1987 Act.
23. Section 28; see *R* v. *Woodspring District Council ex p Walters* (1984) 16 HLR 64; see also *Wincentzen* cited above.
24. *R* v. *South Herefordshire District Council ex p Miles* (1983) 17 HLR 82; *R* v. *Dacorum Borough Council ex p Brown* (1989) 21 HLR 405.
25. See *Kelly* and *Mazzaccherini*, both cited above.
26. See the next section, 'Right to request review of decision'.
27. See 'Challenging decisions generally' on pp. 000–000.
28. Section 35A(3) permits a local authority to allow a longer period. In practice, it may make sense to allow a 'late review' as the only alternative may be to resolve the matter by way of judicial review proceedings. Where a review is rejected as late there is nothing to stop a homeless applicant making a repeat application and preempting a new decision to review (which would no doubt be rejected on the same grounds if there was no material change in circumstances: see *R* v. *Hambleton District Council ex p Geoghegan* [1985] JPL 394 and *R* v. *Ealing London Borough Council ex p McBain* [1986] 1 All ER 13).
29. Section 29(1)(b), 1987 Act.
30. Section 35(B)(1). A similar statutory review procedure in England and Wales was recently held by the House of Lords to be ECHR compliant: *Begum* v. *London Borough of Tower Hamlets*, 13 February 2003 (http://www.publications.parliament.uk/pa/ld200203/ldjudgmt/jd030213/begum-1.htm)
31. Section 35(B)(3) and (5).
32. Section 31, 1987 Act.
33. In terms of s.35(A)(2)(d), 1987 Act.
34. In terms of 'special needs' regard can had to the special needs of a person specified in s.24(2), 1987 Act, which refers to: 'any other person who normally resides with him as a member of his family or in circumstances

in which the local authority consider it reasonable for that person to reside with him'.

35.   In many cases it will be helpful to obtain as much supporting evidence as possible (for example, from a GP, health worker or social worker).

36.   The key principles of judicial review were set out by the House of Lords in the *Council of Civil Service Unions* v. *Minister for the Civil Service* ('the *GCHQ* case') [1985] AC 374. See Aidan O'Neill QC (1999) *Judicial Review in Scotland: A Practitioner's Guide*, London, Butterworths.

15

Welfare Rights

ANNE MACKENZIE

What are welfare rights?

The term 'welfare rights' is commonly used to describe the practice of that branch of law which governs entitlement to social security and local authority benefits.

Although under no duty to provide a welfare rights service, most local authorities fund some welfare rights provision under the duty to provide advice in the Social Work (Scotland) Act 1968. Some authorities choose, as an alternative or in addition to providing their own service, to fund a voluntary organisation such as the Citizen's Advice Bureau.

The aims and objectives of a welfare rights service are, generally, to maximise the income of the client group by assuring that all social security benefits to which they are entitled are received and thus to combat poverty and social exclusion.

In pursuance of these aims, services offer some combination of the following:

- information (including training and publicity designed for fellow professionals)
- advice (to the public and professionals)
- advocacy (with the Department of Work and Pensions or local authority benefits departments)
- representation (at tribunals and with the Commissioners for Social Security).

The extent of provision and the level to which these services are offered will depend on the resources available and the commitment of the individual authority to this kind of work.

Why offer welfare rights services?

Social workers do not necessarily see the relevance of practising welfare rights. It is not 'real social work' and does indeed not address emotional and social problems in a way for which they are trained.[1] Although teams are traditionally located within social work services, few qualified social workers undertake welfare rights work.

Essentially an area of legal practice, welfare rights work is viewed by most lawyers as unprofitable. Legal aid is not available for social security tribunals in Scotland. The onus therefore falls largely on the statutory and voluntary sectors. If an authority is committed to combating social exclusion, there are excellent reasons for funding welfare rights.

Clients served by welfare rights teams are often among the most disadvantaged and excluded in society: those with disabilities, those who misuse drugs or alcohol, people from abroad, lone parents and older people, people with mental health problems. They often feel that they have little control over their own lives and destinies. To take on the system and win can be very empowering. In around 75 per cent of cases clients who are originally denied benefits and who subsequently challenge the decision with the assistance of representatives are successful. Research also shows that providing advice services of this kind can prove beneficial to the health and general well-being of clients.[2]

Due to their close contact with and knowledge of their clients, social workers are particularly well-placed to identify potential benefits issues. Without at least a basic understanding of the benefits system, they cannot hope to give the client a full service. At best some of the most pressing, practical problems will not be addressed; at worst an ill-advised intervention in a welfare rights issue can cause the client to lose much-needed income. A working knowledge of the system can enable a social worker to deal with straightforward issues and be aware of the circumstances in which a referral to a specialist service is more appropriate.

Shortage of money and problems related to benefits can add a great deal of stress to lives already beset with problems, possibly induced by ill health, disability or difficult family circumstances. The removal of one source of difficulty can only make others which are perhaps less tractable easier to cope with. The positive results in monetary terms to individuals and communities are demonstrable. Millions of pounds of benefits lie unclaimed every year. A recent survey done by the Fraser of Allander Institute on the provision of welfare rights services in

Glasgow[3] showed that the money gained in one year for clients amounted to more than £11 million.

As social work services are dedicated to improving the functioning of clients within the community it is perhaps appropriate that they house welfare rights services.

An overview of the social security system

Background

Since the days of the Poor Law and the workhouse, some provision has been made in Britain for the relief of poverty, usually based locally. However it is only since the second decade of the twentieth century that there has been any systematic attempt to address the problems of unemployment, old age, sickness and their attendant lack of resources.

The foundation of the present system was laid, in the immediate post-Second World War period, by the Beveridge Report. The intention was that most areas of need would be addressed by a scheme of social insurance, which would, in rare circumstances, be topped up by means-tested provision.

In the intervening years the system developed according to the thinking of successive governments and under the influence of the law of the European Union. The rate of change has accelerated until the situation has been reached where major changes occur two or three times every financial year.

The labour government at the time of writing is committed to encouraging people into work and this is reflected in the introduction of work-focused interviews for all working-age claimants, the New Deal and the increasing emphasis on tax credits as a means of delivering help. The imminent revolution in support for working people and families discussed below takes this trend further towards its conclusion.

Present system

Social security benefits are administered by the Department of Work and Pensions (DWP). Housing Benefit and Council Tax Benefit are administered by the local authority.

The benefits system is complex, ever-changing and often obscure. Entitlement to one benefit frequently depends upon entitlement to another. Each benefit has its own unique set of rules and, as a result, it is difficult to identify any underlying principle or unifying factor. This difficulty has been exacerbated by the incessant tinkering with the system by successive recent governments. However it remains customary to categorise benefits as follows:

- income maintenance benefits;
- compensation benefits;
- income-related benefits.

It is impossible in a brief chapter to give full details on the rules governing entitlement to every individual benefit. A comprehensive account can be found in the *Welfare Benefits Handbook* published annually by the Child Poverty Action Group. However the following is a short overview.

Income maintenance benefits

Benefits in this category are designed to replace income lost as a result of some occurrence within the life of the claimant which reduces or removes altogether their earning power. They are in general dependent on the payment of National Insurance (NI) contributions and are not strictly speaking related to the claimant's income. However the distinction between income-related and non-income-related benefits has recently been blurred by the introduction of a reduction in the level of Incapacity Benefit paid where a claimant is in receipt of an occupational pension.[4]

Income maintenance benefits include:

- contribution-based Jobseeker's Allowance;
- Statutory Sick Pay and Incapacity Benefit;
- bereavement benefits, for bereaved spouses of either gender;
- retirement pension;
- maternity benefits;
- Invalid Care Allowance, shortly to become known as Carers Allowance, for full-time carers of people on certain disability benefits.

Bereavement benefits and retirement pension can be paid to those in full-time work.

In line with the original purpose of these benefits or their predecessors as the first line of defence against misfortune, they must be claimed by anyone who has entitlement before recourse can be had to income-related benefits. They are counted in full as income in the calculation of such income-related benefits.

Compensation benefits

Compensation benefits are designed to compensate the claimant for some condition or status which normally brings with it additional expenses not shared by the rest of the population. They are not dependent on the payment of NI contributions nor are they related to the claimant's income or savings.

Such benefits are often the key to entitlement to income-related benefits or can lead to an increase in such entitlement. The most important of these are

- Disability Living Allowance;
- Attendance Allowance;
- Child Benefit for people who have the care of children;
- Industrial Injuries Benefit for workers who have been disabled by an industrial injury or disease.

Income-related benefits

Income-related benefits, also known as means-tested benefits, are designed to top up the income of people who, for whatever reason, have few financial resources. They are probably the mostly widely known benefits and are widely claimed but were originally designed to be benefits of last resort.

Two benefits bring up to a minimum level the income of people who are not in work for over 16 hours per week:

- income-based Jobseeker's Allowance for people who are obliged to make themselves available for and to seek work;
- Income Support for those who due to age, illness or disability, caring responsibilities for a person with a disability or, in the case of a lone parent, for children are not obliged to seek work as a condition of receiving benefit.

In addition there are two tax credits for those in low-paid work of over 16 hours per week, namely Working Families' Tax Credit and Disabled Person's Tax Credit. They are not strictly speaking benefits and are administered by the Inland Revenue rather than the DWP. However they form part of the overall scheme to combat low income.

Credits are limited in their application to people with disabilities or those with children. Both are fairly generous and can provide for assistance with the costs of childcare.

Into this category also fall the local authority benefits:

- Housing Benefit to assist tenants on low incomes with the payment of rent;
- Council Tax Benefit to assist with the payment of Council Tax.

They are available to people whether in or out of work.

Entitlement to income-related benefits depends on the composition and resources of the household, that is, the claimant, his or her partner and any dependent children. Where two adults of different gender are living together 'as husband and wife' they are treated as a household and their joint resources are considered. They cannot choose to be treated as single people. The factual situation is used to determine whether or not two people of the opposite gender are 'living together' and the legal status of marriage is important only in determining entitlement to bereavement benefits and retirement pension. Persons of the same gender living together are always treated as single people.

In its simplest form, the government sets a level of income the household needs to live on. The resources available to the household (income, savings and so on) are compared with this minimum income level and provided the basic conditions of entitlement are met the balance is made up with an income-related benefit.

The calculations for tax credits are more complex and, as a matter of policy, some income, such as child maintenance, is ignored for the purposes of calculating entitlement.

Counted among the income-related benefits is the controversial Social Fund. Previously, provision was made by a series of single payments and extra allowances for exceptional expenses incurred by people with disabilities and so on. These were replaced in 1986 by the Social Fund, a much more limited scheme with the emphasis on repayable loans.[5] The Discretionary Social Fund is budget-limited and provides the following:

- Budgeting Loans to meet exceptional expenses and available only to those on Income Support;
- Crisis Loans – minimal amounts to meet emergencies available at least theoretically to all;

- Community Care Grants available only in very limited circumstances to those on Income Support who need extra help to establish themselves or remain in the community.

The Regulated Social Fund provides grants for people on income-related benefits to pay for funeral and maternity expenses and to deal with the effects of unusually cold weather. The amounts payable are strictly defined – there is no element of discretion and payments are not limited by local budgets.

Benefits for different groups

Few people will go through life without claiming a social security benefit. Most parents receive Child Benefit and most older people have entitlement to a retirement pension.

Many will also for some period be totally reliant on the state. While no one who is dependent on benefits lives at anything other than the most basic level of comfort, the generosity with which a particular claimant is treated depends largely on the reason for their dependence. Some people, for example asylum seekers, young people and students, have very little, if any, entitlement.

The government has promised 'Work for those who can: security for those who cannot'. This memorable phrase conceals vast complexities in the situation and poses more questions than it answers, such as:

- How do you ensure that work is available?
- How do you distinguish between those who can and cannot work?
- What constitutes security?

It is worth reiterating that the level of benefit payments, in general, permits at best a very basic standard of living. Therefore to write of a group being treated generously is to use the concept in comparative terms. That said, the lot of those claimants whom most people would unhesitatingly describe as among 'those who cannot' has in general improved somewhat.

Chief among these are pensioners and older people. The recent furore over a minimal rise in the rate of the basic retirement pension hid the fact that the level of Income Support, now renamed Minimum Income Guarantee (MIG), for the poorest pensioners had increased considerably since the late 1990s. The level of MIG remains low, at around 30 per cent of the average wage. However, higher benefit levels and an increase in the level of permitted savings have benefited many pensioners. It may be argued that retired people should not have to depend on means-tested benefits for an adequate standard of living. The alternative of higher state pensions for all is, however, increasingly unaffordable.

The interaction between the introduction of free personal care for people over 65 in Scotland with the existing availability of Attendance Allowance (and in some cases increased MIG) for older people with care needs has gone some way to improving the lot of the frailest older people.

The situation of the poorest people with severe long-term disabilities has also improved, at least on paper. Income-related benefits for adults and families with children with severe disabilities have increased, the problem being increasingly one of identification and proving need. The key to obtaining additional benefits (including income-related benefits) for people with disabilities is usually an award of Disability Living Allowance, particularly at a higher rate. Such an award confirms that the recipient has needs for assistance with mobility and/or personal care in the long term. Although the DLA rules are little changed on paper since their introduction in 1992 most advisers agree that they are now more strictly interpreted. As awards are often made for relatively short periods and are always subject to review, people with disabilities frequently lose income on which they depended and are put through the ordeal of proving that they experience the limitations they claim. As a means of providing security DLA therefore has certain drawbacks.

An even more acute problem of definition occurs in relation to those who claim to be unfit for work. Baffled and daunted by the rising tide of claims for Incapacity Benefit, successive governments have attempted to limit its availability. Benefit levels are low and most claimants have to claim additional income-related benefits.

The test of incapacity for work, which is designed to be objective, takes no account of the individual characteristics of the claimant. As a result many people who because of educational attainment, age and work history have little hope of finding employment are defined as 'fit for work'. They may be sentenced to years claiming the less generous Jobseeker's Allowance and attending inappropriate computer courses.

Those who 'can work' but are unemployed are treated in a manner which verges on the punitive. Basic levels of Jobseeker's Allowance are very low, (20 per cent of average earnings) and lower for young people. Claimants are subject to increasing levels of compulsion, for example the compulsory New Deal for Young People. For all claimants there is an obligation actively to seek work, which is not in itself exceptionable, but is enforced by benefit sanctions, reducing income below minimum living standards.

Despite pledges to eliminate child poverty, families with children, particularly lone-parent families, remain over-represented among the very poorest. Many depend on income-related benefits which are arguably inadequate.[6] Obliged by poverty to borrow from the Social Fund, their repayments force them to subsist on even lower income levels. This remains the case despite the discreet introduction of increases in Income Support for families with children, particularly a child with a disability.

That the government sees the solution to the problem of family poverty as paid employment for parents is shown by the comparative generosity of tax credits and the introduction of the New Deal for Lone Parents. Parents, even lone parents, are thus defined as 'those who can' and the unpaid work of childcare is not valued.

From benefits to credits

At the time of writing in October 2002, major changes are on the horizon for the system of support for people on low to moderate incomes.[7]

The Child Tax Credit will ultimately provide support to all families with children, whether in or out of work, on a sliding scale depending on income. Support for children will thus be separated from support for adults. The present tax relief will cease in April 2003 when the credit becomes available to those in work or not otherwise claiming income-related benefits. From April 2004 it will totally replace increases for children on income-related benefits. For the poorest families the credit will be more generous than the present system and surprisingly some help will be paid to families earning up to £58,000.

In addition a Working Tax Credit will be available to top up low earnings. In a departure from existing schemes, single people with no disability will be eligible if over 25 and working full-time. The scheme will however provide more assistance for those with children or a disability.

These schemes are designed to further the aim to make it easier and more advantageous for people to take up work. The theory is that support for children will transfer seamlessly when a parent starts work.

How successful they are remains to be seen but certain potential problems have been identified:

- Tax credits will be paid into bank accounts. Many people on low incomes have no access to financial services.
- The credits follow a 'benefit' model rather than a tax model in looking at the resources of the whole family rather than the individual. This will bring many working people into possible surveillance of their private life.

From October 2003 a further tax credit will be introduced this time for pensioners. It will replace MIG and in addition will give additional income to people with small occupational and personal pensions and/or modest savings who were previously excluded. This will go some way to addressing the quite legitimate complaints of those pensioners previously just above MIG level that they were penalised rather than rewarded for making provision for their old age. However it may be unduly complex.

Sources of social security law

The bare bones of entitlement to benefits and the rules for making decisions are contained in various Acts of Parliament such as the Social Security (Contributions and Benefits) Act 1992 and the Social Security Act 1998. These bones are fleshed out by delegated legislation, the regulations made by ministers by the authority granted to them under the Acts, for example Social Security (Incapacity for Work) (General) Regulations 1995 and Social Security and Child Support (Decisions and Appeals) Regulations 1999. Many of the most important provisions are contained within these regulations.

Social security is not a devolved matter[8] and all Acts are those of the UK Parliament and apply throughout Great Britain. As a result, social security law is virtually uniform throughout Scotland and England and Wales.

The law of the European Union has direct relevance for social security matters. EU regulations prescribe rules to be followed in relation to workers moving between member states. Other pieces of EU law, for example Council Directive 79/7/EEC, which deals with the equal treatment of men and women, have been applied widely in a social security context. European social security law is a topic in its own right but it is sufficient here to note its importance.

The developing field of human rights is also becoming increasingly influential. The Human Rights Act 1998 imports the European Convention on Human Rights into national law and permits local courts to give it effect where previously an application had to be made to the European Court of Human Rights. In benefits matters the most important articles are Article 6, which deals with the need for speedy and independent hearings of disputes, and Article 8, which protects home and family life. Article 14, which prohibits discrimination, is also likely to prove fertile ground. It is due to the potential application of Article 6 that Housing Benefit appeals have been brought within the scope of the Appeals Service where previously they were determined by a board of the Council. Before the Act, the ECHR was used to challenge the less favourable treatment of widowers as opposed to widows under previous rules.[9]

Contrary to the obvious belief of some officials of the DWP, social security law is part of the general law of the land and does not exist independently. Concepts and definitions from other branches of law apply where these do not directly conflict with the wording of the legislation.

As with most UK law, decided cases from the Commissioners, the higher courts and the European Court form part of the law and can be called in aid to identify the correct interpretation of the rules.

Claims, decisions and appeals

Social security decisions are made by officials of the Department of Work and Pensions, known as Decision Makers. Decisions on Housing and Council Tax Benefit are taken by officials of the local authority and tax credit decisions by officers of the Inland Revenue. Appeals relating to tax credits are heard by the Commissioners for Inland Revenue. With the exception of the Discretionary Social Fund, which has an internal review process, most decisions on social security, housing and council tax benefits can be appealed to a tribunal administered by the Appeals Service, which is ostensibly independent.

The appeal tribunal looks at the whole case again. A claimant can choose to have their case looked at on the papers or can appear in person either on their own or with a representative such as a Welfare Rights Officer. All the evidence shows that claimants who appear and in particular who are represented have a much higher chance of success.[10]

A claimant can only appeal further, to the Commissioners for Social Security, where the tribunal has made a mistake in its application of the law. Thereafter appeal lies to the courts, the Court of Session in Scotland and the Court of Appeal in England and Wales. Their decisions can be appealed in turn to the House of Lords.

Even a basic appeal to a tribunal can take some months. A claimant whose absolute entitlement to income-related benefits is in question, for example he or she is alleged to be living with a working partner or to have disposed of capital, may thus be left without any source of income for a considerable period.

Time limits for appealing are tight and relatively inflexible. The result of a successful appeal is, however, often a major improvement in a client's standard of living. Representation is therefore one of the most immediately practical services offered to clients.

Conclusion

As can be seen the practice of welfare rights is complex and, as with dealing with any large bureaucracy, frequently frustrating. However I hope that it is also evident that social security law can be used as a tool to improve the lot of the most disadvantaged. When successful the result is immensely rewarding.

Notes

1. For an interesting discussion of these issues with an English perspective see P. Burgess (1994) 'Welfare rights', in P. Hanvey and T. Philpot (eds) *Practising Social Work*, London, Routledge.
2. S. Abbot and L. Hobby (1999) *Report No. 99/63*, Liverpool, Liverpool University Health and Community Care Research Unit.
3. Fraser of Allander Institute for Research (2001) *The Impact of Welfare Spending on the Glasgow Economy*, Glasgow.
4. Social Security Contributions and Benefits Act 1992 s.30DD inserted by the Welfare Reform and Pensions Act 1999 s.63 (for new claims for Incapacity Benefit from 6 April 2001).
5. Social Security Act 1986, now codified in the Social Security Contributions and Benefits Act 1992.
6. See, for example, S. Becker (2002) ' "Security for those who cannot": Labour's neglected Welfare Principle', *Poverty*, p. 112.
7. Tax Credits Act 2002.
8. Scotland Act 1998 Schedule 5 Head F.
9. App 365789/97 *Cornwell* v. *UK* and App 38890/97 *Leary* v. *UK*.
10. H. Genn and Y. Genn (1989) *The Effectiveness of Representation at Tribunals*, London, Lord Chancellor's Department.

16

Domestic Abuse: Social Work Practice and the Law

LESLEY-ANNE CULL

Introduction

One woman in four is attacked at some point in her life by a male partner (Economic and Social Research Council, 1998) and every week in the UK two women are killed by a current or former partner (Alabhai-Brown, 1999). In many cases, children are frequently either a witness to or aware of the abuse (Hester and Radford, 1996; Children in Scotland, 1999). In a third of the cases, the abuse (including murder) against these women occurs post-separation (Scottish Office, 1996; Kelly, 1998). These disturbing statistics reveal 'a scale of violence and abuse [which] has many dreadful consequences for individuals, families and the whole community' (Jay, 1999). In this chapter, I will explore how far current law and social work practice in Scotland can offer protection and support to victims of domestic abuse and, where children are involved, what the issues are in relation to child safety and protection.

Defining domestic abuse

Until fairly recently, there was no agreed definition of domestic abuse. In 1997, the report *Hitting Home – a Report on the Police Response to Domestic Violence* (Scottish Office, 1997) recommended that a standard definition be developed. The working group of the Scottish Criminal Statistics Committee (involving the Association of Chief Officers of Probation in Scotland) agreed the following definition:

Domestic abuse is any form of physical, non-physical, or sexual abuse which takes place within the context of a close relationship, committed either in the home or elsewhere. This relationship will be between partners (married, cohabiting or otherwise) or ex-partners. www.scotland.gov.uk/stats/bulletins/00203-00.asp (accessed 17.1.03)

It is recognised that people in same-sex relationships and men in heterosexual relationships also experience domestic violence but in 91 per cent of the 35,800 incidents reported to the Scottish police in 2001, the victim was female and the perpetrator male (www.scotland.gov.uk/stats/bulletins/00203-00.asp). Domestic abuse has been described as 'the most significant problem damaging the health and safety of women (Stanko and Hobdall, 1993). A National Group to Address Domestic Abuse in Scotland was established in June 2001 with a remit which included identifying and disseminating good practice as well as identifying key issues and developing a common national response. A number of specific-issue working groups were set up to look in particular at the legislative provisions relating to domestic abuse, refuge provision, prevention, and training (www.scotland.gov.uk/library5/social/dapr-00.asp).

Women and domestic abuse

Many women experience great difficulty in disclosing the domestic abuse they have suffered. One reason may be located within the legal and popular discourse: women may not identify with the prevailing images of 'battered women' and not define what is happening to them as 'abuse' or 'violence'. It has also been argued that a culture of silence and shame surrounded the issues of domestic abuse during much of the twentieth century and that women might have found it difficult to admit abuse and to acknowledge what was really happening (Radford, 1996). Another reason may be a fear of children being removed from their care and of losing their home. Of those questioned for the British Crime Survey 1998, over half the survivors of domestic abuse had not told anyone about the last attack and of the 47 per cent who had told someone, nearly all had told a relative or a friend.

For some women, pressure and intimidation may be brought to bear to prevent what has happened being reported to the police. Domestic abuse often occurs within the home and there are frequently no adult witnesses who can support the victim of an attack. As part of the government response to the Global Platform for Action conference in Beijing in 1995, the Scottish Office Central Research Unit commissioned a piece of research which took place between October 1996 and October 1997 to examine current service provision for women experiencing domestic abuse. The report's main findings concluded that access to services is constrained by the lack of information and knowledge on the part of both the service providers and the women themselves (Scottish Office, 1998). Further, the report stated that the provision of services across Scotland is spread unevenly, with women in rural communities having the lowest levels of provision overall. Two of the report's findings related to the response of service providers to women seeking support – as well as varying widely in the quality of support provided (with practice ranging from 'good' to 'inappropriate'), there were few multi-agency responses to domestic abuse at a local level in Scotland. It is increasingly being recognised that the effectiveness of preventative work, intervention and continuing support relies upon coordinated work on the basis of an inter-agency approach. Yet women are in some cases sent to as many as ten different places before they get the help that they need, this experience creating a further barrier to effective support (Dominy and Radford, 1996). Following the work and recommendations of the National Group to Address Domestic Abuse in Scotland, however, all local authority areas now have multi-agency domestic abuse groups, with membership from police, Women's Aid, Victim Support, health boards and trusts, and council officers representing social work, housing, education and community safety forming the 'core' of these groups (www.scotland.gov.uk/library5/social/dapr-00.asp).

The police response to domestic abuse generally and in relation to the quality of police intervention at the first report of abuse in particular is crucial in determining whether the victim will continue to seek help. There were also differences in the way in which situations were monitored and whether or not local authorities were contacted as a matter of routine where children were involved (whether or not they were on the premises at the time of the abuse). In some areas, the police have developed policies with local authorities and work with refuges and the relevant voluntary agencies, such as Scottish Women's Aid, with the aim of working together to ensure that women receive prompt and appropriate help. However, there needs to be a change in police practice if women are to receive the support and understanding they need when reporting domestic abuse. Too often, the police see such abuse as a private dispute and even serious assaults are

treated as being minor. In some cases, women are told that the man cannot
be arrested if there was no witness to the violence. Criminal prosecutions
are rare, occurring only in a minority of cases (Radford *et al.*, 1999). The
British Crime Survey (Mirlees-Black *et al.*, 1998) results showed that only
11 per cent of domestic assaults occurring in the previous year had been
reported to the police, suggesting that calling the police is the last resort for
many women who are attacked in the home. Certainly, Women's Aid see
many victims who have never reported their experience of violence to the
police (Scottish Office, 1997). A Canadian study found that, on average,
women had been assaulted 35 times before contacting the police (Scottish
Office, 1997).

Social work practice and domestic abuse

Domestic abuse is rarely a 'one-off' event. Physical and sexual abuse
tend to increase in frequency and severity over time, and other forms of
abusive behaviour may be part of an ongoing pattern. A recent sample
of Scottish victims indicated that 49 per cent said they had been injured
more than once in a year and 20 per cent said that force had been used
against them at least once a week (Scottish Office, 1997). Studies in
Scotland and elsewhere point out that it is important therefore for
professionals to realise that it may not be the severity of the particular
attack which has led to its being reported:

> Rather it may be the cumulative effect of persistent abuse and intimida-
> tion, decreasing acceptance of the man's justification for violence and
> repeated failure to solve the problem alone. (Scottish Office, 1997, p. 3)

A woman seeking help and support may be doing so after months or
years of abuse and find the prospect of leaving the abusive relationship
as frightening as the prospect of staying. Women are at particular risk
just before or immediately after leaving a violent relationship, and are
right to feel vulnerable at this point. Therefore the way in which a social
worker responds when first approached by a woman who has experienced domestic abuse is crucial.

Listening to the woman and believing her is the first step. The next
step is to respond in a way that is appropriate to the situation. It is, for
example, essential to consider her immediate safety and that of any children in the family, as their safety and welfare are paramount. Women

need to be given privacy so that they can feel able to discuss what has happened to them, and it is particularly important that this should be offered at a pace they feel comfortable with. As well as offering emotional support, social workers should be able to provide information about protection, access to voluntary agencies that support the survivors of domestic violence, relevant health services, police powers, housing and how to obtain legal advice from a solicitor experienced in family law. If a woman's situation has reached crisis point, she may need access to several of these agencies, for example the police, the emergency accommodation services and the courts.

Women in the *Hitting Home* study were found to have contacted a wide range of support, with the most common being Women's Aid, housing departments, solicitors, the benefits agency, friends, neighbours, GPs and the police. The services they sought were broadly around accommodation and refuge, their own and their children's protection and around finding emotional support from informal contacts. The report highlights the difference in the women's experiences of the service provided to them, with 91 per cent of those using Women's Aid finding it helpful, but only 48 per cent of those in contact with the Housing Department or social services finding their response helpful. The common issues arising from poor service provision related to none being offered as well as to a failure by service providers to understand the issues and consequently offering inappropriate responses. Women also felt that there was a lack of any or accessible information about services and that the 'daunting nature of the help seeking process and fear of discovery' was a deterrent to obtaining support and advice.[1]

After the immediate crisis has passed, the woman may need assistance with long-term arrangements for housing, advice on benefits or counselling. It is important to remember that many women who have experienced domestic abuse assume that they are to blame for the violence. Social workers need to emphasise to women the appropriateness of seeking help and stress that violence in the home is a criminal offence, that expert help is available and that legal intervention is possible (South and East Belfast Trust, 1998).

The legislation and domestic abuse

Research in the UK and elsewhere has also shown that perpetrators of domestic abuse do not readily see their conduct as criminal and that many victims feel blameworthy in some way for the abuse. The act of charging an offender sends a clear message to both parties, that an independent person believes that the conduct of the accused was criminal. Victims who insist that they do not want charges to be preferred, or who make claims that the injuries resulted from an accident, may be so disturbed by the trauma of the situation, or so afraid of repercussions from the perpetrator, that they need to be seen at a later date (Scottish Office, 1997). It is important for professionals such as the police and social workers, however, to be sensitive to the complexity of balancing the need for intervention (for example where there are child protection issues) with the need to allow women to take control of their lives.

Whether or not the police use criminal law provisions (for example common assault) against an abusive person, individuals may still use civil law in order to obtain protection. Under the Matrimonial Homes (Family Protection) (Scotland) Act 1981, a court can grant an exclusion order to prevent a spouse from entering the matrimonial home in order to protect the other spouse (and any children of the family) from conduct which would injure them either physically or mentally. The order effectively suspends the occupancy rights of the spouse, but there are two requirements to be met before the court can grant the order. First, the order must be necessary to protect the applicant or any child of the family from actual or threatened conduct of the other spouse and, second, it must not be unjustified or unreasonable for the court to make such an order. The court also has the power to grant a matrimonial interdict. This restrains or prohibits the conduct of one spouse against the other (and any children of the family) and may also prohibit the spouse from entering or remaining in the matrimonial home. The court can attach a power of arrest to a matrimonial interdict, which gives the police the power to arrest without warrant if there is reasonable cause to suspect that a breach of the interdict has taken place. However, if the matrimonial interdict is granted at the same time as an exclusion order, the court *must* attach the power of arrest. Breach of a matrimonial interdict carries with it a penalty of up to two years' imprisonment. The Act also applies to heterosexual cohabiting couples who are 'entitled' – that is, they have occupancy rights in the home. However, a 'non-entitled' applicant must apply to the court for occupancy rights (and be granted these) before they can apply for an exclusion order, so this can lead to some weeks' delay. The Protection from Abuse (Scotland) Act 2001 has extended the law generally on who can apply for an interdict with a power of arrest attached. The Act covers divorced couples and same-sex couples, but there is no requirement to prove any sort of relationship between the parties, so it provides protection for any person who is being abused by someone else.

The Protection from Harassment Act 1997, in its application in Scotland, has strengthened both the civil and criminal law. Under the Act, victims are able to obtain a non-harassment order to prevent harassment and the breach of such an order is a criminal offence punishable by up to five years' imprisonment. However, the order can only be made if there is evidence of a 'course of conduct', that is, relevant conduct on at least two occasions.

It is possible that some victims of domestic abuse are reluctant to report incidents if they feel that this might ultimately lead to their children being taken into care. This perception has to be acknowledged in the way in which social workers and other professionals deal with information-sharing, whilst ensuring that the safety of any children of the family remains paramount. The Scottish Office Police (CC) Circular 3/1990 states that the social work department should advise the Reporter to the Children's Panel of cases where children are present in a home where an assault has been committed (in some regions, police officers routinely inform the Reporter of such cases). The priority must be to consider whether child protection procedures need to be put in place and to ensure that any children should be assessed by the relevant agencies. Under the Children (Scotland) Act 1995 the courts, on application by the local authority, have powers to order the exclusion of a member of the household 'where a child has suffered, is suffering or is likely to suffer significant harm as a result of any conduct of the named person' (s.77). This legislation strengthens the need for good information flows between social services and the police (Scottish Office, 1997).

When women do approach social services for advice about an abusive situation, they may feel extremely anxious about applying to the court for an order and want to look at other options. Taking time to listen to what they want and to respect their wishes is therefore important. Good practice is about being sensitive and enabling women to discuss their fears, as well as exploring with them ways to maximise their safety. Understanding the potential danger of further violence towards women living in abusive situations is essential. There is a large body of evidence that shows convincingly that women are at greatest risk of harm when they leave the relationship (Scottish Office, 1996; Barnett, 1999).

Children and domestic abuse

Abuse in the home has a significant impact on children. Children are frequently witness to, or are aware of, abuse and violence against their mother. Studies have indicated that up to 90 per cent of children of domestic abuse victims have been in the same room or in a nearby room when the abuse occurs (Children in Scotland, 1999). Exposure to domestic abuse has a significant consequence for children's health, development, self-esteem and confidence in both the short and the long term (Humphreys, 1999). However, children's experience needs to be understood not only in terms of the effects of witnessing or being implicated in conflict and abuse, but also in the context of their perception of the emotional climate of the family. In most (although not all) cases, they will have experienced a family atmosphere that is characterised by stress and conflict, and that can affect their development in a number of ways. Young children in particular are likely to experience feelings of self-blame and fear.

The welfare of the children where domestic abuse is an issue therefore must clearly be of concern. Given it is increasingly recognised that children themselves are being emotionally abused by being witness to the abuse against their mothers, this must be an issue of concern for all professionals encountering domestic abuse (Neville, 1999). Children in Scotland supports Scottish Women's Aid's call for greater recognition and services for children affected by domestic abuse, emphasising that local authorities must have services that address the needs of children affected by domestic abuse identified within their service plans and implemented. They also recommend that services such as housing, health and education must recognise and address the needs of children affected by domestic abuse (Children in Scotland, 1999).

Conclusion

Providing women with a safe environment in which to explore the options, both legal and practical, available to them is a vital part of the social work service. Social workers should be able to offer advice about securing safe accommodation, whether that be in the woman's home or in a refuge, and on how to pursue civil or criminal proceedings. Some women leave and return to abusive partners many times before they feel able to make a final decision to leave. Their wishes and right to choose should be respected and protected on their behalf. Where child protection is an issue in domestic abuse, it is important that social workers do not lose sight of the woman's needs but work in partnership with her. This does not imply that children's needs should be conflated with those of their mothers but instead that supporting women, rather than admonishing them for their 'failure to protect', is an important underlying principle (Humphreys *et al.*, 2000). It is also important to recognise the emotional, psychological and financial costs attached to escaping from abuse and the effects of having been in a relationship characterised by long-term abuse. Social work in relation to domestic abuse is a skilled and demanding task. That task should be seen as part of a multi-agency commitment in all local authority areas to developing a framework of best practice and creating an effective response to domestic abuse.

Note

1. The Domestic Abuse Helpline offers access to services for women and children by providing a freephone number (0800 027 1234) which, as well as providing an opportunity to speak in confidence about what has happened to them, provides relevant information, for example about legal matters, housing or benefits. Calls to the helpline are not recorded on telephone bills. From 2002 the Helpline has been available from 10.00 a.m. to midnight every day of the year.

References

Alabhai-Brown, Y. (1999) 'At home with fear', *Community Care,* 12–18 August, p. 12.

Barnett, A. (1999) 'Disclosure of domestic violence by women involved in child contact disputes', *Family Law,* February, p. 105.

Children in Scotland (1999) *Children and Domestic Violence: Policy Briefing*, www.childreninscotland.org.uk/brdomviol.htm (accessed 17 January 2003).

Domestic abuse recorded by the police in Scotland, 1 Jan.–31 Dec. 2001: www.scotland.gov.uk/stats/bulletins/00202-00.asp (accessed 17 January 2003).

Dominy, N. and Radford, L. (1996) *Living without Fear,* London, Cabinet Office Women's Unit.

Economic and Social Research Council (1998) *Violence Research programme,* Middlesex, Brunel University.

Henderson, S. (1998) *Service Provision to Women Experiencing Domestic Violence in Scotland* in Scottish Office Central Research Unit, Scottish Office Crime and Criminal Justice Research findings No. 2, Edinburgh, Scottish Office.

Hester, M. and Radford, L. (1996) *Domestic Violence and Child Contact Arrangements in England and Denmark,* Bristol, Policy Press.

Humphreys, C. (1999) 'Judicial Alienation syndrome: failures to respond to post-separation violence', *Family Law,* May, p. 313.

Humphreys, C., Hester, M., Hague, G., Mullender, A., Abraham, H. and Lowe, P. (2000) *From Good Intentions to Good Practice,* Bristol, Policy Press.

Jay, M. (1999) *Living without Fear: An Integrated Approach to Tackling Violence Against Women,* London, Home Office.

Kelly, L. (1998) *Domestic Violence Matters: An Evaluation of a Development Project* London, Home Office.

Mirlees-Black, C., Mayhew, P. and Percy, A. (1998) *The 1998 British Crime Survey, England and Wales,* London, Home Office Research and Statistics Directorate.

Neville, E. (1999) 'Domestic violence: a police perspective', unpublished seminar report.

Radford, L. (1996) '"Nothing really happened"; the invalidation of women's experiences of sexual violence', in M. Hester, L. Kelly and L. Radford (eds) *Women, Violence and Male Power,* Buckingham, Open University Press.

Radford, L., Sayer, S. and AMICA (1999) *Unreasonable Fears? Child Contact in the Case of Domestic Violence: A Survey of Mothers' Perceptions of Harm,* Bristol, Women's Aid Federation of England.

Scottish Office (1996) *Scottish Crime Survey*, Edinburgh Scottish Office Centre Statistics Unit.

Scottish Office (1997) *Hitting Home – Report on the Police Response to Domestic Violence* 1997, Edinburgh, Scottish Office.

South and East Belfast Trust (1998) *Domestic Violence Guidelines in Good Practice: An Interagency Response,* Belfast, South and East Belfast Trust.

Stanko, E.A. and Hobdall, K. (1993) 'Assault on men – masculinity and male victimisation', *British Journal of Criminology*, vol. 33, no. 3, p. 400.

www.scotland.gov.uk/stats/bulletins/00203-00.asp (accessed 17 January 2003).

www.scotland.gov.uk/library5/social/dapr-00.asp (accessed 14 March 2003).

17

Special Educational Needs: Working with Children and Families

MARION McLARTY AND MOYRA HAWTHORN

Introduction

The legal framework which governs educational provision often seems complicated and inaccessible, even sometimes to those employed in education themselves, and this can lead to confusion and misunderstanding. This is particularly likely to be the case at a time of great change such as the current situation in Scottish education in 2003.

It is the intention of the authors of this chapter to give an overview of recent legislation and some which is still in draft form at the time of writing, and to alert readers to some of the areas which are most problematic to pupils with special needs and disabilities and to their families and carers.

It is important to emphasise at the outset that the Scottish education system is quite distinct from that in England and Wales. Due to the UK-wide nature of a great deal of our media, viewers, listeners and readers in Scotland are often informed of developments in education which apply only south of the border and they are sometimes unaware that rights and requirements in Scotland are somewhat different. An example of this confusion was seen recently during interviews for applicants to the Bachelor of Education course at a Scottish university. When applicants were asked to discuss recent educational initiatives of which they were aware, five out of a group of twelve mentioned only English issues.

While always separate from England and Wales the system in Scotland often displays parallel initiatives to those in the south; for example, the modern system in England and Wales was set in place by the Education Act of 1870 while the modern Scottish system was instituted in 1872 with the Education (Scotland) Act of that year. It was not for another 102 years, however, that all Scottish children gained the right to education when the Education (Mentally Handicapped Children) (Scotland) Act 1974 brought Scottish education in line with the system in England and Wales. Those interested in the early developments in special education in Scotland will find this usefully covered in Dockrell *et al.* (1978) and Thomson (1983).

Current attitudes to and provision for children with special needs were influenced significantly by two reports which were published in what is often referred to as 'the watershed year' of 1978. The wide-ranging Warnock Report (Committee of Enquiry into the Education of Handicapped Children and Young People, 1978) was a significant event for special education throughout the UK (except N. Ireland), while the HMI report on pupils with learning difficulties (Her Majesty's Inspectors of Schools, 1978) identified practice in Scottish mainstream schools as a major cause of educational failure for many pupils. The Education (Scotland) Acts of 1980 and 1981 following these reports established processes and practices which are largely unaltered at the time of writing.

The establishment of the new Scottish Parliament was followed closely by fresh legislation on education. Two important Acts were passed, the Standards in Scotland's Schools etc. Act 2000 and the Education (Disability Strategies and Pupils' Educational Records) (Scotland) Act 2002. Although there was a gap of almost twenty years between the Education Acts of the 1980s and those of the new Parliament, this is not to say that there were no developments or innovations during the period. New curricular frameworks were developed, (5–14 and Higher Still) which are designed to include all learners, however profound and complex their difficulties, and the Scottish Office Education Department (later the Scottish Office Education and Industry Department) regularly issued guidelines on a range of educational issues.

Legislation

Recent legislation that provides the legal structure for what happens in education in Scotland includes:

- the Standards in Scotland's Schools etc. Act 2000;
- the SEN and Disability Act 2001. This is a UK Act which applies to all Scottish education.
- the Education (Disability Strategies and Pupils' Educational Records) (Scotland) Act 2002.
- The Education (Additional Support For Learning) (Scotland) Bill will be published in 2003.

These Acts of the Scottish and UK parliaments set out what pupils, parents and professionals can expect from the education system in Scotland and allow them to be aware of what might be expected of them. The full text of the Acts can be accessed on the internet at http://www.hmso.gov.uk/legislation/scotland/acts.

The Standards in Scotland's Schools etc. Act 2000 is a wide-ranging Act which sets out to address how education should be provided in the twenty-first century. It emphasises the rights of every child to a school education and indicates the education authority's responsibility to ensure that this is of a high quality.

One particular section which caused a great deal of controversy during the consultation period was Section 15, 'Requirement that education be provided in mainstream schools'. This was due to the fact that, after stating this 'requirement' the Act then goes on to state three acceptable reasons for not providing education in a mainstream school, these being that the school:

(a) would not be suited to the ability or the aptitude of the child;
(b) would be incompatible with the provision of efficient education for the children with whom the child would be educated; or
(c) would result in unreasonable public expenditure which would not ordinarily be incurred. (Section 15(3) Standards in Scotland's Schools etc. Act 2000)

Although the Act then goes on to state 'it shall be presumed that those circumstances arise only exceptionally', concern was, and continues to be, expressed about the power to exclude a variety of children which is presented to education authorities and school management. The Education (Disability Strategies and Pupils' Educational Records) (Scotland) Act 2002 might be said to redress the balance here and is discussed below.

Another important issue in the welfare of children and young people is addressed in Section 16, 'No justification for corporal punishment'. The significance of this section is its potential effect on issues of restraint of disruptive and challenging pupils. Already many local authorities are reviewing their policies and procedures in this area and it seems realistic to presume that the relationship between punishment and restraint may provide some interesting discussion for some time to come.

Section 40, 'Education outwith school', lays a duty on education authorities to 'make special arrangements for the pupil to receive education elsewhere than at an educational establishment' for those who are unable to attend school due to health reasons. Where a pupil has been excluded or has withdrawn from a school, the authority must 'without undue delay' provide education in another school or make special arrangements. A potential problem might lie in the concept of 'undue delay', which may be viewed differently by pupils, their parents and local authorities.

Towards the end of the Act (ss.56 and 57) reference is made to sex education and medical matters and the power of the Executive in this is made clear. This section reminds us of the public controversy (and homophobic backlash) which surrounded the repeal of the notorious 'Clause 28'. At that time, the Executive gave an undertaking that it would reserve the right to decide how sex education was taught in Scottish schools. Recent information from teachers and pupils, however, indicates that little has actually changed and teachers are still unsure and lacking in confidence as to how to deal with issues of homosexuality.

The Special Educational Needs and Disability Act 2001 which is an Act of the UK Parliament was designed to correct the shortcomings of the Disability Discrimination Act 1995 which did not provide protection against discriminatory practice in education. This Act applies to all Scottish educational provision (including Community Education). This means that a pupil with a disability at school is protected by this Act and the Education (Disability Strategies and Pupils' Educational Records) (Scotland) Act 2002.

The Education (Disability Strategies and Pupils' Educational Records) (Scotland) Act 2002 is a much shorter and more focused piece of legislation which came into force on 1 October 2002. The guidance documentation which accompanies the legislation includes a list of the types of impairments which would cause a pupil to be regarded as disabled within the meaning of the Act and it is interesting to note that the impairments listed, which include specific impairments such as deafness and autism as well as the more vague, moderate learning difficulties, are essentially those which are currently associated with the concept of special educational needs. This is particularly significant in view of the changes contained in the proposed Education (Additional Support For Learning) (Scotland) Bill which is discussed below.

The Disability Strategies legislation requires the preparation and implementation of 'strategies relating to the accessibility, for pupils with a disability, of school education', as well as legislating on administrative details regarding pupils' educational records. The legislation creates three clear duties for education authorities, these being in line with and following from the section in the Special Educational Needs and Disability Act 2001, parts of which already apply to Scotland (see above).

The guidance defines the 'three duties' which accessibility strategies will require of local education authorities as being those of ensuring:

* access to the curriculum;
* access to the physical environment of schools; and
* improving communication with pupils with disabilities.

The firm belief in inclusion and the rights of disabled children and young people is clear in these guidelines and recommendations are uncompromising and leave little space for manoeuvre for authorities tempted to offer excuses, for example:

> If no capital building work is planned for the near future, the responsible body [the local authority] will have to consider bringing forward its own refurbishment projects. (Scottish Executive, 2002, p. 1)

The proposed Education (Additional Support For Learning) (Scotland) Bill displays a fundamental change to the way that support needs in education have been regarded since 1980. What it aims to do, as this section will explain, is to separate the concepts of support needs and disability which have been regarded as one and the same for a very long time. This might be seen as rather controversial particularly as the connection between the two concepts is emphasised at a UK level in the SEN and Disability Act 2001. Before considering the proposed legislation it is important to be clear about the original term 'special educational needs'.

The term 'special educational needs' is set out in Section1(5)(d) of

the Education (Scotland) Act 1980 and then restated in the SOEID
Circular 4/96 *Children and Young Persons with Special Educational
Needs: Assessment and Recording.*

> Children and young persons have special educational needs if they
> have a learning difficulty which calls for provision for special educa-
> tional needs to be made for them. Learning difficulty is said to be
> present if children and young persons:
>
> (a) have significantly greater difficulty in learning than the majority
>   of the same age: or
> (b) suffer from a disability which either prevents or hinders them
>   from making use of educational facilities of a kind generally
>   provided for those of their age in schools managed by their
>   education authority; or
> (c) who are under the age of 5 years old and, if provision for special
>   educational needs were not made for them, are or would likely,
>   when over that age to have a learning difficulty as defined above.
>   (SOEID, 1996)

The change from 'special educational needs' to 'additional support
needs' which is contained in the draft bill is designed to include children
for whom English is an additional language, refugees and asylum seekers, children with social, emotional and behavioural difficulties and
gypsy/traveller children; and may also include gifted or more able children. It may well be argued that, with disability legislation to protect the
interests of the traditional group of pupils with SEN, the way is now
clear to formalise the position of those who have always required extra
support but who have not enjoyed the benefits of having their needs offi-
cially recognised.

The planned changes mean that responsibility for the identification,
assessment and provision for pupils with difficulties will be an in-house
matter for schools and the new process is designed to make use of a
number of systems already in place, like Personal Learning Plans and
Individual Educational Programmes (IEPs). It is only when a pupil has
complex needs which require support by more than one agency (that is,
not just education) that a Coordinated Support Plan (CSP) will be put in
place. This emphasis on the role of health and social services is new and
is likely to involve social workers much more in the work of schools.

The Act, when it is passed, will place new statutory duties on education authorities and on social work departments, the former being required to seek advice and information on the pupil and the latter to provide it. There is also the suggestion that agencies other than education be fully involved in the drawing up and regular review of both long- and short-term aims in the Coordinated Support Plan. At the conclusion of the process the pupil and parents will receive the entire document while individual agencies will receive only relevant parts in order that confidentiality may be maintained. Where a young person already has a Record of Needs (RoN), the change to the new system will be phased in.

Clearly these changes will have major implications for social work departments, even if only in increased workloads. There will be a need to collaborate much more closely with education and health services, not just in the drawing up of the new plans but also in the regular review of long- and short-term targets. During the period of consultation concerns have been voiced about the extra workload and the need for staff development in collaborative working if the new system is going to work effectively.

The Future Needs Assessment is to be discontinued under the proposed changes with the recommendation from the Executive that forward planning is to be a normal part of the move from school for all pupils. This echoes recommendations from the Beattie Report (Scottish Executive 1999) which recommends that key workers be available to help young people at this time.

The views of children, young people and families

The legal framework of the educational provision for children and young people with SEN is complex and it can be daunting for parents and young people who wish to understand the system and possibly query decisions that have been taken. A number of organisations in Scotland offer help and support to parents and families and one in particular, Enquire, has been set up specifically to provide such advice.

This organisation reports that the Standards in Scotland's Schools etc. Act 2000 has been generally welcomed as having defined the purpose of education and tightened up some of the 'loopholes' in the 1980 and 1981 Acts. It has embedded in law some of the good practice previously recommended by HMI and evident only in some schools, such as the involvement of the pupils in planning educational programmes. In spite of this Enquire notes that there are still occasions where legal duties are not observed in practice and parents feel confused or dissatisfied.

A major concern of parents centres on issues surrounding their child's RoN. Under the Education (Scotland) Act 1980 (updated in Circular 4/96), local authorities must open a RoN for any child over two years but under school-leaving age who has SEN which are 'pronounced, specific or complex' and 'require continuing review'.

The draft Bill proposes that the RoN will be phased out and replaced by a system of Coordinated Support Plans but concerns have been expressed that while the present system is far from perfect this has generally been due to inadequate resources and there is no guarantee that a new system will be an improvement.

One factor of the RoN process has been the recognition of the rights of parents and carers to initiate action if they have concerns over a child's progress. In the past parents have been able to approach GPs or psychological services directly if they did not wish to work through the school. It is clear that parental/carer rights in this area will be in no way diminished by the new system.

A particular concern that has arisen during the consultation process on the draft Education (Additional Support For Learning) (Scotland) Bill is that there are likely to be some children who currently have a RoN and very complex disabilities who may find themselves regarded as not qualifying for a Coordinated Support Plan. One parent at a recent seminar described the situation of her son who is likely to be in this situation. He currently has a RoN as he has severe autism and is a non-verbal communicator. He attends his local school with a great deal of support and has input from speech and language therapists who are employed by the local authority. The extended family is very supportive and no input is required from social services. All this means that this pupil is supported by just one agency, education, and therefore would not require a CSP. Were this pupil to attend a school in another area where speech and language therapy is provided by health services, however, he would then be supported by two agencies and qualify for a CSP. Clearly this is an anomaly which will be addressed but it demonstrates the need for all agencies to be aware of those who may 'slip through the net' in the new system.

Another worry for parents is the 'presumption of inclusion in mainstream education' introduced in the Standards in Scotland's Schools etc. Act. While this is commonly held to be a very positive move, providing that supports are in place, concern has been expressed at the lack of consultation with parents and young people. While many will undoubtedly benefit, concerns and doubts are expressed as to its suitability for all; the normal noise level of a busy school can trigger epileptic seizures or provoke acutely distressed behaviour in some people on the autistic spectrum. The Act seems, however, to recognise the specific needs of low-incidence groups and provide for their needs in s.15 (above).

Exclusion is another cause of concern for families and young people. The legal process which schools must go through before excluding a pupil is clear but sometimes an informal exclusion may occur due to behaviour which challenges the system or even because of staff absence causing a lack of support resources. Parents sometimes do not wish a formal exclusion to appear 'on the child's records' but it is important that they indicate the less favourable treatment which they are experiencing and request that the exclusion be formalised and details be put in writing. Sometimes this is sufficient to bring about a return to school. It is also important in cases of exclusion to note that responsibility for the pupil lies with the last school attended until alternative provision is made. Section 40 of the Standards in Scotland's Schools etc. Act 2000 (above) should be consulted on this.

Related to these concerns are those involving children and young people who receive part-time education. This may occur for a number of reasons: they may be awaiting transfer to a setting more appropriate to meeting their needs on account of health, emotional or behavioural issues. Legally, the length of the pupil's school year is 190 days and to receive less may be perceived to be discriminatory. Educational provision may be a combination of home tutors, work assigned for completion at home, educational outings in the community and/or part-time placement in an educational establishment. The new legislation and information from the Executive stress the centrality of young people and parents to decisions on educational provisions and they should feel confident in making their views heard on this, as on all other matters.

Pre-school education raises concerns for some parents of children with disabilities. While for many children best provision is undoubtedly with their peers in local resources, parents report little in the way of specialist support in these settings, although a RoN can be opened for pre-school children. Parents of children with disabilities also report difficulty in securing appropriate pre-five provision to allow them to return to work.

Sources of support

In many instances, the provision of education for children with SEN runs smoothly, with professionals working in partnership with parents, children and young people. All education authorities should have written information regarding provision in their area, including early intervention. They have a duty to ensure that this information is open, accessible and available in a variety of languages and mediums (for example Braille). When difficulties arise, however, and parents and young people feel that they have achieved as much as they can independently, it can be helpful to use the services of an outside agency. A range of organisations exist in Scotland offering advice and practical support to families, some have been existence for many years (for example, the Royal National Institute for the Blind, the Royal National Institute for the Deaf, Capability Scotland) while others are relative newcomers, (for example, SENSE Scotland, Equity, Enquire). Enquire was set up and is funded by the Scottish Executive and aims to provide information, advice and mediation services to families affected by disabilities, to young people themselves or to those who work on their behalf. They offer a telephone helpline, a range of guides, fact sheets and other publications, and training to professionals and families in some parts of the country. This agency would be a good first contact even for those who might require more specialist support.

Provision of face-to-face advocacy and mediation services vary across regions and agencies but new developments are ongoing. Advocacy services are particularly helpful for those who have difficulty communicating with service providers while mediation provides a neutral third person in any disagreement.

Working in partnership with young people

In the course of their school life some young people experience a change in circumstances which requires a change of educational arrangements to meet their needs effectively. The new legislation, along with increasing numbers of professionals in the field, recognises the importance of working in multi-agency partnership with children, young people and their families. This is particularly important when exclusion from school is a possibility. The new Coordinated Support Plans are likely to be a valuable vehicle for addressing a range of issues in the lives of young people, not just those surrounding their education. Because of the way in which services for children are organised, support packages are likely to involve not just education and psychological services but a range of professionals from health, social work services and voluntary agencies. While this can be complex to coordinate, such a group will be a rich resource in developing and implementing support procedures. Good intra-agency working is essential, not only to ensure consistency for young people but also to ensure that 'what works' is shared. A range of up-to-date literature is available on strategies and approaches for working with young people under stress.

Conclusion

Those involved in education in Scotland, whether as practitioners, consumers or legislators, are currently 'living in interesting times', the full results of which will not be clear for some years yet. The year of 1978 which saw the publication of both the Warnock Report and the HMI report on pupils with learning difficulties is generally viewed as a watershed year which brought about a change from the old model of pupil deficit and handicap to new attitudes and approaches in learning support and providing for special educational needs. The first two years of the twenty-first century, which have seen a raft of new educational legislation, might be hailed as the next watershed which sees legislation and general attitudes move from a model based on needs to one firmly established on rights. The rights of children and young people are fundamental to the new Scottish legislation and whatever glitches might be experienced in the settling-in period, this is an important principle on which to base professional practice.[1]

Note

1. The authors are grateful to a number of people and organisations for their help and advice with this chapter; in particular they would like to thank the staff of Enquire and Equity.

References

Committee of Enquiry into the Education of Handicapped Children and Young People (1978) *Special Educational Needs* (Warnock Report), London, HMSO.

Dockrell, W.B., Dunn, W.R. and Milne, A. (1978) *Special Education in Scotland*, Edinburgh, Scottish Council for Research in Education.

Her Majesty's Inspectors of Schools (1978) *The Education of Pupils with Learning Difficulties in Primary and Secondary Schools in Scotland*, Edinburgh, HMSO.

Scottish Executive (1999) *Implementing Inclusiveness, Realising Potential: The Beattie Committee Report*, Edinburgh.

Scottish Executive (2000) *Standards in Scotland's Schools etc. Act 2000*, http://www.hmso.gov.uk/legislation/scotland/acts.

Scottish Executive (2002) *The Education (Disability Strategies and Pupils' Educational Records) (Scotland) Act*, http://www.hmso.gov.uk/legislation/scotland/acts.

SOEID (1996) *Children and Young Persons with Special Educational Needs: Assessment and Recording*, Edinburgh, Scottish Office.

Thomson, G.O.B. (1983) 'Legislation and provision for the mentally handicapped child in Scotland since 1906', *Oxford Review of Education*, vol. 9, no. 3, pp. 233–40.

18

The Law and Practice Relating to Freeing for Adoption and Adoption

JANICE WEST

This chapter will explore the development of the legal framework in relation to the permanent placement of children within adoptive placements. The process of adoption from application to the granting of the order will be set within the current context of practice. Adoption and 'freeing' will be discussed as potential routes to permanence and the lessons learned from research will be examined. It is beyond the scope of this chapter to provide a detailed account of the legislation – that is best obtained from the authoritative source (McNeill, 1998).

Social policy context

Legislation in relation to adoption first appears in the Scottish context with the passing of the Adoption (Scotland) Act 1930. This was seen as a legislative response to the 'problem' of children born outwith marriage and also helped regulate the redistribution of such children (Ball, 1995). Throughout the twentieth century, adoption policy and practice have evolved in response to the changing nature of Scottish society, a process that is likely to continue as has been recognised by the Labour government in their review of the legislation in England and Wales.

The shifts in adoption trends need to be widely recognised and acknowledged; adoption of children from care in the 21st century is

less about providing homes for relinquished babies and more
concerned with providing secure, permanent relationships for some
of society's most vulnerable children. (Cabinet Office, 2000,
Executive Summary, p. 1)

While this statement represents a shift in emphasis on the part of
policy-makers, there is still a clear implicit message of 'rescue' for children in public care. Marsh and Thoburn (2002) have suggested that the
increased priority currently being given to adoption reflects a desire by
politicians to use it as a 'quick exit from care'. This appears to be in
response to the research suggesting poor outcomes over a range of indi-
cators for such children and the concerns expressed about 'corporate
parenting' (Jones *et al.*, 1998; Francis, 2000). It also reflects the preoccupation of policy-makers with the shaping of society within accepted
and acceptable parameters.

Within social work practice since the 1970s there has been an ongoing concern about the planning processes for children in public care.
While continuing to endorse the view that children should, where possible, grow up within their family of origin, social workers became increasingly concerned about 'drift' in the planning process (Rowe and Lambert,
1973). There was a growing interest in creating permanent solutions for
children. It is difficult within social work literature of that period to find
any consensus on a definition of what constitutes 'permanency planning'.
It tends to be associated with alternative family placements, through
either adoption or fostering arrangements (Maluccio *et al.*, 1986), thereby
excluding those young people for whom the plan will be to prepare them
for independence outwith a close family network (Biehal *et al.*, 1995).
For the purposes of this chapter, however, the rather narrow definition
related to fostering and adoption is being used in order to explore the
range of legislation related to adoption and 'freeing' for adoption.

Current perceptions of adoption

Adoption began as a legal remedy characterised by the breaking of ties
with birth families: processes which are cloaked in secrecy and where the
relationship created by adoption is seen as excluding the birth family (Hill,
1991). During the 1990s however, this began to change. There was a
move away from the 'straightforward' baby placement towards the placing of children with complex needs. There were also increasing numbers

of children being placed with adopters where there was a clear expectation of some degree of ongoing involvement with the birth family. For most children, this will mean some degree of contact by letter between the two families, usually mediated by the adoption agency. This process of 'open adoption' falls far short of the New Zealand model (Ryburn, 1994) but does begin to engage with the research evidence that suggests that children who are adopted often have an intense curiosity about their family of origin (Triseliotis, 1973). Adoption has, therefore, moved from being a service providing children for families to one of providing families for children. It should be noted, however, that the changing expectations made of adopters have implications for their availability to undertake this complex parenting task. The recruitment of suitable prospective adoptive parents is a challenge faced by all adoption agencies.

Adoption in Scotland is currently regulated by the Adoption (Scotland) Act 1978 as amended by the Children (Scotland) Act 1995. There are also regulations, guidance and Rules of Court that help to define the parameters of practice. Freeing for adoption, although part of the overall pattern of permanent placement and covered by the same primary legislation, raises particular issues and will be dealt with separately within this chapter. At the time of writing, the Scottish Executive is undertaking a review of adoption practice (Scottish Executive, 2002) which, while not as far-reaching as that in England and Wales (Department of Health, 2000), is likely to bring about a number of changes to current legislation and practice.

Routes to adoption

The current legislation allows for the adoption of children under three different categories:

- step-parent adoptions;
- other biological relatives;
- adoption agencies and societies.

It is not possible for children to be placed for adoption through any form of 'private' arrangement and it is unlawful for payment to be made directly for the purpose of securing agreement to adoption (section 51 of the Adoption (Scotland) Act 1978). In 2001, the majority of adoption petitions in Scotland (approximately 60 per cent of the total) were adoptions where neither petitioner was related to the child (Scottish Executive, 2002). The overall number of adoption petitions coming before the Scottish courts has decreased dramatically since the early 1980s with only 420 petitions in 2001. There are many possible reasons for this decline in numbers. The changing nature of the social policy context has made it easier for women to contemplate raising a child alone. While still a difficult task, the social stigma of illegitimacy has lessened and access to resources such as housing, employment and finance is less complicated. This has altered the profile of children being placed for adoption, with fewer 'straightforward' baby placements and an increase in the number of children aged 2–11 years who have been unable to remain in their birth family due to pressures that lead to social work intervention.

Adoption process: who can adopt?

Who is eligible to be considered suitable to adopt is a matter of ongoing debate. Historically, when adoption was viewed primarily as a resource for adults seeking to adopt babies, selection criteria were based predominantly on material considerations. The logic appears to have been that the primary responsibility of adoption agencies was to provide the best possible physical environment for the child. This was frequently supported by birth parents whose reasons for placing the child for adoption often included financial and social betterment. As the children available for adoption changed, so too did the potential adopters. They began to be more representative of the population at large although it would be fair to say that the most stringent selection criteria are still applied to those seeking to adopt 'straightforward' babies. The legislation allows for the possibility that a single carer can meet the needs of a child through adoption. Given that it remains impossible for two same-sex adults to jointly petition for adoption, it would be necessary for one partner to lodge a petition under this section of the legislation. While this has been the subject of discussion within the English adoption law review, to date the Scottish courts have declined to adjudicate on this matter.[1]

Assessment of prospective adopters

The introduction of National Care Standards for Adoption Agencies

(Scottish Executive, 2002) is an attempt to ensure some degree of quality assurance over the adoption process and these standards make specific reference to the process of assessment. The expectation is of a 'full and thorough' assessment of the prospective adopter(s) that will be conducted in an open and inclusive manner. The exact form that the assessment will take remains subject to interpretation but there is a clear expectation of involvement throughout by the applicants. In keeping with the spirit of the Children (Scotland) Act 1995, this new framework assumes that delay will be kept to a minimum and that the process of assessment will be completed within six months (Standard 23). While it is clearly an important development to have a framework within which the process of assessment is managed, there are wider issues about the nature of assessment that are not addressed. A standards framework tends to collude with the notion that there is a clear scientific way of assessing suitability and does not take account of the inherent value-laden and subjective nature of the task. It does not, for example, seem to be particularly helpful to suggest that risk can be anything more than minimised by assessment and that the possibility of applicants being selective about the information they share must be acknowledged.

The traditional means of assessment has been through the creation of a home study report, often using the British Agencies for Adoption and Fostering Form F as a proforma. Recently, some agencies have begun to assess potential adopters utilising a competence framework which they consider allows for a clearer consideration to be made of the direct parenting capacities of the applicants. Given the relative newness of the competence framework for assessment, there is no clear evaluation of the comparative strengths and weaknesses of each approach. It is clear, however, that prospective adopters require to be offered an assessment process that encompasses knowledge and understanding of the task as well as direct scrutiny of them as people. Adoption panels are similarly charged with responsibilities to ensure that the decision-making process is both transparent and timeous. The task of parenting a child through adoption is complex and this needs to be reflected in the process of selection of potential carers.

Petitioning the court for an adoption order

After a child has been placed with prospective adopters, they will at some point require to formalise the situation by applying to the court for an adoption order. Most adoptions in Scotland are processed through the Sheriff Court with only a very small proportion being heard by the Court of Session at first instance. For many children who come to adoption from a background of instability and distress, there may be no sense of urgency about this formal process. Social workers providing support to families during this period can help both adults and children appreciate that the child may need time to settle into this new environment before being able to decide whether adoption seems to be the best outcome. The child's life history, age and patterns of attachment will all influence when is the appropriate time to petition the court, as will the confidence of the adopters in their new role. It is therefore essential to balance the need to enable all concerned to be involved in deciding the timing of this legal decision with the legislative principle of avoidance of delay.

Having had the petition lodged, the court will appoint a curator *ad litem* and Reporting Officer to advise on a range of issues (see Chapter 25, 'The role of the curator *ad litem* and reporting officer in adoption proceedings', by Janice West). Once all the paperwork is in place and all relevant explorations have been completed, the Sheriff will set a date for a court hearing where evidence will require to be led in order to satisfy the court on points of law. In some situations, the decision to grant an adoption order may be contested by parent(s) of the child although the court, having heard the objections, may dispense with consent if the appropriate legal grounds can be satisfied (s.5 of the 1978 Act). With the introduction of the Human Rights Act 1998, there have been a number of reported challenges to adoption proceedings on the grounds that the permanent severing of legal links between parents and children is in breach of Article 8 of the European Convention on Human Rights which emphasises the 'right to respect for private and family life'. To date, the courts have rejected such challenges but this does raise issues for social work practice as it is now particularly important that evidence can be presented to the court which demonstrates that every possible effort has been made to sustain the child within their birth family before adoption is considered.

Adoption planning and the children's hearings system

The children's hearings system now plays a significant role in the adoption process. Legislative changes introduced by the Children (Scotland) Act 1995 s.73 have created a requirement for panels to be consulted in any situation where adoption may become the plan for a 'looked after' child. While this applies in fairly small numbers to children who are the subject of straightforward petitions to the court, it is an important change in the legislation. The involvement of the hearings system is, however, more common in relation to children where the plan is 'freeing' for adoption. This change to the legislation has helped social workers explore more openly their plans for children in public care within the hearings system. Prior to this change in legislation, it was difficult for panel members to discuss any potential adoption plans as this was considered to be at odds with the rehabilitative ethos of the hearings system. Issues such as contact can now be more openly addressed and can be incorporated into adoption plans in whatever manner best meets the needs of the child. This can create tensions between social workers and panel members whose perspective on the child's situation may differ. The children's hearings system is predicated on assumptions of rehabilitation and frequent review. This means that panel members are unlikely to wish to consider adoption as an option until they are satisfied that every possible attempt at rehabilitation has been explored. This can present difficulties for social workers as there is a fine line between ensuring that full rehabilitative efforts have been made and leaving a child in a potentially harmful environment for longer than is helpful to their development and well-being. It is often the role of the safeguarder to provide an independent opinion in such situations.

Freeing for adoption

The history of the legal remedy of 'freeing' is interesting as the legislation was originally enacted with a different purpose in mind to that which has evolved as its main use. The Houghton Committee (HMSO, 1972) identified that there was a problem for relinquishing mothers in the adoption process. Consent by the parent(s) is given in respect of particular petitioners and the child remains the legal responsibility of the birth parent until all parental rights and responsibilities are transferred via adoption. What the Houghton Committee reported was that these mothers were unable to begin rebuilding their lives for many months as they awaited the outcome of the court proceedings. It was considered appropriate to allow birth parents to consent, in principle, to the proposed adoption at an early stage.

Sections 18–20 of the Children Act 1975 introduced the possibility that the courts could be asked to decide upon the principle of adoption even when no new carers had been identified: the safeguard being that the court required to be satisfied they were likely to become available within a year. This opened up a route to adoption for many children and young people previously not considered 'suitable for adoption'. Social workers began to identify situations where the barrier to adoption was the combination of legal uncertainty and complex personal needs. It became clear that prospective adopters were more able to begin to establish emotional bonds with children when the uncertainty of parental agreement had been removed (Lambert *et al.*, 1990).

In terms of social work planning, 'freeing' provides an opportunity for the adoption proposal to be tested in court at an early stage before long-term relationships have been created. The contest is between the adoption agency and the birth parents which means that the adoptive parents do not have to enter into direct competition over the care of the child. It can also ease the process of resource-finding as children can seek new families with their legal availability already resolved.

Section 16 of the Adoption (Scotland) Act 1978, as amended, enables local authorities to seek to free a child for adoption against the expressed wishes of the birth parent(s). The grounds are essentially the same as those that apply to dispensing with parental agreement elsewhere in the adoption legislation. The legal tests of which the court requires to be satisfied are that such grounds are established and that placement is likely to safeguard and promote the child's welfare throughout his or her life. Such decision-making, while radical in terms of outcome, is consistent with the UN Convention on the Rights of the Child and the European Convention on Human Rights as both place the child's right to family life within a context which suggests that the preference would be that this should be the birth family but the emphasis is on 'family'.

Freeing for adoption, in situations where agreement is forthcoming, can provide a helpful release to birth parents. They can rebuild their lives without undue concern about the child's future. In 'contested freeing' situations, the extent of opposition can vary considerably from birth parents who cannot bring themselves to sign an adoption agreement but who are content with the plan for their child (Lambert *et al.*, 1990) to those who contest the process throughout. The emotional impact of giving agreement to adoption should not be underestimated. Some parents will be prepared to accept that while they 'care about' their child, they cannot 'care for' him or her. In such circumstances, it can be very difficult to take the next step to agreeing that the child should grow up as part of another family (Mason and Selman, 1996).

Research suggests that this is one of the major areas of concern to relinquishing mothers who fear that the child will not understand the reasons for their decision (Sawbridge, 1988; Mason and Selman, 1996). Part of the difficulty for social workers working within the adoption process is how to maintain some degree of relationship with birth parents in a context where the social work role may involve gathering evidence which may be used in court to justify a decision to permanently remove the child from parental care. Once a decision has been made to seek a permanent new family for a child, it may become difficult for the social worker to sustain a working relationship with birth parents. It has become evident from the testimony of relinquishing parents and from adopted adults that the process of accepting the status of adoption can be considerably assisted when children are comfortable with their understanding of their personal history. Recent policy reviews both in Scotland and the rest of the UK have highlighted the need for better post-placement support to all concerned in the 'adoption triangle' (Department of Health, 2000; Scottish Executive, 2002).

Conclusion

This chapter has sought to highlight that creating a new family for a child through adoption is a skilled and complex task that requires social workers to develop awareness of the need for coherent and consistent planning throughout the process. It demands a clear understanding of the legislative options available together with an awareness of the research evidence that supports the need to minimise delay at every stage. In terms of legislation and policy in Scotland, it is not yet clear how this will develop. It seems clear, however, that if adoption is to continue to be regarded as a viable legislative choice for children it needs to reflect the aspirations of society that all children should be able to benefit from the opportunity to grow up as part of a family, however 'family' is defined.

References

Ball, C. (1995) 'Adoption: a service for children?', reprinted in M. Hill and M. Shaw (eds) (1998) *Signposts in Adoption: Policy Practice and Research Issues,* London, British Agencies for Adoption and Fostering.

Biehal, N., Clayden, J., Stein, M. and Wade, J. (1995) *Moving On: Young People Leaving Care Schemes,* London, HMSO.

Cabinet Office (2000) *Review of Adoption: Issues for Consultation,* London, Performance and Innovations Unit.

Department of Health (2000) *Adoption: A New Approach?,* Cmnd 5017, London, HMSO.

Francis, J. (2000) 'Investing in children's futures: enhancing the educational arrangements of "looked after" children and young people', *Child and Family Social Work,* vol. 5, no. 1, pp. 23–33.

Hill, M. (1991) 'Concepts of parenthood and their application to adoption', *Adoption and Fostering,* vol. 15, no. 4 (also in M. Hill and M. Shaw (eds) (1998) *Signposts in Adoption,* London, British Agencies for Adoption and Fostering).

HMSO (1972) Report of the Departmental Committee on the Adoption of Children (Houghton Report), Cmnd 5107, London, HMSO.

Jones, H., Clark, R., Kufeldt, K. and Norrman, N. (1998) 'Looking after children: assessing outcomes in child care: the experience of implementation', *Children and Society,* vol. 12, pp. 212–22.

Lambert, L., Buist, M., Triseliotis, J. and Hill, M. (1990) *Freeing Children for Adoption,* London, BAAF.

McNeill, P. (1998) *Adoption of Children in Scotland,* 3rd edn, Edinburgh, W. Green/Sweet & Maxwell.

Maluccio, A., Fein, E. and Olmstead, K.A. (1986) *Permanency Planning for Children,* New York, Tavistock.

Marsh, P. and Thoburn, J. (2002) 'The adoption and permanence debate in England and Wales', *Child and Family Social Work,* vol. 7, pp. 131–2.

Mason, K. and Selman, P. (1996) *Parents Without Children, Evaluation and Research Report,* University of Newcastle, Department of Social Policy.

Rowe, J. and Lambert, L. (1973) *Children Who Wait: A Study of Children Needing Substitute Families,* London, Association of British Adoption Agencies.

Ryburn, M. (1994) *Open Adoption: Research, Theory and Practice,* Aldershot, Avebury.

Sawbridge, P. (1988) 'The Post Adoption Centre – what are the users teaching us?', *Adoption and Fostering,* vol. 12, no. 1 (also in M. Hill and M. Shaw (eds) (1998) *Signposts in Adoption,* London, British Agencies for Adoption and Fostering).

Scottish Executive (2002) *National Care Standards for Adoption Agencies,* Edinburgh, Stationery Office.

Triseliotis, J. (1973) *In Search of Origins: The Experiences of Adopted People,* London, Routledge & Kegan Paul.

Part III

Service User and Practice Perspectives

19

The Role of the Mental Health Officer

KATHRYN MACKAY

Introduction

This chapter will focus on the present remit of the Mental Health Officer (MHO) under the Mental Health (Scotland) Act 1984 and how it will broaden under the Mental Health (Scotland) Bill 2002. It will also cover the duties under the Adults with Incapacity (Scotland) Act 2000. The wider legal and policy context has been addressed elsewhere so it will only be touched on here.

MHO practice varies across Scotland due to resource and structural difficulties in local authorities (Ulas, 1999) but also as to how the MHO role is defined by local authorities (Mental Welfare Commission, 2002). Some will fulfil their statutory duties only. Others take a broader 'spirit of the Act' approach, offering advice and support to all people who become subject to compulsory measures of care as opposed to the statutory minimum involvement.

MHO role

This section will address key legal duties and powers of MHOs under current legislation and practice issues arising from them, as well as considering how new legislation might change these.

To consider consent to detention in hospital when requested to do so by a medical practitioner

The MHO role is to determine whether the person has a mental disorder and whether it is necessary, for the health and safety of that person or of

215

others, for him or her to be detained in hospital. In order to do this the MHO should try to communicate with the person and speak to the doctor and other appropriate people. The Act identifies where an MHO will be or may become involved in decision-making in relation to detention of a person. For example:

- s.24: emergency detention order lasting 72 hours where the person is presently in the community. A doctor should seek the consent of an MHO or relative where practical.
- s.25: emergency detention order lasting 72 hours where the person is currently a voluntary hospital patient. Consent as per s.24.
- s.26: 28 day short-term order that can only follow s.24 or s.25 orders. An approved medical practitioner should seek the consent of either the nearest relative or MHO where practical.
- s.18: long-term order that lasts initially up to six months and can be renewed for another six months and thereafter yearly. This requires an MHO or nearest relative to formally lodge an application to the Sheriff Court supported by two medical recommendations. A hearing must take place to consider the grounds for the application.

Further, under s.117 of the existing Act, an MHO can gain a warrant, from a Justice of the Peace, to access premises, with a doctor in attendance and where appropriate remove the person to a place of safety for up to 72 hours. This will remain but will be modernised to ensure non-hospital-based options are pursued.

The view of the MHO as to whether a patient should be detained does carry significant weight, as doctors will not proceed if the MHO refuses consent to an emergency or short-term detention under ss.24–6. The MHO may be required to submit an s.18 court application whether they agree that it is needed or not; but they can state their reasons for opposing this course of action. It is my experience as an MHO that in these applications the MHO's opinion will not be given as much weight as medical opinion. There is evidence that some MHOs do not feel confident in their role and therefore do not feel able to oppose applications effectively, although conversely others have persuaded psychiatrists not to pursue an application in the first place (Bean *et al.*, 2001).

Under the proposed Bill, the MHO will have to submit a care plan for every application for a compulsory treatment order. This builds on a similar requirement that was first introduced in the Mental Health (Patients in the Community) Act 1995.

The Bill also lays greater emphasis on the MHO involvement in the review of orders. Previously there was no such statutory duty though in practice some local authorities encouraged MHOs to request a part in the process which otherwise could be a routine affair between the responsible medical officer (RMO), usually the psychiatrist, and the nurses. An MHO presence can ensure that due process is followed, a wider context can be brought into the discussion and the detained person and the nearest relative have the opportunity to speak about their situation and explore their legal rights in more depth. This discussion can often highlight issues to be addressed about the current care of the patient as well as whether there are still grounds for them to be detained.

Providing advice and assistance

The MHO has a duty to inform people about the legal processes and their rights of representation and appeal, and to facilitate their access to legal representation. More broadly the MHO should provide information about health and community services and offer ongoing involvement as appropriate. There is also a particular duty to protect the detained person's property; this may involve securing a house, removing possessions from a hostel for safe keeping and finding temporary lodgings for pets.

Research has highlighted that GPs and junior psychiatrists have limited training and therefore limited knowledge of the mental health legislation (Humphreys, 1994; Morgan *et al.*, 1999). Therefore many MHOs will see providing advice to medical practitioners as part of their role.

Social circumstances reports

Where a person is detained in the short or long term, an MHO provides a social circumstances report for the RMO and the Mental Welfare Commission. The social circumstances report should provide personal and social details, consider the circumstances that led to the detention and make recommendations for future intervention. It informs the RMO of relevant information and allows the Mental Welfare Commission to consider any issues about the appropriateness of the detention that they might further pursue.

The MHO should at least see the person being detained, a member of their family or carer and discuss the situation with the RMO and nursing staff. My experience as an MHO is that interviews, once the initial crisis of hospital admission is past, afford the person and their relatives the opportunity to talk about their experience and to receive advice and information about mental health, liaising with health professionals and community support.

Social circumstances reports provide another example of variations in practice. Some authorities are only doing such reports where there has been no MHO consent; others argue it is good practice to provide them for all people who are detained under ss.18 and 26. The Mental Welfare Commission is concerned that some areas are not even fulfilling their statutory requirement. Again the Mental Health Bill continues to allow some leeway in exceptional circumstances where the report would serve no practical purpose. It does however require individual MHOs to justify this in writing to the RMO and Mental Welfare Commission.

MHO role under the Adults with Incapacity (Scotland) Act 2000

This Act concerns people who do not have the capacity to act, make decisions, communicate decisions, understand decisions or retain the memory of decisions. It has modernised the institutional approaches to intervention for financial and welfare reasons which should be based on minimal intervention and the person's best interest. It has increased the ability of relatives, carers and friends to be more involved in financial and personal welfare than previously.

The Act also increases the role of many local authority officers: assessment and care management workers, chief social work officer, legal and financial staff. As a general rule MHOs will have a role to play with people who are seen to have incapacity due to mental disorder (Scottish Executive, 2001). They may be asked to undertake a range of activities, including:

- Investigating circumstances where the personal welfare of an adult is at risk. This requires a full assessment, report and, in complex situations, case conferences to determine whether the person lacks capacity and whether action is required to safeguard their welfare. There is also a duty to investigate complaints in relation to the use of existing orders.
- Supervising welfare attorneys and guardians. This is to ensure that they are carrying out the functions ascribed by the order and whether

there may be a need to vary the order due to changing circumstances. The supervisor should assess also whether they are working within the principles of the Act. There is a process to remove an attorney or guardian if they are not fulfilling their role in the best interests of the person.

- Providing a report to the Sheriff relevant to applications for welfare intervention or guardianship orders. This report comments on the appropriateness of the order sought and the suitability of the nominated person to carry out the proposed actions.

Summary

At the time of writing the role of the MHO is undergoing another intense period of change and enlargement. It is possible to argue that many of the proposed mental health statutory changes have confirmed what has been good practice in the 'spirit of the Act', for example MHO involvement in the review of all long-term orders. The future involvement of an MHO will be more significant given increased rights for the person, the establishment of mental health tribunals and the emphasis upon individual care planning. This will provide a stronger platform for MHOs to be involved in a more meaningful way. MHOs should become more confident in using their independent voice within the psychiatric services to the benefit of the people who are or may be subject to compulsory measures of care.

References

Bean, A., McGuckin, A. and Macpherson, S. (2001) *An Evaluation of Section 18 of the Mental Health (Scotland) Act 1984*, Edinburgh, Scottish Executive Central Research Unit.

Humphreys, M. (1994) 'Junior psychiatrists and emergency compulsory detention in Scotland', *International Journal of Law and Psychiatry*, vol. 17, no. 4, pp. 421–9.

Mental Welfare Commission (2002) Annual Report 2001–2002 Edinburgh, Mental Welfare Commission.

Morgan, J.F., Schlich, T. and Flakowski, W. (1999) 'Application of the powers of compulsory admission to psychiatric hospital by general practitioners, approved social workers and psychiatrists', *Medicine, Science and the Law*, vol. 39, no. 4, pp. 325–31.

Scottish Executive (2001) *Adults with Incapacity (Scotland) Act 2000: Code of Practice for Local Authorities Exercising Functions under the Act,* Edinburgh, The Stationery Office.

Ulas, M. (1999) 'Research issues in mental health social work: the problem of continuity of care and a consistent role', in M. Ulas and A. Connor (eds) *Mental Health and Social Work,* Research Highlights in Social Work No. 28, London, Jessica Kingsley.

20

The Role of the Reporter to the Children's Panel

JACKIE ROBESON

Origins of the Reporter

The office of Reporter was first conceived in the Kilbrandon Report[1] and created with the introduction of the children's hearings system in Part II of the Social Work (Scotland) Act 1968. The functions and responsibilities of the Reporter are now to be found in the Children (Scotland) Act 1995 and related legislation.

Context of the Reporter within the children's hearings system

The Reporter was envisaged as an independent officer with a key role in the administration of the system and in determining which children required to enter into the system. The Reporter was to be pivotal in ensuring that the other key principles of the system – the welfare basis, universality of access, separation of function (between resolution of disputed facts and disposal) and the involvement of lay members of the community in disposal – were real and effective.

Structure and organisation

The Scottish Children's Reporter Administration (SCRA) exists as a non-departmental public body, overseen by a board whose chief officer is an official known as the Principal Reporter. Day-to-day functions are delegated to Reporters[2] in terms of the organisation's Scheme of

Delegation. Reporters are located within areas that accord with current local authority boundaries. The number of Reporters in each area relates to the size of the authority area. An Authority Reporter heads each Reporter area. Each Reporter has responsibility for a defined geographical area within each authority so that every child has an identifiable Reporter for his or her home address. The SCRA has chosen this structure to allow Reporters to have local knowledge of a child's environment and services available and so that Reporters can contribute to local developments, for example Children's Services Plans,[3] to improve services for children.

Key functions of the Reporter

The Reporter's functions can be roughly grouped into five roles.

Receiver of referrals

The legislation makes both general and particular provision for bringing children to the attention of the Reporter. Any person can refer, if he or she believes that a child may be in need of compulsory measures of supervision. The local authority and police have a statutory responsibility to refer a child where a child may be in need of compulsory measures. The police have additional responsibilities to refer children who may have committed offences. Statutory emergency action such as the granting of a child protection order must prompt referral to the Reporter.

Any child can be referred to the Reporter: the term 'child' covering a child or young person from birth to 16; over 16 if still of school age; or up to 18 if still subject to a supervision requirement.

The majority of referrals come from the police and social work services. Incidents and concerns about children are referred. A significant amount of referrals come from health and education and other caring agencies working with children.

There is no standard referral form. Most referrals are sent or confirmed in writing. The Reporter has a duty to record referrals and to inform the referrer of the outcome of referrals. Referrals are recorded in the Reporter's administration database (RAD) and statistical information about referral rates and trends are published annually in SCRA's Annual Report.

Investigator

When a Reporter receives information from any source as described, they are required to investigate the child's situation. The legislation is no more descriptive than that the Reporter must make 'such initial investigation as he thinks necessary'. The Reporter will investigate to the level necessary to decide whether the particular child needs compulsory measures of supervision.

The Reporter's powers of investigation are wide. The Reporter will usually obtain written reports from agencies already involved with a child or make contact with agencies or professionals to get information, for example an assessment of health or risk. The request for reports and format of reports are not strictly prescribed but are agreed with the main agency providers. Information or reports provided for investigation purposes only will be kept confidential.

National standards for timescales for the provision of reports from key agencies exist and annual reporting on performance against standards applies.[4]

Decision-maker

The decision to be made by the Reporter is whether grounds for referral exist and are sustainable in law (that is, there is a *prima facie* case in law) and there is a need for compulsory intervention. If the Reporter decides that intervention is required and can be provided to the child without the need for compulsion then the reporter can arrange for the child and family to receive assistance from the local authority on a voluntary basis. The Reporter may decide that the criteria for compulsory measures are not met or that there is no need for any further action or involvement on the part of the Reporter. The child and family are usually told of the referral and the decision and whilst the Reporter would normally write to the child and family, they may relay the decision through personal contact.

The Reporter's decision is completely independent and there is no appeal against the decision made. Ultimately, if the Reporter's decision is to refer the child to a children's hearing, it is the children's hearing that decides whether or not compulsory measures are required.

Information about a child lies within the Reporter's files and database and remains confidential. Once a decision about a referral has been made, the referral can not be raised again unless further or new information is available.

If the Reporter's decision is to refer the child to a hearing they are responsible for drawing up 'grounds for referral' which are a formal statement of the concerns that have prompted the hearing.[5]

Administrator

When a children's hearing is required to consider the need for compulsory measures of supervision for a child it is the Reporter who is responsible for making arrangements. They provide the premises for the hearing, set the date and time, invite all persons who are entitled to be there, provide the necessary papers, attend the hearing and keeps a record of the proceedings.

The Reporter plays no role in the decision-making at the hearing, however, and although available to clarify procedure in a general sense, can take no part that is or could be perceived to influence the outcome of the hearing.

Following the hearing, the Reporter is responsible for the administrative process so that the correct action is taken, for example referring the matter to court for proof or notifying persons that a supervision requirement has been made. The Reporter will schedule any further hearings to be arranged for a child. They have the responsibility to ensure that any hearing required because of a request for a review (necessary within a year from last review) or emergency action occurs with proper notice and notification.

Legal agent

Where the grounds for referral (the formal statement of concerns) are not accepted, either because these are denied or because the child is unable to understand them, the hearing must decide whether to refer matters to the court for proof or to discharge the referral. It is the Reporter who will act as legal agent if the case is referred to court.

Where a disposal of a hearing is challenged by appeal to the Sheriff Court, the Reporter will act as legal agent in that legal forum. Other court processes can also necessitate the Reporter's involvement, for example an application to recall or vary a child protection order or application for an exclusion order or child assessment order.

The Reporter is responsible for all necessary paperwork for court, for preparation for the court, including preparation of witnesses, and for the conduct of the case at court, including examination and cross-examination of witnesses. Reporters are not required to have a legal qualification to appear in court, although many do. Internal and external training for court is provided for Reporters when they become Reporters and during their service as Reporters.

At court, proceedings are in private. Wigs and gowns are not worn. The proceedings are highly specialised and there is a large amount of important case law relating to these proceedings that Reporters have been instrumental in developing.

The court process has become more complex and it is not uncommon for court cases to take place over several weeks with multiple senior legal representation for families. Where appeals occur to the Sheriff Principal or Court of Session, advocates would normally represent the SCRA in the presentation of cases at that level.

General

A Reporter would typically be involved on a daily basis with a variety of the above functions. Most Reporters would be involved in one or two hearing sessions a week (a hearing session would on average contain three cases lasting approximately 45 minutes per case). Involvement in court cases can range from one a fortnight to three or four a week. Investigation and decision-making account for the majority of reporter time. Reporters are regularly involved in their local communities, attending local meeting and liaising with agencies in the development of services for children.

Notes

1. *Report of the Committee on Children and Young Persons, Scotland* (1964), Cmnd 2306, Edinburgh, HMSO.
2. Local Government etc. (Scotland) Act 1994, s.128(5).
3 Children (Scotland) Act 1995, s.19.
4. Blueprint for the Processing of Children's Hearing Cases, Inter-agency Code of Practice and National Standards, 2nd edn 2001, The Scottish Executive.
5. Reporter decision-making has been the subject of research (Hallett, C. and Murray, C. with Jamieson, J. and Veitch, B. [1998] *The Evaluation of Children's Hearings in Scotland*, 4 vols., 1998–2000, Edinburgh, Scottish Central Research Unit).

21

Independent Advocacy: A Practice Perspective

ANGELA FORBES

Although independent advocacy has been around for quite some time now, it is only since the early 1990s that the movement has blossomed in Britain. Its support by government is principally due to the emergence of two different, and not necessarily complementary, philosophies that underpin the promotion of greater user involvement in and control of services. The first is the consumerist approach that influenced much of the community care reforms of the 1990s. The second focuses on the empowerment of individuals and extending democratic principles to the provision of services to bring about social change. However, it is not within the scope of this chapter to explore the social or policy context of the growth of independent advocacy.[1] Rather, we will focus on how independent advocacy works in practice. The independent advocacy service I work for, Advocacy Service Aberdeen (ASA), has been around since early 1996 and provides independent advocacy to users of health and social care services. What follows is a personal perspective of independent advocacy: how it works at ASA and why I believe it is important for social justice, equality of opportunity and 'empowerment'.

What is independent advocacy?

Most professionals in the 'caring' field would consider themselves to be, at appropriate times, advocates for their clients, users or patients. Indeed, independent advocates recognise this and do not wish to interfere with that important part of the professionals' role. However, professionals who provide any other type of service cannot provide

226

independent advocacy. This is because of three central tenets of independent advocacy: independence; absence of conflicts of interest; and advocates not having 'professional' views. These three are inextricably connected and recognised as fundamental by everyone involved in independent advocacy. The Scottish Executive's guidance to commissioners of services explains the reasoning behind this succinctly:

> advocates have to be structurally and psychologically independent of the service system. Independent advocates – whether paid or unpaid – can be entirely clear that their primary loyalty and accountability is to the people who need advocates, not to the agencies providing health and social services, and not to the government. (Scottish Executive, 2000, p. 10)

They go on to outline the problems for independent advocacy with conflicts of interest and 'professional views'. Professional workers have to make judgements about who should receive services based on the resources available, eligibility and their own professional view about what is best for the person. Consequently, there are times when there are personal and professional risks to being entirely on the side of the service user. A professional may not agree with the service user's view about what is best; or be constrained by what they know about the availability of resources or what their managers are saying:

> Because advocates do not have this sort of power over people and do not control access to resources they are in a better position to see things from the person's point of view rather than the system's point of view. (Scottish Executive, 2000, p. 10)

From the above it can be seen that an independent advocate approaches work in a different way from other caring professionals. Because advocates do not have a view about what is 'best' for someone, nor do they have a vested interest in any particular service, they do not give advice or therapy and do not mediate. An independent advocate provides people with information about their rights, services and the options that are available. Most importantly, they *listen* to what the person is saying, empathise with the person (try to understand their situation from their point of view) and they support the person to make an informed choice and to argue for it – including supporting them to argue for something the advocate may not agree with. They do this by supporting them to express themselves or by speaking on their behalf at their request. They do not try to influence the person if presented with arguments from more powerful people: they are on their client's side and their client is always in control of the relationship.

There are of course some people who, for a variety of possible reasons, find it difficult to communicate verbally or express their wishes to others. Independent advocates can work with people whose views are difficult to ascertain, but the work they do is subtly different. It would be impossible to demonstrate convincingly that a person with limited communication skills is 'in control' of the advocacy relationship, or, indeed, that the advocate is clearly expressing their view. The advocate would not attempt to do this. In this relationship, the advocate would get to know the person by spending time with them, speaking to all the important people in the person's life and trying to put themselves into the person's situation. In these circumstances, the advocate's input would be to ensure that decisions were being based on the likes and dislikes of the person and what was objectively in their 'best' interests, rather than on what resources were available or what was convenient for staff.

Who needs it?

Although there are times in everyone's life when they could do with the type of support given by an independent advocate, there are some people who, because of their life experience, vulnerability or society's prejudices, use 'support services' frequently (sometimes continuously) and, as such, may particularly benefit from independent advocacy. As the Scottish Executive's guidance notes, 'Individuals who rely on ... service systems often have limited personal power and resources to argue their case' (Scottish Executive, 2000, p. 8). Because some people's power has been eroded, access to independent advocacy is important in order to redress the power imbalance and give vulnerable people a voice. Recognition of this is reflected in how independent advocacy has developed (most projects being specifically for vulnerable people – in particular, people with learning disabilities or mental health problems) which in turn reflects current national priorities for who should access independent advocacy. I am hopeful that, because of growing appreciation of the efficacy of independent advocacy, greater funding will be forthcoming to support other vulnerable groups.

Advocacy Service Aberdeen (ASA)

ASA is an independent advocacy service based in the City of Aberdeen. At the time of writing we have nine paid staff members and 18 volunteers. We provide 'crisis advocacy' (that is, we work on a one-to-one basis with people to address specific issues – which can involve short- or long-term relationships) and support self-advocacy groups. We do not provide citizen advocacy which normally involves unpaid advocates having a long-term relationship with one person with the aim of helping the person to feel more included in the community and encouraging the community to be more supportive and inclusive. Staff and volunteers have varied backgrounds but all must undergo our advocacy skills training, be committed to working to our principles and share the belief that independent advocacy can change lives. Although ideally, and in theory, we work with anyone who uses health and social care services, in practice most of our work is with people diagnosed with mental health problems or people with a learning disability. This reflects the fact that we have a number of projects dedicated to specific groups. We are actively seeking to ensure that our service develops so that other groups have equal access to it.

Most of the people who use our service either feel overwhelmed by the position they are in, that they are not being listened to, that they do not understand their rights and options, that they are being prevented from doing what they wish, or that they have been treated unfairly, negligently and, on occasion, abusively. Unfortunately, some people describe feeling all these things. Some, although by no means all, of the people who use our service are socially isolated and report that days go by when the only person they speak to is their advocate.

As explained above, it is our job to help people express what they are feeling and what they want and to ensure that they understand their options and rights. Of course, having an advocate does not mean that a person will get what they want – people do not always get what they want. What it does ensure is that people are given the opportunity to express themselves, are listened to and are given answers to their questions and explanations for actions and opinions – many people report that this is enough to make them feel more 'in control' and powerful. We recently conducted a survey of our service users' views about what they thought of our service. The results were extremely positive and some of the answers express far more eloquently than I can why independent advocacy is important:

I can honestly say had it not been for my advocate I would not be here today. She has been there for me for a long time now, and thanks to her I can cope and speak up for myself. Feeling her presence is a great comfort, and she instils me with great confidence, something I never had until she came into my life.

Advocacy helped, as I'm not very good at talking to professionals (especially social work) – they often take me up wrong. They seem to take much more notice when my advocate is with me – even though we're saying the same thing – they don't fob her off.

My advocate doesn't give me advice – she lets me speak the way I want to and doesn't interrupt. I feel I can say things better 'cos she's there.

It is the hope of ASA that the work we do with people will 'empower' them: that in time we will be redundant and the people we work with will be effective self-advocates. There are of course some people we support who, because of their disability, will always need an advocate; but many of our service users can be supported to develop the skills and confidence to assert themselves without our help. For some, this may take a long time, but one of the most highly valued (by our service users) features of independent advocacy is the commitment to 'be there' for as long as it takes.

Social care/health staff and independent advocates

Caring professionals can feel threatened by advocates. They can feel they are being personally criticised or that the fact an advocate is involved reflects badly on their practice or their relationship with the service user. This is rarely the case: people need advocates because of 'the system' and its inequalities and because of their own personal history. Advocacy is not about criticising individuals. Professionals who understand and accept the need for independent advocacy are demonstrating to the people who use their services that their views are important and that it is acceptable to comment on or even criticise services and ask for change. While there are times when there will be tensions between independent advocates and other professionals (this is to be expected and not feared), independent advocacy can only make a difference to people's lives if advocates and the staff who support people respect and understand one another.

Note

1. For further reading on independent advocacy, please refer to the following: Atkinson, D. (1999) *Advocacy: A Review*, Brighton Pavilion; Bateman, N. (2000) *Advocacy Skills for Health and Social Care Professionals*, London, Jessica Kingsley; Gray, B. and Jackson, R. (2002) *Advocacy & Learning Disability*, London, Jessica Kingsley; Mind (1994) *The Mind Guide to Advocacy in Mental Health*, London, MIND; Sang, B. and O'Brien, J. (1984) *Advocacy: The UK and American Experiences*, London, King's Fund; Simons, K. (1994) *Citizen Advocacy: The Inside View*, Bristol, Norah Fry Inst.

Reference

Scottish Executive (2000) *Independent Advocacy: A Guide for Commissioners*, Edinburgh, Scottish Executive.

22

The Work of the Scottish Child Law Centre

KATY MACFARLANE

Brief history

In the early 1980s, experts from the fields of law and social work formulated a proposal to create an independent, accessible source of information on child law in Scotland. The Social Work Services Group commissioned a study to look into the creation of a Scottish Child Law Centre. The study concluded that 'the lack of an expert information and advice service in Scotland presents difficulties and frustrations to professionals dealing with young people and the law'. As a result, the Scottish Child Law Centre came to life in June 1988.

Throughout the early part of the 1990s, the centre increased its work in promoting knowledge of law relating to the rights of children and young people in Scotland. The centre was instrumental in monitoring the implementation of the United Nations Convention on the Rights of the Child. At the same time, the number of advice calls increased to such an extent that a dedicated telephone advice line was set up. The centre was also actively involved in the consultation process that led to the introduction of the Children (Scotland) Act 1995 and set up an extensive training programme subsequent to its implementation.

Over the years, the role of the Centre has settled into five main areas: advice, information, education, representation and consultation.

1. The advice line deals with a wide variety of legal queries from all over Scotland. Calls come from children, parents, social workers, children's rights officers, solicitors – even a Sheriff or two!

2. Information is in the form of leaflets, briefings on new law and publications. Data gathered from the telephone advice line about subject matter and geographical areas of calls can then be collated to help identify areas of unmet need. Information leaflets are then specifically targeted to meet those needs.
3. Demands for education and training are increasing. The majority of training courses being delivered is to adults working with and caring for children and young people, but a significant amount is being requested by young people's groups themselves.
4. The Centre currently represents children through the children's hearings system.[1] Since March 2002, children have had the right to legal representation at a hearing.[2] This brings the children's hearings system in line with Article 6 of the European Convention on Human Rights, now enshrined in the Human Rights Act 1998.[3]
5. Staff at the Centre are regularly asked by the Scottish Executive to consult and comment on proposals for new legislation affecting children. This ranges from initiatives in delivering healthy school meals to the law relating to smacking. One of the most important and exciting consultations concerned proposals to introduce a Children's Commissioner to Scotland – a proposal very much welcomed by the Centre. Discussions were conducted at every level with the views of children and young people being of paramount importance to the ultimate decision. The consultation has resulted in a decision to set up the office of Children's Commissioner. It is proposed that the Bill will be published in December 2002 with the Act being brought into force in November or December 2003. Consultation with both the Scottish Executive and other agencies ensures that children's views can be voiced and their opinions included in the discussion process. This must lead to a more equal, child-centred society.

Never had it so good!

For the first time in history, children in Scotland have more rights than they have ever had – the right to have a voice in proceedings affecting them, the right to an education, the right to consent to medical treatment where they have capacity. However, it has become increasingly apparent through the work of the Centre that there has been little corresponding increase in knowledge about rights. Some, but by no means all, adults who work with and care for children receive in-service training.

Promoting knowledge of children's rights and giving children and young people the confidence to use their rights is essential to a child-centred society.

So how can children's knowledge of their legal rights be improved? During 2002, the Centre has devised a 'Children's Rights Roadshow' – a 90-minute lesson that teaches pupils about their legal rights and responsibilities within society. This fits into the personal and social education (PSE) curriculum currently taught in Scottish schools and complements the teaching of 'citizenship' within the subject. The majority of the 32 local authorities in Scotland have welcomed the venture. However, a few have expressed reservations about the implications of children knowing their rights! The 'Roadshow' is aimed at children of around 12 years of age – the age at which most legal rights take effect. Pupils are taken through a scenario involving a 13-year-old boy who, amongst other things, works as a paperboy, gets in trouble with the police, wants advice from the doctor and talks to his school guidance teacher in confidence. Feedback from schools has been positive at all levels and has led to education departments requesting training sessions for groups of probationer teachers as well as guidance teachers and others involved in the PSE course. Keen to build on this success and certain of the fact that a knowledge of children's legal rights should be part of the core curriculum in teacher training, the Centre is currently forging links with colleges so that presentations can be made to trainee teachers. The result will be that new teachers enter the profession with at least a basic knowledge and respect for children's rights.

So, what's new?

The two fastest growing areas of concern for the Centre are (1) children and confidentiality and (2) education, especially special educational needs. Why?

First, with more and more coverage of child protection issues in the press and on television, local authorities and agencies working with children and young people are under pressure to update or, in some cases, create child protection policies and to issue good-practice guidelines to those working directly with children. This is laudable, but, in the opinion of the Centre, these policies must include references to the right of a child or young person to confidentiality. From the number and nature of calls that the Centre receives on worries by children of alleged breaches of confidentiality by adults, it would seem that the right to confidentiality of children and young people is being bypassed by the adults who are there to protect them. Recognition has to be given to the possibility that, in some cases, a child or young person can be exposed to more severe danger, even suicide, where information is divulged against their wishes. It has to be said that the Centre vehemently supports the right of children and young people to be protected by those who look after, care for and work with them, but it also is very much in favour of children and young people being involved in the process of protection. They have a right to be involved in the decision to pass their case on to a counsellor or adviser and to expect that disclosure is on a strict 'need to know' basis. Of course, there will be extreme situations where this is not possible and emergency help and protection must be sought urgently whether or not the child or young person agrees. The Centre supports this without question. Further, the current level of inconsistency amongst the different child protection and confidentiality policies requires to be addressed. At present, there is no predictability and no expectation of consistency amongst policies and this only serves to increase the confusion for children and young people. The Scottish Child Law Centre is currently working with several local authorities to address these problems.

Second, more and more parents are contacting the Centre because they feel that their children's needs are not being met within the current education system in Scotland.[4] The reasons for this are obvious: (a) children have increased rights in education and (b) parents and children are becoming more aware of these rights. Since the implementation of the Standards in Scotland's Schools etc. Act 2000, children of school age have, for the first time ever, a legal right to an education,[5] the local authority has a duty to secure that 'the education is directed to the development of the personality, talents and mental and physical abilities of the child or young person to their fullest potential',[6] and local authorities have a duty to take account of the views of the child or young person in significant decisions affecting them.[7] These new rights, combined with the growing knowledge and, especially, the growing expectations of parents, have resulted in challenges to the system at all levels. Since the 2000 Act came into force, there has been an unprecedented increase in the number of calls from parents who feel that their child is not getting the type and quality of education that the Act promises.

Conclusion

The Scottish Child Law Centre is unique because it is the only service in Scotland dealing specifically with the provision of legal advice for children and young people and those working with and caring for them.

Children and young people are keen to have their voices heard and their views and opinions are important and valid. If we, as a society, want to do the best for our children, then we must learn to listen to what they have to say.

Notes

1.   This was set up as a result of the Kilbrandon Committee Report in 1968.
2.   Children's Hearings (Legal Representation) (Scotland) Rules 2002.
3.   The right to a fair trial. See Schedule 1 to the Human Rights Act 1998. See also *S* v. *Miller* 2001 SLT 1304.
4.   13 per cent of all calls relate to education issues.
5.   Section 1, Standards in Scotland's Schools etc. Act 2000.
6.   Section 2(1), Standards in Scotland's Schools etc. Act 2000.
7.   Section 2(2), Standards in Scotland's Schools etc. Act 2000.

23

The Sheriffs and the Sheriff Court: The Judicial Function

BRIAN KEARNEY

The Sheriff

A Scottish Sheriff does not, like an American sheriff, carry a gun, nor, like an English High Sheriff, wait, in lace-bedecked robes, on the High Court judges on circuit. A Scottish Sheriff is the judge of the local court with authority to deal with almost all forms of civil dispute and all but the most serious criminal cases. There are now some 137 full-time Sheriffs in Scotland. All are qualified lawyers who have spent at least ten years in practice, and generally much longer. They come from varying social and educational backgrounds, some from professional families, others the sons and daughters of factory workers, clerks and typists. You may still see a Sheriff or two on the golf course or even at Lords, but you are at least as likely to meet one amongst the crowd at Celtic Park or Ibrox or, male as well as female, at the supermarket check-out. Sheriffs hold a commission signed by the Queen. Of course the Queen only acts on the advice given to her. Until recently that advice was in effect given by the Lord Advocate. In 2002 a Judicial Appointments Board was set up and it advises the Scottish Ministers who in turn advise the Queen.

Judicial independence

On taking up his or her appointment a Sheriff, like any other judge, makes an oath or affirmation to do justice to all 'without fear or favour,

affection or ill will'. The purpose in setting up the Judicial
Appointments Board was to try to make it transparent that judges were
independent in the sense of not being appointed as a political or other
favour and therefore perhaps tempted in making a judicial decision to
repay that favour rather than conform to the judicial oath. Some have
doubted whether this would often be a real temptation. In Western
democracies it is generally difficult to remove a judge and this security
of tenure is a marvellous recipe for independence of judgement. In the
United States, where the appointments to the Supreme Court are, within
certain conventional restraints, overtly political, loyalty to the appointing President cannot be relied on. In 1956 President Eisenhower
appointed William J. Brennan to the Supreme Court as a safe, conserv-
ative, pair of hands. Thereafter Justice Brennan handed down a series of
liberalising opinions which shook and shocked the right. Eisenhower is
reported as saying that 'appointing Bill Brennan was one of the two
dumbest things I ever did'.

Judges and Sheriffs cherish their independence not because it enables
them to 'get their own way' without fear of unpleasant consequences but
because independence of judgement in the sense of impartiality is at the
heart of the judicial function. There would be little point 'going to law'
if you were not confident that the judge would listen to the evidence,
listen to what you or your representative had to say, and then decide the
case in accordance with law on the basis of a fair view of the evidence.
So precious is the independence of the judiciary that the mere appearance of the possibility of bias can imperil a decision even at the highest
judicial level. In 1999 the highest appeal court in the United Kingdom,
the House of Lords, found itself in this position when it was realised that
one of the Lords of Appeal in Ordinary (as the 'Law Lords' are formally
called) who had sat in relation to the case involving General Pinochet
had an indirect connection with one of the parties to that case and it was
thought necessary to rehear the case before other Law Lords.

Hearing both sides

It is an elementary aspect of impartiality that the judge or Sheriff should
give each side the chance to say their piece. The Human Rights Act of
1998 incorporated the European Convention on Human Rights into our
law. Article 6 of the Convention includes the provision that 'everyone
is entitled to a fair and public hearing within a reasonable time by an

independent and impartial tribunal established by law' and these words are often quoted and the impression given that they are saying something new. This is true only in the limited sense that they give statutory force to an ancient principle which, when lawyers scattered Latin tags (which they are now discouraged from doing), was embodied in the words *'audi alteram partem'* ('hear the other party'). I ultimately have the responsibility of deciding the case and if there is something which concerns me that has not been addressed in argument or evidence then I will try to raise it with the parties in such a way as to indicate what my concern is without giving the appearance of having already made up my mind. Sometimes this needs a bit of care, since the normal idioms of speech are sometimes cast in an emphatic mode. One often asks a question introduced by words such as 'Surely you can't mean that . . .?' That is all right for day-to-day conversation, but coming from a judge on the bench these words may give the impression that his or her mind has been almost made up.

Our adversarial system – expert and other evidence

Intervening from the bench when evidence is being given has to be done with special care because our system of letting each side say their piece involves giving each side the opportunity to develop the case in the way they choose. The judge is rather like the umpire in a cricket match – seeing that the rules are kept, responding to any cry of 'How's that?' and ruling on disputed issues, but not playing an active role in the game. It can sometimes be a little frustrating, particularly when one side is represented by a highly experienced and skilled pleader and the other side by a mediocre one. The rule is that we should only interrupt in order to clarify an answer. Of course such a rule is capable of being interpreted narrowly or broadly and some judges take a more interventionist role than others, but we all acknowledge that there are limits and that it would be wrong for us to 'take over' the questioning from one side.

Having mentioned the limited function of the judge during the conduct of the case it is right to emphasise the paramount position of the judge when sitting alone in a civil case or a summary (that is, a non-jury) criminal case. The judge is the person who decides what the evidence is worth, what conclusions of fact are to be drawn and what are the legal consequences for the parties. The position of the 'expert witness' illustrates this. Generally witnesses are only allowed to give evidence about what they saw and heard and not give opinions. Expert witnesses, that is, those qualified by special academic qualifications and/or experience in a special subject such as engineering or some branch of medicine, are allowed to give their opinion as to what factual conclusion may properly be drawn from certain facts. The expert, however, should only be asked for their opinion, not what they think the result of the case should be. Nor is the court bound to accept the opinion of the expert. There was a famous case in 1948 wherein one side led three experts and the other side led a number of informed but not 'expert' witnesses and the court decided for various reasons that the experts were not acceptable and that, using its common sense, it should decide the case against the opinion of the experts.

The primacy of the Sheriff on the matter of assessing the value of evidence was strongly asserted in *F* v. *Kennedy (No. 2)* 1993 SLT 1284 which was a case wherein evidence of statements by children was adduced and it appeared that the *Cleveland* guidelines had not been observed by those interviewing the children. Lord Justice-Clerk Ross observed: 'but the mere fact that the guidelines had not been followed did not mean that the Sheriff was not entitled to accept the evidence of the children as reliable'.

Fact and opinion

Professional witnesses, including social workers, will frequently find themselves called either as witnesses to fact, or witnesses to opinion, or both. When preparing to give evidence as to fact it is important to have 'worked up' the case in advance by refamiliarising oneself with the files. The solicitor, reporter or procurator fiscal preparing the case should go through a similar process. In an ideal world there should, at a reasonable time before the proof or trial, be a meeting between the legal professional and the social worker witness at which the key issues will be identified and any documents required traced and handed over for lodging in court. This is particularly important in criminal jury trial procedure where there are strict rules about the lodgement in advance of documents which are to be relied upon. Of course we do not live in an ideal world and sometimes, particularly in civil cases and referrals under the children's hearings system, such a meeting is rushed or even non-existent. In that event the social worker witness can only do their best and become thoroughly familiar with the file and bring it to court. If at all possible the *original* file and reports should be brought to court and not, for example, an abstract thereof which has been specially prepared for the purpose of giving evidence.

Social workers are professionals who are entitled to give evidence on such fields of expertise as may be within their competence. For example, in addition to more routine social work matters, a social worker may have a specialised qualification in the identification of child physical and/or sexual abuse. If the social worker expects to be asked to give opinion evidence then it is essential that they be ready to lay before the court the details both of their general qualifications and in relation to any specialised certificates, diplomas *or experience in the field* (for the courts recognise that there is more to being an 'expert' than having letters after your name!) which the witness may possess. It is no bad idea for the social worker witness to have prepared a written 'CV' setting out formal qualifications, experience in practice, and, if applicable, the approximate number of times they have given evidence in relation to cases of the type involved: this CV can be given to the legal professional before the proof or trial so that they can 'take it from' the witness at the outset of their evidence so as to establish the relevant degree of expertise.

It is of course open to the social worker 'expert' as to any other expert witness to rely on published research.[1] In this event it is essential for the witness to be ready to produce the work of research for the judge to see. Once again this should ideally in all cases, and this is a near essential in jury cases, be prepared for along with the legal professional well before the proof or trial.

The social worker 'expert' may be called along with one or more experts and indeed sometimes a joint report may have been prepared. There is no harm in having discussed a case with another expert but care must be taken when giving evidence to make clear where any factual basis for opinion evidence has come from, that is, does it derive from one's own observations, from the 'brief' from the legal professional, or from information supplied by the other expert.

Some practical hints

When in the witness box there are some practical points which should be kept in mind.

- Listen to the question and answer it fully and fairly but not elaborately.
- Listen to the question that is being asked and answer that question – not the question you would like to have been asked.
- Do not become argumentative.
- Remember that although called by one party you are ultimately there to assist the court. Your standing with the court will rise, not fall, in so far as you are, and are seen to be, objective.
- Stick to your last. Do not be tempted to comment on matters on which you are not expert. Do not be afraid to say 'I do not think I am qualified to comment on that'.
- Be particularly careful of innocent-sounding questions about the facts of the case. You will have been 'briefed' as to the supposed factual background and your opinion will of necessity have been based on that briefing. You may be asked what that briefing was and, if so, you must obviously answer frankly. You should make clear that your knowledge of the facts of the case is limited by the information you have been given and not be tempted to guess on a matter which you have not been briefed upon.
- Do not get flustered. Keep 'cool' as they say – or, as we say in my part of the West of Scotland: 'Keep the heid!'

Where witnesses follow this advice, they should find the task of giving evidence less of an ordeal and they will certainly help the judge!

Formality and informality

Judges are also sometimes criticised for being excessively formal and even ridiculed for wearing wigs and gowns. Opinions differ as to whether we should continue to wear the wig in particular. This is not the place to examine the detail of these arguments, but I would simply say that a degree of formality has its place. Judges have to take some far-reaching decisions, some of which, at least for some parties, have very unpleasant consequences.

I go back to where I started. Our essential feature is our independence. We are appointed by the Queen, nowadays on the advice of a board set up by the government, but we do not take orders from any of these. The formalities of the court, such as standing when the judge comes in and rises and the wearing of gown and wig by the judge and gown by solicitors (wig and gown by advocates) are symbols of this special position and I think they have some value. Informality has its place also; and when it seems appropriate we can relax formality. Particularly nowadays, I think many of us make every effort both to inform ourselves on the needs of vulnerable witnesses and to adapt our court manner to allow for these needs. Our Scottish Judicial Studies Committee, of which I have the honour to be a member, tries to keep us up to date not only with changes in the law, but also on the latest thinking on such matters as how best to deal with cases involving vulnerable witnesses such as children and the special considerations which apply in cases involving ethnic minorities. I find that it is as well to start from the formal position and, when appropriate, relax. I do not think many people would appreciate it if the judge came in, parked his jacket over the back of the chair, introduced himself by his first name and then proceeded to try, say, a case of alleged child abuse which might ultimately result in the imprisonment and/or the deprivation of parental rights of the accused.

Conclusion

When I was asked to contribute this chapter it was suggested that it might take the form of 'A day in the life of a Sheriff' and it has contained much about judicial independence and deportment and some thoughts on the law and practice in relation to the giving of evidence. These, however, are significant issues which underlie our daily work and inform our decisions. I should add that we do not only work 'on the bench' but spend as much or more time writing judgments, reading up on the law and thinking about pending cases. While by no means unable to enjoy ourselves whether on the golf course or the football park, in the concert hall or at family picnics, we tend to maintain some of the reserve which seems inseparable from our professional responsibilities. Judging is not just a job, but also a way of life – and one which can bring unending interest and satisfaction.

Note

1. For example a witness may say 'This has been established by well-accepted research', and then cite the relevant reference(s).

24

ENABLE

ELIZABETH CRAIGMYLE

ENABLE Legal Services and ENABLE Trustee Services Ltd have existed since 1988. ENABLE is Scotland's largest national voluntary organisation for people with learning disabilities and their families and carers and it was formed in 1954 by parents of people with learning disabilities. ENABLE is a voluntary organisation, which is controlled and managed by people with learning disabilities, carers and volunteers from across Scotland. ENABLE has around 4,000 members in 68 local branches. There are local and national membership schemes and two-thirds of ENABLE's national members are people with learning disabilities. ENABLE carries out a similar function to Mencap in England and Wales. ENABLE has also formed a number of separate charitable companies to deal with various aspects of its work such as ENABLE Scotland Ltd, which provides a range of services for adults and children with learning disabilities, including supported employment, small care homes, supported living services, community day-care services, short breaks and out-of-school care for children, and Ace Advocacy, a new charitable company which deals with the support and management of advocacy schemes for people with learning disabilities. ENABLE also provides a Legal and Information Advice Service and campaigns on behalf of people with learning disabilities and their carers.

One of my visions for the future would be to try to encourage larger voluntary organisations to assume in-house legal assistance rather than utilise firms in private practice, in the hope that distinct specialities can grow and ultimately Scotland can offer a community legal service offering legal advice and assistance to the public over the full range of social welfare law. I carried out a considerable amount of work in this regard in the early part of 1999 which was started by my predecessor Colin McKay in partnership with the Scottish Association of Law Centres

(SALC), of which ENABLE is an associate member, and the Scottish Consumer Council, and a detailed research paper was produced in March 1999, 'The unmet legal needs of the disabled'. Since this time there have been further advances by SALC and others, and the Aslan Manifesto for a Community Legal Service was published in July 2000 (see SCOLAG Legal Journal, no. 277, November 2000), but it still appears that there is quite a long way to go until a community legal service is formed. If there is a formation of such a service there is no doubt that those involved will require to pull in expertise from social welfare lawyers throughout Scotland and such a service will require to be independent and unfettered, and rely on leading-edge IT technology to provide advice to those in the more rural areas of the country.

Access to legal advice within ENABLE is available in a variety of ways. Existing clients can contact me or my colleagues on a direct basis as can fellow professionals such as independent solicitors, doctors, social workers, advocates, and so on. New legal enquiries tend to come via the Legal and Information Inquiry Line which is open from 1.30 p.m. until 4.30 p.m. Monday to Thursday and from 1.30 p.m. until 3.55 p.m. on a Friday (tel. 0141 226 4541). Legal Services and the Information Service work very closely together, having weekly surgeries to discuss enquiries and issue responses. Legal advice is also available at any training event conducted by legal services and such events are frequent and can be carried out anywhere in the country. Requests for training are received from social work departments, the law society, carers' groups, the health service, speech therapists, other voluntary agencies, and so on. The subjects most commonly requested for training purposes are the Adults with Incapacity (Scotland) Act 2000, wills and trusts and disability discrimination. Training events often take the form of a general talk followed by individual surgeries for people. Legal advice is also provided to the various branches throughout Scotland. Various leaflet publications are available free of charge on most major legal topics; these are regularly updated and can be obtained by contacting the Information Service.

My job is very diverse. I have around 190 current private client cases. The range of advice sought by my clients is in many ways similar to any small private practice and in other ways it is much more specialised. For example, I have current cases involving tenancy and housing provision, sexual abuse, transitional housing benefits, charging for services, special educational needs, appointments under the Adults with Incapacity (Scotland) Act 2000, drafting wills and trusts, winding up executry estates and a fatal accident inquiry relating the sad circumstances of the death in hospital of a middle-aged man who had lifelong learning disabilities and mental health problems. The fatal accident inquiry is unlikely to finish until January 2003 at the earliest and it has been ongoing since July 2002. It is the second fatal accident inquiry in which I have represented the family of a deceased person with learning disabilities over the last eighteen months. In one way I feel that this is extraordinary but in another way I feel society is changing and with the advent of the Disability Discrimination Act 1995 and the Human Rights Act 1998 people are becoming much more aware of the law and of the services and provisions their learning-disabled relatives should receive and they are prepared to litigate to achieve their desired outcome. However, I have never come across a client of ENABLE Legal Services who is financially driven; normally the family is seeking the truth, an apology, if justified, and an undertaking to improve any system which has failed it or their relative. Unfortunately the courts have not been known to make high awards to families for the loss to society of someone with profound lifelong learning disability and/or mental health problems who had never worked and had no dependants.

Devolution has played a major role in my job as the new Scottish Parliament, as one of its first enactments, placed the Adults with Incapacity (Scotland) Act 2000 onto the statute book. This Act is the culmination of many years of lobbying by ENABLE and other organisations and individuals involved in incapacity and mental health law to achieve an integrated up-to-date Act dealing with the welfare and financial legal needs of adults with incapacity. ENABLE was a founding member of the Alliance for the promotion of the then Incapable Adults Bill. The Act is an empowering piece of legislation covering the whole range of incapacity and introducing welfare and financial attorneyship, a new form of guardianship, a new authority of doctors to treat, a new withdrawer's scheme for people wishing to apply to withdraw money from an incapable adult's bank account and a new office of the Public Guardian which monitors attorneys and guardians and provides safeguarding measures for adults with incapacity and provisions for managing residents' finances. The Act replaces very archaic disjointed laws and is being phased in commencing April 2001; only Part 4 remains outstanding, 'Managing residents' finances', which is due to begin in April 2003. The terms of the new Act have created a considerable amount of work for both my colleagues and me and have involved us in multidisciplinary training events throughout Scotland since March 2001.

The Act's gateway principles of benefit, minimum intervention, consideration of an adult's past and present wishes, communicating by any possible means and the encouragement and enhancement of skills go to the very core of ENABLE's ethos and aims. For the first time we have a statutory framework which recognises that incapacity is not an all-or-nothing concept and an obligation is placed upon those involved in the adult's life to ascertain the adult's capabilities as well as the areas of life the adult needs support and help with. The Act respects the adult as an individual and places an emphasis on capacity, rather than incapacity. It is individualist, specific and flexible in its terms and, once implemented, it aims to offer the adult the benefits of the type of support and protection aimed at the adult's personal needs. I anticipate that these training events will continue for some time to come as the Act affects all of us, not just people with learning disability and their families and carers, and it has raised the profile of incapacity as an issue.

ENABLE has also been involved in giving evidence to the Justice Committee relative to the Mental Health (Scotland) Bill. The Bill follows detailed consultation with ENABLE and others by the Millan Committee, which was in charge of the review. One of ENABLE's goals is for there to be a piece of legislation which deals solely with learning disability. ENABLE disagrees with the continuation of a combined approach of mental health and incapacity law. The legal areas are distinct. It is unlikely that this will happen in the new Mental Health Act review despite the fact that there are specific areas in the 1984 Mental Health (Scotland) Act which deal only with learning disability, in particular ss.106 and 107: these deal with matters relating to sexual relationships as far as women with learning disabilities are concerned. Both Sections 106 and 107 in terms of the current Bill have been amended to reflect both men and women and to introduce new statutory offences for sexual abuse, and ENABLE supports the terms of the new Bill. ENABLE does accept that there will always be cases of dual diagnosis where individuals with learning disabilities also have mental health problems but ENABLE welcomes the Adults with Incapacity Scotland Act 2000 as it goes a considerable way towards emphasising the distinct areas where an adult can become incapacitated through learning disability, dementia, mental health problems or head injuries.

Finally I wish to say a little about ENABLE's will-writing service and Trustee Service. Many years ago ENABLE realised the need for people with learning disabilities and their relatives and carers to have support in relation to their finances. Parents and carers worried about the fact their sons or daughters with learning disability would become adults and lose benefit entitlement if monies were left to them from any source as their own individual capital. ENABLE gives advice to the effect that if a will were drawn up in the correct way legally incorporating a discretionary trust provision then this would offer protection and peace of mind. The Trustee Service manages around 140 trusts and has 200 trusts registered in total. ENABLE offers support to independent solicitors and other organisations and agencies in relation to the drawing up of trust deeds. ENABLE also receives referrals from the Criminal Injuries Compensation Authority, social work departments and solicitors in private practice. ENABLE has leaflets available which emphasise the importance of making a will and also leaflets relative to the work of the Trustee Department. The leaflets are available free of charge by calling ENABLE's Information department on 0141 226 4541.

25

The Role of the Curator *ad litem* and Reporting Officer in Adoption Proceedings

JANICE WEST

Curators *ad litem* have a long history in civil law proceedings in Scotland, working across a range of situations where the interests of children require to be safeguarded. As Cleland (1996) has noted, 'the curator is not a representative for the child in any traditionally understood sense'. The appointment is made by the court in any situation where it is perceived that the interests of the child require to be protected. This could include issues of residence, education, financial management or any other matter being considered by the court. The powers of the curator *ad litem* are wide-ranging and he or she is an officer of the court. This chapter presents an account of the role and task of the curator *ad litem* in adoption proceedings within the Sheriff Court together with the associated role and responsibilities of the Reporting Officer. The legislative authority for each of these roles is located within the Adoption (Scotland) Act 1978 and the associated Act of Sederunt.[1] While some aspects of the responsibilities are prescriptive, there is also scope for some individual discretion and interpretation in the precise execution of the roles.

Who can be a curator *ad litem* or Reporting Officer?

Curators *ad litem* and Reporting Officers are appointed by and are responsible and accountable to the court, not the child or family. In the majority of adoption petitions, the geographical location of all parties enables both tasks to be undertaken by the same person. There are, however, circumstances where separate appointments are made. Appointment is made by an interlocutor from the relevant court and it is necessary to remind the prospective appointee that they cannot act in any proceedings where this may potentially lead to a conflict of interests. It would, for example, be incompatible with the independence of the role for a curator *ad litem* to be appointed if he or she was employed by the same local authority that is the placing adoption agency. Appointees are usually drawn from a Panel of Curators *ad litem* and Reporting Officers maintained by local authorities[2] and while there are no specific qualifications laid down by statute, most tend to have either a social work or legal background (Curran, 1988; McKellar and West, 1994).

Responsibilities of the curator *ad litem*

The full range of responsibilities placed upon the curator *ad litem* are contained within the Act of Sederunt previously mentioned but there are some which it may be of interest to explore here as they are at the very heart of the role:

Investigating the facts contained in the adoption petition and advising the court as to the accuracy of the information

In most situations, this will be a very straightforward matter with the curator *ad litem* confirming the accuracy of the information provided. Where a factual error exists (for example, a date or place wrongly recorded) this should be brought to the attention of the court. It is for the court to decide how best to proceed and it does not fall within the authority of the curator *ad litem* to conduct any fuller investigations.

Investigating the circumstances of the prospective adopters and providing an opinion to the court as to whether adoption is likely to safeguard and promote the welfare of the child throughout his life

The curator has a responsibility to provide the court with information which will allow a decision to be made which reflects the welfare of the child 'throughout his life' as specified by s.6 of the Adoption (Scotland) Act 1978. When considering the extent to which adoption is likely to 'safeguard and promote' the child's welfare, the curator will require to take account of a number of factors to arrive at an opinion which will assist the court in its decision-making. Although most petitioners now attend the court hearing, it is not always possible for the Sheriff to gain any real insight into the quality of the relationship which exists between the child and the prospective adopters.

This is an area which can be fruitfully explored by the curator through discussion with both the child and prospective parents. In proceedings, for example, where the petitioner is the new husband of the child's mother who is seeking to gain full parental rights and responsibilities, the primary motivation may be to exclude the birth father from the child's life on an ongoing basis. It may be that the child's mother feels that she needs to end all ties with her past life in order that she can concentrate on the future. This, however, is unlikely to be in the best interests of the child who, particularly as a young adult, may wish to maintain some degree of contact with the birth father. While this 'fresh start' approach is understandable in terms of the needs of the adults concerned, research would suggest that the identity needs of children are very different (Triseliotis *et al.*, 1997).

Ascertaining whether the child wishes to express any views as to the proposed adoption

Adoption legislation, like other legislation relating to children, places a significant emphasis on the inclusion of children and young people in decision-making processes where appropriate. This is clearly a skilled activity and one which is vital if the principle that the child's interests are paramount is to be upheld. Taking into consideration the wishes and feelings of the child does not mean responding positively to the child's wishes. Rather it requires that the curator *ad litem* listens to the child and presents his or her views within the report. Providing a safe environment in which a child can speak freely to a stranger is not easy and can be particularly difficult to achieve for those children involved in inter-family adoptions. Curators *ad litem* require to be skilled in the process of direct work with children and have a clear commitment to the rights of children to participate at an appropriate level in decisions which affect their lives. Given the importance of this task, it is perhaps surprising that no specific training is required to fulfil this role, a concern which echoes that of safeguarders in the children's hearings system (Hill *et al.*, 2002).

Ascertaining that the prospective adopters understand the nature and effect of the granting of an adoption order

One of the overarching principles of the Children (Scotland) Act 1995, often referred to as the 'no order principle', requires any decision-making body to be sure that whatever legal intervention is being considered will be of greater value to the child's welfare than taking no action. This requires the curator *ad litem* to explore with the prospective adoptive parent(s) that they have a clear understanding of the legal implications of adoption. In the case of a birth mother giving her agreement to her new husband becoming the full legal parent of her child, she may need to be encouraged to examine both the potential advantages and disadvantages of such a decision for her child. The mother also needs to carefully consider her own changing status – moving from being the sole legal parent to sharing that status with her husband.

Where the petition seeks to have parental agreement dispensed with, advising the court as to whether the case has been made for such a decision

While it is primarily the responsibility of the petitioners and their legal representatives to fully present the case for dispensation of parental agreement, the curator *ad litem* should provide the court with as much information on this matter as possible. Given the responsibility to ensure that options other than adoption have been considered, the curator *ad litem* should explore with the birth parent what alternative solutions they may wish to propose to the court. It has been my experience that birth parents may withhold agreement because they do not wish to be seen by the child as having actively engaged in the adoption process. They are not in a position to suggest an alternative outcome or may have a timescale for such an alternative plan which is unrealistic in terms of the needs of the child. The decision about what constitutes 'unreasonable' in this context is for the court to decide and has been well argued in existing case law.[3] The role of the curator *ad litem* is to provide the court with as much factual information as is available and to offer an opinion on the position being taken by the birth parent.

Responsibilities of the Reporting Officer

The primary responsibility of the Reporting Officer in adoption proceedings is the witnessing of agreements by relevant parties. Where a child is 12 years old or more, the consent of the child is required before an adoption order will be granted. It is part of the role of the Reporting Officer to ensure that such written consent has been freely given. The consent may have been witnessed by the solicitor acting for the petitioner(s) and it is important to ascertain that no undue pressure has been exerted or financial inducements offered to obtain this consent.

It is also part of the role to witness the agreement of the legal parent(s) to the granting of an adoption order. In so doing, the Reporting Officer must ensure that the person signing the form is fully aware of the nature of the decision they are making. This would include checking to ensure that he or she knows something about the prospective adopters, that alternatives to adoption have been explored and that any agreement is being given freely and unconditionally. In terms of this last point, it is important in more open placements that the birth parent is clear that they cannot bargain in terms of the agreement. Even if statements have been made by the adoption agency about ongoing 'postbox' contact, this cannot be considered as a condition of agreement.

While the curator *ad litem* and Reporting Officer are officers of the court, responsible to the court and not any of the other parties, the roles do require an understanding of the adoption process as a whole. It would therefore be unhelpful to assume either a totally legal or social work perspective. Fulfilling these duties on behalf of the court requires an awareness of the range of perspectives and sensitivities involved with the primary focus placed clearly on the welfare of the child as the paramount consideration.

Notes

1. For a detailed discussion, see P. McNeill (1998) *Adoption of Children in Scotland*, 2nd edn, Edinburgh, W. Green/Sweet & Maxwell.
2. Curators *ad litem* and Reporting Officers (Panels) (Scotland) Amendment Regulations 1985.
3. *L.* v. *Central Regional Council* 1990 SLT 818; *Lothian Regional Council* v. *A* 1992 SLT 858.

References

Cleland, A. (1996) 'The child's right to be heard and represented in legal proceedings', in A. Cleland and E. Sutherland (eds) *Children's Rights in Scotland*, Edinburgh, W. Green/Sweet & Maxwell.

Curran, J. (1988) *Survey of the Administrative Arrangements for Curators* ad litem, Central Research Unit, Social Work Services Group, Edinburgh, Scottish Office.

Hill, M., Lockyer, A., Morton, P., Batchelor, S. and Scott, S. (2002) *The Role of Safeguarders in Scotland*, Centre for the Child and Society and Department of Politics, University of Glasgow.

McKellar, P. and West, J. (1994) *The Representation of Children: Curators' Perceptions of Current Issues*, Glasgow, Glasgow Caledonian University.

Triseliotis, J., Shireman, J. and Hundlebury, M. (1997) *Adoption: Theory, Policy and Practice*, London, Cassell.

26

Code of Practice for Social Service Workers and Code of Practice for Employers of Social Service Workers

SCOTTISH SOCIAL SERVICES COUNCIL

Introduction

This document contains agreed codes of practice for social service workers and employers of social service workers describing the standards of conduct and practice within which they should work. This introduction, which is also reproduced in the Code of Practice for Social Service Workers, is intended to help you understand what the codes are for and what they will mean to you as a social service worker, employer, service user or member of the public.

The Scottish Social Services Council began its work on 1 October 2001, at the same time as the General Social Care Council, the Northern Ireland Social Care Council, and the Care Council for Wales. The Councils have a duty to develop codes of practice and have worked together in developing these codes as part of their contribution to raising standards in social services.

The two codes for workers and employers are presented together in this document because they are complementary and mirror the joint responsibilities of employers and workers in ensuring high standards.

What are the codes?

The Code of Practice for Social Service Workers is a list of statements that describe the standards of professional conduct and practice required of social service workers as they go about their daily work. This is the first time that standards have been set in this way at national level, although many employers have similar standards in place at local level. The intention is to confirm the standards required in social services and ensure that workers know what standards of conduct employers, colleagues, service users, carers and the public expect of them.

The Code of Practice for Employers of Social Service Workers sets down the responsibilities of employers in the regulation of social service workers. Again, this is the first time that such standards have been set out at national level. The code requires that employers adhere to the standards set out in their code, support social service workers in meeting their code and take appropriate action when workers do not meet expected standards of conduct.

The codes are intended to reflect existing good practice and it is anticipated that workers and employers will recognise in the codes the shared standards to which they already aspire. The Councils will promote these standards through making the codes widely available.

How will the codes be used?

The codes are a key step in the introduction of a system of regulation for social services in the four countries of the UK. The Councils are responsible for the registration of those working in social services. The register will be a public record that those registered have met the requirements for entry onto the register and have agreed to abide by the standards set out in the Code of Practice for Social Service Workers.

The Councils will take account of the standards set in the Code of Practice for Social Service Workers in considering issues of misconduct and decisions as to whether a registered worker should remain on the register.

What will the codes mean to you?

As a social service worker you will have criteria to guide your practice and be clear about what standards of conduct you are expected to meet.

You are encouraged to use the codes to examine your own practice and to look for areas in which you can improve.

As a social service employer you will know what part you are expected to play in the regulation of the workforce and the support of high quality social services. You are encouraged to review your own standards of practice and policies in the light of the standards set in the code.

As a user of services or a member of the public the codes will help you understand how a social service worker should behave towards you and how employers should support social service workers to do their jobs well.

CODE OF PRACTICE FOR SOCIAL SERVICE WORKERS

The purpose of this code is to set out the conduct that is expected of social service workers and to inform service users and the public about the standards of conduct they can expect from social service workers. It forms part of the wider package of legislation, practice standards and employers' policies and procedures that social service workers must meet. Social service workers are responsible for making sure that their conduct does not fall below the standards set out in this code and that no action or omission on their part harms the well being of service users.

Status

The Scottish Social Services Council expects social service workers to meet this code and may take action if registered workers fail to do so.

Employers of social service workers are required to take account of this code in making any decisions about the conduct of their staff.

Social service workers must:

1. Protect the rights and promote the interests of service users and carers;
2. Strive to establish and maintain the trust and confidence of service users and carers;
3. Promote the independence of service users while protecting them as far as possible from danger or harm;
4. Respect the rights of service users while seeking to ensure that their behaviour does not harm themselves or other people;
5. Uphold public trust and confidence in social services;

6. Be accountable for the quality of their work and take responsibility for maintaining and improving their knowledge and skills.

1. As a social service worker you must protect the rights and promote the interests of service users and carers.

This includes:

1.1 Treating each person as an individual;
1.2 Respecting and, where appropriate, promoting the individual views and wishes of both service users and carers;
1.3 Supporting service users' rights to control their lives and make informed choices about the services they receive;
1.4 Respecting and maintaining the dignity and privacy of service users;
1.5 Promoting equal opportunities for service users and carers; and
1.6 Respecting diversity and different cultures and values.

2. As a social service worker you must strive to establish and maintain the trust and confidence of service users and carers.

This includes:

2.1 Being honest and trustworthy;
2.2 Communicating in an appropriate, open, accurate and straightforward way;
2.3 Respecting confidential information and clearly explaining agency policies about confidentiality to services users and carers;
2.4 Being reliable and dependable;
2.5 Honouring work commitments, agreements and arrangements and when it is not possible to do so, explaining why to service users and carers;
2.6 Declaring issues that might create conflicts of interest and making sure that they do not influence your judgement or practice; and
2.7 Adhering to policies and procedures about accepting gifts and money from service users and carers.

3. As a social service worker you must promote the independence of service users while protecting them as far as possible from danger or harm.

This includes:

3.1 Promoting the independence of service users and assisting them to understand and exercise their rights;

3.2 Using established processes and procedures to challenge and report dangerous, abusive, discriminatory or exploitative behaviour and practice;

3.3 Following practice and procedures designed to keep you and other people safe from violent and abusive behaviour at work;

3.4 Bringing to the attention of your employer or the appropriate authority resource or operational difficulties that might get in the way of the delivery of safe care;

3.5 Informing your employer or an appropriate authority where the practice of colleagues may be unsafe or adversely affecting standards of care;

3.6 Complying with employers' health and safety policies including those relating to substance abuse;

3.7 Helping service users and carers to make complaints, taking complaints seriously and responding to them or passing them to the appropriate person; and

3.8 Recognising and using responsibly the power that comes from your work with service users and carers.

4. As a social service worker you must respect the rights of service users while seeking to ensure that their behaviour does not harm themselves or other people.

This includes:

4.1 Recognising that service users have the right to take risks and helping them to identify and manage potential and actual risks to themselves and others;

4.2 Following risk assessment policies and procedures to assess whether the behaviour of service users presents a risk of harm to themselves or others;

4.3 Taking necessary steps to minimise the risks of service users from doing actual or potential harm to themselves or other people; and,

4.4 Ensuring that relevant colleagues and agencies are informed about the outcomes and implications of risk assessments.

5. As a social service worker you must uphold public trust and confidence in social services.

In particular you must not:

5.1 Abuse, neglect or harm service users, carers or colleagues;

5.2 Exploit service users, carers or colleagues in any way;

5.3 Abuse the trust of service users and carers or the access you have to personal information about them, or to their property, home or workplace;

5.4 Form inappropriate personal relationships with services users;

5.5 Discriminate unlawfully or unjustifiably against service users, carers or colleagues;

5.6 Condone any unlawful or unjustifiable discrimination by service users, carers or colleagues;

5.7 Put yourself or other people at unnecessary risk; or

5.8 Behave in a way, in work or outside work, which would call into question your suitability to work in social services.

6. As a social service worker you must be accountable for the quality of your work and take responsibility for maintaining and improving your knowledge and skills.

This includes:

6.1 Meeting relevant standards of practice, and working in a lawful, safe and effective way;

6.2 Maintaining clear and accurate records as required by procedures established for your work;

6.3 Informing your employer or the appropriate authority about any personal difficulties that might affect your ability to do your job competently and safely;

6.4 Seeking assistance from your employer or the appropriate authority if you do not feel able or adequately prepared to carry out any aspect of your work or you are not sure about how to proceed in a work matter;

6.5 Working openly and co-operatively with colleagues and treating them with respect;

6.6 Recognising that you remain responsible for the work that you have delegated to other workers;

6.7 Recognising and respecting the roles and expertise of workers from other agencies and working in partnership with them; and

6.8 Undertaking relevant training to maintain and improve your knowledge and skills and contributing to the learning and development of others.

CODE OF PRACTICE FOR EMPLOYERS OF SOCIAL SERVICE WORKERS

The purpose of this code is to set down the responsibilities of employers in regulating social service workers. The purpose of workforce regulation is to protect and promote the interests of service users and carers. The code is intended to complement rather than replace or duplicate existing employers' policies and it forms part of the wider package of legislation, requirements and guidance that relate to the employment of staff. Employers are responsible for making sure that they meet the standards set out in this code, provide high quality services and promote public trust and confidence in social services.

Status

Relevant regulatory bodies in Scotland will take this code into account in their regulation of social services.

1. To meet their responsibilities in relation to regulating the social service workforce, social service employers must:

1. Make sure people are suitable to enter the workforce and understand their roles and responsibilities;
2. Have written policies and procedures in place to enable social service workers to meet the Scottish Social Services Council (SSSC) Code of Practice for Social Service Workers;
3. Provide training and development opportunities to enable social service workers to strengthen and develop their skills and knowledge;
4. Put in place and implement written processes and procedures to deal with dangerous, discriminatory or exploitative behaviour and practice; and

5. Promote the SSSC's Code of Practice to social service workers, service users and carers and co-operate with SSSC's proceedings.

As a social service employer you must make sure people are suitable to enter the social service workforce and understand their roles and responsibilities.

This includes:

1.1 Using rigorous and thorough recruitment and selection processes focused on making sure that only people who have the appropriate knowledge and skills and who are suitable to provide social services are allowed to enter your workforce;
1.2 Checking criminal records, relevant registers and indexes and assessing whether people are capable of carrying out the duties of the job they have been selected for before confirming appointments;
1.3 Seeking and providing reliable references;
1.4 Giving staff clear information about their roles and responsibilities, relevant legislation and the organisational policies and procedures they must follow in their work; and
1.5 Managing the performance of staff and the organisation to ensure high quality services and care.

2. As a social service employer you must have written policies and processes in place to enable social service workers to meet the SSSC's Code of Practice for Social Service Workers.

This includes:

2.1 Implementing and monitoring written policies on: confidentiality; equal opportunities, risk assessment; substance abuse; record keeping; and the acceptance of money or personal gifts from service users or carers;
2.2 Effectively managing and supervising staff to support effective practice and good conduct and supporting staff to address deficiencies in their performance;
2.3 Having systems in place to enable social service workers to report inadequate resources or operational difficulties which might impede the delivery of safe care and working with them and relevant authorities to address those issues; and

2.4 Supporting social service workers to meet the SSSC's Code of Practice for Social Service Workers and not requiring them to do anything that would put their compliance with that code at risk.

3. As a social service employer you must provide training and development opportunities to enable social service workers to strengthen and develop their skills and knowledge.

This includes:

3.1 Providing induction, training and development opportunities to help social service workers do their jobs effectively and prepare for new and changing roles and responsibilities;
3.2 Contributing to the provision of social service and social work education and training, including effective workplace assessment and practice learning;
3.3 Supporting staff in posts subject to registration to meet the SSSC's eligibility criteria for registration and its requirements for continuing professional development; and
3.4 Responding appropriately to social service workers who seek assistance because they do not feel able or adequately prepared to carry out any aspects of their work.

4. As a social service employer you must put into place and implement written policies and procedures to deal with dangerous, discriminatory or exploitative behaviour and practice.

This includes:

4.1 Making it clear to social service workers that bullying, harassment or any form of unjustifiable discrimination is not acceptable and taking action to deal with such behaviour;
4.2 Establishing and promoting procedures for social service workers to report dangerous, discriminatory, abusive or exploitative behaviour and practice and dealing with these reports promptly, effectively and openly;
4.3 Making it clear to social service workers, service users and carers that violence, threats or abuse to staff are not acceptable and having clear policies and procedures for minimising the risk of violence and managing violent incidents;

4.4 Supporting social service workers who experience trauma or violence in their work;

4.5 Putting in place and implementing written policies and procedures that promote staff welfare and equal opportunities for workers; and

4.6 While ensuring that the care and safety of service users is your priority, providing appropriate assistance to social service workers whose work is affected by ill health or dependency on drugs and alcohol, and giving clear guidance about any limits on their work while they are receiving treatment.

5. As a social service employer you must promote the SSSC's Codes of Practice to social service workers, service users and carers and co-operate with the SSSC's proceedings.

This includes:

5.1 Informing social service workers about this code and your responsibility to comply to it;

5.2 Informing social service workers about the SSSC's Code of Practice for Social Service Workers and their personal responsibility to meet that code;

5.3 Making services users and carers aware of this code and the Code of Practice for Social Service Workers and informing them about how to raise issues through your policies and if necessary contact the SSSC in relation to the Codes;

5.4 Taking account of the SSSC's Code Practice for Social Service Workers in making any decision that relates to the conduct of workers;

5.5 Informing the SSSC about any misconduct by a registered social service worker that might call into question their registration and inform the worker involved that a report has been made to the SSSC; and

5.6 Co-operating with SSSC investigations and hearings and responding appropriately to the findings and decisions of the SSSC.

Author Index

Subject Index